# Approaches to Teaching the Works of Ralph Ellison

# Approaches to Teaching the Works of Ralph Ellison

Edited by

*Tracy Floreani*

The Modern Language Association of America
New York   2024

© 2024 by The Modern Language Association of America
85 Broad Street, New York, New York 10004
www.mla.org

All rights reserved. MLA and the MODERN LANGUAGE ASSOCIATION are trademarks owned by the Modern Language Association of America. To request permission to reprint material from MLA book publications, please inquire at permissions@mla.org.

To order MLA publications, visit www.mla.org/books. For wholesale and international orders, see www.mla.org/bookstore-orders.

The MLA office is located on the island known as Mannahatta (Manhattan) in Lenapehoking, the homeland of the Lenape people. The MLA pays respect to the original stewards of this land and to the diverse and vibrant Native communities that continue to thrive in New York City.

Approaches to Teaching World Literature 177
ISSN 1059-1133

Library of Congress Cataloging-in-Publication Data

Names: Floreani, Tracy, editor.
Title: Approaches to teaching the works of Ralph Ellison / edited by Tracy Floreani.
Description: New York : The Modern Language Association of America, 2024. | Series: Approaches to teaching world literature, 1059-1133 ; 177 | Includes bibliographical references.
Identifiers: LCCN 2024000949 (print) | LCCN 2024000950 (ebook) | ISBN 9781603296717 (hardcover) | ISBN 9781603296724 (paperback) | ISBN 9781603296731 (EPUB)
Subjects: LCSH: Ellison, Ralph—Study and teaching. | Ellison, Ralph—Criticism and interpretation. | LCGFT: Literary criticism. | Essays.
Classification: LCC PS3555.L625 Z54 2024 (print) | LCC PS3555.L625 (ebook) | DDC 813/.54—dc23/eng/20240126
LC record available at https://lccn.loc.gov/2024000949
LC ebook record available at https://lccn.loc.gov/2024000950

# CONTENTS

## PART ONE: MATERIALS

| | |
|---|---|
| Primary Sources | 3 |
| Biographical Materials | 4 |
| Contextual Materials | 5 |
| Critical Studies | 6 |
| Other Resources | 9 |

## PART TWO: APPROACHES

Introduction — 15
*Tracy Floreani*

### *Invisible Man* in the Twenty-First Century

Layers of Identity: Learning to Teach *Invisible Man* — 26
*John F. Callahan*

Resisting Black-Lack Readings of *Invisible Man* — 35
*Sherry Johnson*

Can the Joke "Slip the Yoke"? *Invisible Man* and the Knot of Black Humor — 45
*Kirin Wachter-Grene*

"Punking" *Invisible Man*: Reading Race, Queerness, and Disability — 53
*Alvin J. Henry*

*Invisible Man* and the Urban Uprising — 67
*J. J. Butts*

Claiming the Lens of Love: Reading *Invisible Man* through
1 Corinthians 13 — 76
*Martha Greene Eads*

### Broader Contexts

Historicizing Ellison: Politics and Pedagogy — 88
*Barbara Foley*

The Democratic Ideal of Ellison's Jazz-Shaped America — 97
*Sterling Lecater Bland, Jr.*

Listening for the Invisible — 106
*Jake Johnson*

vi    CONTENTS

## Short Works

The Voices of History: Narrating the Past in Ellison's Short Fiction    112
  *Keith Byerman*

Teaching Intergenerational Conflict and Technology in "Flying Home"
    and "Cadillac Flambé"    122
  *Paul Devlin*

Is Resistance Futile? Exploring "King of the Bingo Game"
    in a Secondary ELA Classroom    133
  *Aimée Myers*

Navigating Freedom with "Uncertainty and Daring": Reading Ellison
    and Writing Memoir in a Prison Classroom    142
  *Agnieszka Tuszynska*

Epistolary Ellison: Letter Writing as Pedagogy    153
  *Clark Barwick*

## Versions of the Second Novel

Reflecting on the Mysteries of Ellison's "Unfinished" Project    162
  *Keyana Parks*

An Episodic Writing-as-Inquiry Approach
    to *Three Days before the Shooting . . .*    173
  *Tracy Floreani*

**Notes on Contributors**    183

**Survey Participants**    187

**Works Cited**    189

*Part One*

# MATERIALS

# Primary Sources

Since Ralph Ellison's death in 1994, much more of his writing has become readily available. *Invisible Man* remains the go-to Ellison text in the classroom and has been consistently in print within the imprints of its original publisher, Random House, since it was first published in 1952. The most recent (2012) Vintage International edition is the preferred classroom edition when the work is taught in full form. Those unable to fit the entire novel into a course schedule often opt for the "battle royal" scene and sometimes also the prologue; these appear as excerpts in many literature anthologies. A couple of Ellison's short stories have appeared in anthologies for years (often, "King of the Bingo Game"), but since the 1996 posthumous publication of *Flying Home and Other Stories*, several more of them now appear regularly in a variety of literature anthologies. A few anthologies also include one or two of Ellison's essays, but, as becomes clear throughout the essays in this volume, most instructors choose specific essays from either *Shadow and Act* (also reprinted as a Vintage International title in 1995 and still in print as a stand-alone book) or *The Collected Essays of Ralph Ellison*, edited by John F. Callahan, which has a helpful new index in its 2024 reissue. Ellison's other book-length collection of essays, *Going to the Territory*, is also still in print as part of the same series, but most people tend to keep *The Collected Essays* on the shelf because it includes both of those books of essays as well as other separately published or recently discovered essays, transcripts of speeches, previously unpublished notes and ancillary materials, an interview, and the elegiac preface by Saul Bellow. Ellison's writings on jazz are also collected in a single volume, titled *Living with Music* and edited by Robert O'Meally.

Ellison's unfinished second novel, edited by Callahan, was published five years after the author's death as *Juneteenth*, which is now available as a 2021 reissue with a new introduction and a preface by the novelist Charles Johnson. This second novel was also released in another form under a different title in 2011; almost three times the length of *Juneteenth*, *Three Days before the Shooting . . .* reads as the uncut version of *Juneteenth* and includes all the excerpts and multiple versions of the narrative pieces that were to compose the second novel. The two versions present very different and fascinating reading experiences, each in its own right.

Other primary sources that provide access to Ellison's own perspectives on his body of work are interviews and letters. *Conversations with Ralph Ellison*, edited by Maryemma Graham and Amritjit Singh, collects a majority of the published interviews with Ellison. Ranging in topic from writing and the arts to race and American culture, many of the interviews were conducted by literary scholars, but the collection includes two by writers with whom he had mentoring friendships, James Alan McPherson and Leon Forrest. *Conversations* is still in print and readily available in many college libraries. The most recent addition to the Random House series of Ellison books is *The Selected Letters of Ralph*

*Ellison*, which was released in 2019 and quickly garnered a lot of excitement from both readers and scholars. The letters provide eloquently written insights on many topics and span six decades of the author's life. An exchange of letters between Ellison and his novelist friend Albert Murray appeared in 2000 as *Trading Twelves*, and a few select letters were published in a 1999 issue of *The New Republic*, but the expansive quality of the *Selected Letters*—and their stand-in as an Ellison autobiography of sorts—seems to have created a buzz that has the letters making their way pretty quickly into the classroom. Finally, for those interested in intertextual studies, Ellison's own photographs are now available in a 2023 art book titled *Photographer*, from the German publisher Steidl.

# Biographical Materials

The book-length biographies of Ellison by Arnold Rampersad and Lawrence Jackson have remained close at hand for those wanting information about the author's upbringing, artistic coming-of-age, personal life, and career trajectory. For quick visual context, the PBS *American Masters* documentary *Ralph Ellison: An American Journey* is a popular classroom mainstay, in full or in segments. Some Ellison scholars find that each of these biographical sources has a lot to offer—but each also has its limits. For this reason, the editor of this volume advises against relying on just one biographical resource about Ellison.[1] Many of the essays in this volume include helpful pieces of biographical information relevant to the teaching of the specific texts. Some collections of critical essays include chapters that deepen study of Ellison the person and author, which educators may also find helpful, including portions of *The Cambridge Companion to Ralph Ellison*, edited by Ross Posnock, and *Ralph Ellison in Context*, edited by Paul Devlin. Adam Bradley's *Ralph Ellison in Progress* offers a fascinating exploration of Ellison's methods in terms of both his technical approach and the influence of the vernacular in his composition process. Timothy Parrish's monograph *Ralph Ellison and the Genius of America* integrates biography and critical study in an illuminating reassessment of the importance of Ellison's work beyond *Invisible Man*, within the context of the American civil rights movement and in conversation with other major contemporary writers and thinkers. To explore in more focus the role of Ellison as public intellectual in the long civil rights era, see "Being Ralph Ellison: Remaking the Black Public Intellectual in the Age of Civil Rights," by Sterling Lecater Bland, Jr., and "The Confederacy of Sages and the Agon of Black Power," by John S. Wright, in the 2015 *American Studies* special issue on Ellison (Calihman et al.).

# Contextual Materials

Most of the books that offer historical context and references for Ellison's works lean heavily toward *Invisible Man*, understandably. Though not currently in print (but still available in most academic libraries), Eric Sundquist's *Cultural Contexts for Ralph Ellison's* Invisible Man is an oft-cited resource, probably because of its succinct but comprehensive and accessible breakdown of key allusions within the novel. Lena Hill and Michael Hill's *Ralph Ellison's* Invisible Man: *A Reference Guide* also approaches historical and cultural contexts and expands into ideas, thematics, and the original critical reception of the novel—also in a very accessible form for undergraduates.

A *Historical Guide to Ralph Ellison*, edited by Steven Tracy, moves beyond *Invisible Man* into broader contexts of the author's work and worldviews. It presents a handful of essays by top Ellison scholars that offer more critical interpretations of specific contextual topics, including gender and sexuality, Ellison's views on the politics of integration, the literary canon, and music. It concludes with a handy bibliographic assessment of the previous fifty years of criticism of Ellison's work (as of 2004). Mentioned earlier in relation to biography, Ross Posnock's edited collection *The Cambridge Companion to Ralph Ellison* similarly contains contextual studies that many classroom instructors excerpt. Available more recently from Cambridge University Press, Paul Devlin's 2021 edited collection *Ralph Ellison in Context* should likewise prove helpful, especially in that it includes even more on Ellison's posthumously published works and is accessible to undergraduate audiences. Both of these Cambridge volumes contain a rich variety of perspectives from more of the top Ellison scholars in the world, including contextual insights on music, gender, geographical sites, visual arts, philosophy, relationships with other artists and literary movements, technology, digital humanities, and politics. Three semibiographical monographs may also prove helpful in tracing in great depth Ellison's intellectual and aesthetic interests: *Shadowing Ralph Ellison*, by John S. Wright (who was himself an Ellison protégé); *Ralph Ellison and Kenneth Burke at the Roots of the Racial Divide*, by the Burke expert Bryan Crable; and *Ralph Ellison, Temporal Technologist*, by Michael Germana. Finally, for broader sociohistorical contexts beyond Ellison-specific criticism, the decade-by-decade Cambridge University Press series American Literature in Transition may prove useful for young students with limited knowledge of the cultural history of the era in which Ellison came of age and wrote many of his major works—especially those volumes devoted to the thirties, forties, and fifties. Most of these include overviews of what was happening in the ethnic literatures of each decade and provide succinct explanations of such helpful cultural contexts as national demographic shifts and regional changes, the importance of radio in the 1930s, attitudes about the beginning of World War II, the vogue for psychoanalysis in the 1950s, and the escalation of the Cold War.

# Critical Studies

The majority of the materials listed in this section are titles and resources that have become available since the 1989 publication of the MLA's *Approaches to Teaching Ellison's* Invisible Man, edited by Susan Resneck Parr and Pancho Savery, so as not to duplicate the resources listed in that volume. While hundreds of high-quality critical studies of Ellison and his work have been written since that edition, the discussion of materials here focuses mostly on resources published since Ellison's death in 1994 and highlights those that may be most helpful to developing or deepening an instructor's background study and understanding of Ellison's work for the purposes of classroom teaching. Each of the essays in part 2, "Approaches," offers suggestions for relevant, helpful materials as well.

As readers will notice in the essays in this volume, those who regularly teach Ellison often turn to his essays for perspectives that inform study of his works. For a critical approach to Ellison's essays in their own right, Cheryl Wall's chapter on Ellison in her book *On Freedom and the Will to Adorn: The Art of the African American Essay* offers one of the most insightful studies of Ellison's work in the genre and within the tradition of African American essayists. The posthumous reissues of his primary works also contain helpful critical introductions to frame an understanding of the texts, and the introduction Ellison wrote for the thirtieth anniversary edition of *Invisible Man* remains a useful critical framework from his own retrospective thinking on the novel.[2]

One has no trouble finding good articles on *Invisible Man* through library databases, and there are too many strong readings of the novel to list here. As a starting point for those less familiar with the novel or new to teaching it, the contextual materials resources listed above are recommended and may be supplemented by some of the book-length critical editions on the novel: *Ralph Ellison's* Invisible Man: A Casebook, edited by John Callahan, or *New Essays on* Invisible Man, edited by Robert O'Meally.

To move beyond the first novel into deeper and wider studies of Ellison's work and career, a few more recent editions prove helpful. *The New Territory: Ralph Ellison and the Twenty-First Century*, edited by Marc C. Conner and Lucas E. Morel, is a thoughtful assessment of Ellison's work in the context of the current era and brings together some all-star Ellison scholars to reassess his work. Of particular use in the volume are Tim Parrish's essay on *Three Days before the Shooting . . .* , which embraces the unfinished second novel in all its incompleteness, and Robert Butler's essay "*Invisible Man* and the Politics of Love," which persuasively rebuts many of the myths about Ellison and assesses why Ellison has—more so than any of his African American writer peers—had to "labor under the weight" of consistent misinterpretations of his engagement with contemporaneous social issues and an ongoing "assault on [his] work and character" (41). Because the body of scholarship on Ellison's unfinished second novel remains relatively small, this book's section on the posthumous novel is also especially helpful for those new to *Juneteenth* or *Three Days*, allowing them to

CRITICAL STUDIES 7

become more familiar with the sprawling, incomplete manuscript from a variety of literary historical and thematic perspectives.[3] Melanie Masterton Sherazi's article "The Posthumous Text and Its Archive: Toward an Ecstatic Reading of Ralph Ellison's Unbound Novel" also offers a helpful overview as well as an expansive approach to the second novel.

For those wanting to expand their critical apparatus to consider Ellison's work within broader studies of African American literature, important critical or comparative frameworks for many classroom instructors may be found in classic studies like Robert Stepto's *From Behind the Veil: A Study of Afro-American Narrative* and Hortense Spillers's 1987 essay "Mama's Baby, Papa's Maybe." More recent studies that provide effective broader contexts for Ellison's work are Farah Jasmine Griffin's *"Who Set You Flowin'?": The African-American Migration Narrative*; Toni Morrison's *Playing in the Dark*; *The Routledge Introduction to African American Literature*, edited by D. Quentin Miller; and James Smethurst's *The African American Roots of Modernism*.

For those especially interested in the political element in Ellison's body of work, Barbara Foley's *Wrestling with the Left* and Morel's edited collection *Ralph Ellison and the Raft of Hope: A Political Companion to* Invisible Man both offer nicely detailed and thought-provoking studies of the first novel, from distinctly different political perspectives. Kenneth Warren's *So Black and Blue: Ralph Ellison and the Occasion of Criticism* considers *Invisible Man* and Ellison's essays as part of his larger discourse on American politics and culture and considers the potential and limits of the novelistic form to serve as a meaningful platform for marginalized peoples. More recently, Bland's *In the Shadow of Invisibility: Ralph Ellison and the Promise of American Democracy* takes on the daunting task of tracing the evolution of Ellison's political and intellectual ideologies over the course of his life and entire writing career and attempts to extend the application of Ellison's legacy to the twenty-first-century context. Strong works with more specific political focus as well as contexts for important comparative possibilities include J. J. Butts's extensive study of Ellison's politically inflected work with the Federal Writers' Project, which can be found in Butts's book *Dark Mirror: African Americans and the Federal Writers' Project*. William J. Maxwell's fascinating study of the shaping of African American literature through the lens of FBI surveillance includes Ralph Ellison within the Cold War period (*F.B. Eyes*), and the FBI files of Ellison and his peers can be viewed through the book's companion *F.B. Eyes Digital Archive* website.

Among his many interests, Ellison maintained an acquisitive curiosity about new technologies of all sorts, both within his home and as a narrative element. Bradley's *Ralph Ellison in Progress* again proves helpful here, if one is interested in exploring the technologies with which Ellison composed (typewriters, Dictaphones, early home computers), as does Jeff Noh's more recent article "Ralph Ellison's Computer Memory." Given the growing interest in Afrofuturism, instructors may want to approach *Invisible Man* within that context, with the help of Lisa Yaszek's "An Afrofuturist Reading of Ralph Ellison's *Invisible Man*."

8    CRITICAL STUDIES

For additional approaches to the technology motifs within Ellison's works, there are a few particularly useful articles, including "Ellison's Technological Humanism" and "Alternating Currents: Electricity, Humanism, and Resistance," by Jennifer Lieberman; Scott Selisker's combination of the sociological and technological in "'Simply by Reacting?': The Sociology of Race and *Invisible Man*'s Automata"; and Johnnie Wilcox's intriguing application of theories of the cyborg in his article "Black Power: Minstrelsy and Electricity in Ralph Ellison's *Invisible Man*." In this volume, Jake Johnson considers sound technology as an abstract concept within Ralph Ellison's daily life, and Paul Devlin explores thematics of technology's role in intergenerational relationships in the short stories.

Discussions of Ellison and his works often eventually come to the topic of gender. Students have perennially been intrigued by the limited role of women characters in his fiction and by the depictions of sexuality and interracial relationships. Additionally, elements of his work have invited new readings of the depictions of masculinity as well as homosocial and homosexual elements. The biographies and many of the critical-context resources already mentioned here contain useful considerations of gender. The earlier Approaches to Teaching volume on *Invisible Man* includes an essay on women in the novel, Mary Rohrberger's "'Ball the Jack': Surreality, Sexuality, and the Role of Women in *Invisible Man*," and some critical works from the 1970s through the early 1990s also focus on the novel's women characters, leaning into second-wave-feminist readings of the semiotics of representation and gender stereotypes. The best-known of these are probably Claudia Tate's "Notes on the Invisible Women in Ralph Ellison's *Invisible Man*" and, building off Tate's work, Catherine E. Saunders's "Makers or Bearers of Meaning? Sex and the Struggle for Self-Definition in Ralph Ellison's *Invisible Man*." Beyond the novel, Keith Byerman's essay in the special Ellison issue of *American Studies* provides one of the few comprehensive readings of the women characters in the short stories, and Smethurst's essay in Tracy's *Historical Guide*, "'Something Warmly, Infuriatingly Feminine': Gender and Sexuality in the Work of Ralph Ellison," offers a broader exploration. More recent feminist takes on Ellison and gender still tend to focus on *Invisible Man* more than any of his other works but offer more problematized or updated readings, such as Meina Yates-Richard's assessment of the novel as falling in line with Black nationalism when it comes to issues of gender and Hyo-seol Ha's intersectional reading in "'I Should Have Gone to Mary's.'" Several essays in this volume touch briefly on gender; particularly helpful in this regard is Martha Greene Eads's essay, which offers an empathetic reconsideration of the stripper character in the famous battle royal scene.

Some helpful works that read the novel through the lenses of masculinity and queer theory are Douglas Steward's queer, psychoanalytic interpretation in "The Illusions of Phallic Agency"; Roderick A. Ferguson's chapter "The Specter of Woodridge: Canonical Formations and the Anticanonical in *Invisible Man*" in his *Aberrations in Black* (54–81); Michael Hardin's broader-scope take in "Ralph Ellison's *Invisible Man*: Invisibility, Race, and Homoeroticism from Frederick

Douglass to E. Lynn Harris"; and the sections on Ellison in Daniel Y. Kim's monograph *Writing Manhood in Black and Yellow: Ralph Ellison, Frank Chin, and the Literary Politics of Identity*. Finally, rethinking the novel through the intersections of genderqueer identity and disability, Alvin Henry's essay in this volume extends his work on Ellison from his monograph *Black Queer Flesh* and offers an innovative rethinking of the protagonist's trajectory with clear lesson plans to help students contextualize readings of queer and disabled characters in the story.

# Other Resources

Literary intertexts often used in the classroom include relevant passages that capture Ellison's conversations—literal and figurative—with other writers, thinkers, and "race men" committed to centering African American culture as part of the effort toward social equity. Passages from W. E. B. Du Bois's *The Souls of Black Folk* on his concept of "double-consciousness," Richard Wright's *Twelve Million Black Voices* and "Blueprint for Negro Writing," essays by James Baldwin (*Collected Essays*), and Amiri Baraka's *Blues People* remain relevant as "conversations between" texts in Ellison studies. Many instructors continue to employ the important canonical intertexts by European and Euro-American authors as well, such as sections of T. S. Eliot's *Waste Land* or *Four Quartets*, Fyodor Dostoyevsky's *Notes from Underground*, Herman Melville's novella *Benito Cereno*, and occasionally Mark Twain's *Adventures of Huckleberry Finn*.[4]

Beyond these works directly alluded to or influential to the novel, many teachers have found great success in teaching Ellison by putting him in conversation with current works. Contemporary novels that contain overt Ellisonian echoes are worth exploring, of course, such as Paul Beatty's *The Sellout*, Percival Everett's *Erasure*, Colson Whitehead's *The Intuitionist*, and Viet Thanh Nguyen's *The Sympathizer*. Essayists less overtly calling to Ellison but addressing relevant topics include Ta-Nehisi Coates, on personal and collective experiences of the trickle-down effect of historical race relations within contemporary American culture; Hanif Abdurraqib, who writes in fascinating new ways about Black performance; and Eula Biss, whose essay "Time and Distance Overcome" is a provocative work of creative nonfiction that explores the parallel courses of technological progress and racist terror. Segments of Griffin's genre-blending memoir *Read until You Understand: The Wisdom of Black Life and Literature* could also fuel engaging conversations about the contemporary relevance of Ellison's thought and aesthetics. Likewise, contemporary films that probe issues of race in American culture provide for stimulating comparative study, such as Boots Riley's *Sorry to Bother You*, as described in Kirin Wachter-Grene's essay in this volume, and Spike Lee's satire of modern minstrelsy, *Bamboozled*, which can be paired with the scene in *Invisible Man* of Tod Clifton selling Sambo dolls to inspire larger explorations of performativity, ambition, and success in American popular culture.

10    OTHER RESOURCES

For those interested in engaging students through arts-integrated pedagogy, a lot has been written on Ellison's relationship with music—as a listener, critic, improvisational composer of words, and musical thinker. O'Meally's edition of Ellison's jazz writing, *Living with Music*, contains a useful critical perspective as well as an interview with Ellison about music. Horace Porter's *Jazz Country: Ralph Ellison in America* assesses the author's cultural perspectives through the lens of the jazz idiom and its influences on Ellison's artistic agenda, philosophy, and writing style. Paul Allen Anderson's "Ralph Ellison's Music Lessons" in *The Cambridge Companion to Ralph Ellison* is a popular classroom supplement, and the volume *Ralph Ellison in Context* includes three insightful essays on not only jazz but also blues and southwestern swing. In this volume, Sterling Lecater Bland offers a practical guide to approaching jazz and blues in the literature lesson. On sound in the abstract, see Herman Beavers's "The Noisy Lostness: Oppositionality and Acousmatic Subjectivity in *Invisible Man*" and Jake Johnson's essay on sound in this volume.

Ellison's interest in visual culture and its influence on his thinking and writing is nicely handled by Lena Hill's chapter on Ellison's fine art collecting in her book *Visualizing Blackness and the Creation of the African American Literary Tradition*. The photography specialist Sara Blair has done important work on Ellison as a visual thinker in her essay "Ellison, Photography, and the Origins of Invisibility" in Posnock's *Cambridge Companion* volume as well as in her book *Harlem Crossroads: Black Writers and the Photograph in the Twentieth Century*.

Any study of visual arts intertexts ought to be extended into primary source explorations as well through two photographic collections. Ellison's collaboration with the photographer Gordon Parks for *Life* magazine in 1952 is replicated in its original layout in the rich catalog curated and edited by Michal Raz-Russo and Jean-Christophe Cloutier and published in conjunction with the 2016 Art Institute of Chicago exhibit *Invisible Man: Gordon Parks and Ralph Ellison in Harlem*. As noted earlier, Ellison's own photography is also now available in print as the Steidl volume *Photographer*. Thinking through relationships between the photographic and the writerly is also nicely assisted by Cloutier's chapter on Ellison and Wright's work on the Lafargue Clinic in Harlem in his book *Shadow Archives: The Lifecycles of African American Literature*.

Students are intrigued by how Ellison's writing has inspired visual artists of later generations, too, so works by artists such as the sculptor Elizabeth Catlett; the painters Jack Whitten, Hank Willis Thomas, and Kerry James Marshall; and the photographer Jeff Wall make for engaging conversations about inspiration and representative versus abstracted depictions of Ellison's influence. Nicole Rudick's *New York Times* article on this topic in relation to *Invisible Man's* lasting inspiration provides a nice overview and visuals to help introduce the idea of visual-literary intertexts to undergraduates.

Other primary source intertexts have been used by instructors throughout the years to enhance study of Ellison's work. These include the text of the 1954 Supreme Court opinion *Brown v. Board of Education of Topeka*, Green Book

OTHER RESOURCES    11

travel guides, biblical verses, portions of Sigmund Freud's *Totem and Taboo*, Booker T. Washington's 1895 speech at the Atlanta Exposition, and various historical documents that help to contextualize specific elements within Ellison's creative works (e.g., contemporaneous news articles on lynchings as a supplement to the story "A Party Down at the Square"). Again, excellent additional primary source materials are described and suggested in various essays in the "Approaches" section of this volume.

Of course, the digital age offers much at our fingertips, not just handy video clips of speeches and songs relevant to Ellison's work and ready-to-use, adaptable online teacher resources, curriculum guides, and book group discussion questions but also deeply engaged and engaging digital humanities projects that may enhance classroom study. Jolie A. Sheffer's *Digital Public Library of America* primary source set, for example, provides audio and visual sources to enhance multimodal contextual and intertextual study of the author as well as a helpful teacher's guide for use. Pushing further, J. D. Porter's essay "Ellison and Digital Humanities" sorts through consternation as to why there is not already more digital humanities (DH) engagement with the author's work, given how well that work lends itself to DH projects and Ellison's own interest in evolving technologies. Providing a model and case study, Porter's essay may inspire educators to engage students in similar projects and contribute to future collaborative study of both Ellison's published writings and his archived manuscripts.

NOTES

1. In an upper-level seminar on Ellison, the editor once tried an experiment in which students were asked to choose and acquire one of the two book-length biographies. (About two-thirds of them chose the Rampersad, the other third the Jackson.) They were to read in sections on their own, and then we would have periodic biographical sessions interwoven into our study of Ellison's works. They compared what they were learning, how the biographies might be influencing their reading of Ellison's work, and how each biographer approached his subject and subtly revealed his own interests and biases in a way that shapes a reader's sense of Ellison. This method led to some fascinating conversations and helped students see how no one biographical approach is inherently authoritative. This strategy is recommended to anyone who plans to use biography in the classroom, even if only through excerpts from each biographical work.

2. Ellison's introduction to the thirtieth anniversary edition of *Invisible Man* has been reprinted in most copies of the novel since, and it is also available in the *Collected Essays* (473–89).

3. For perspective, at the time of this book's publication, the *MLA International Bibliography* lists just over eighty articles and book chapters on the second novel (in both of its published forms) and over 750 on *Invisible Man*.

4. Teaching *Adventures of Huckleberry Finn* remains controversial, but the Norton Critical Edition effectively leans into teaching it through the controversies.

*Part Two*

# APPROACHES

# Introduction

*Tracy Floreani*

As the twentieth century came to a close, Ralph Ellison's 1952 novel *Invisible Man* appeared on almost every list that attempted to catalog the literary century with concocted parameters like the one hundred most important books of the past one hundred years or the top twenty American books of the twentieth century. The novel's significance had been marked along the way with a Franklin Library Bicentennial edition in 1976 and Random House's thirtieth and fiftieth anniversary commemorative reissues, accompanied by the expected symposia and public events in various locations around the country. The list of "greatests" was revived by the Public Broadcasting Service's 2018 series *The Great American Read*, which saw public television programming dovetail with community read-alongs sponsored by public libraries, and Ellison's most famous novel was once again among the titles in circulation. *Invisible Man* remains a popular text in many high school advanced placement and university literature courses.

Influential in his writing style and his thinking, Ralph Ellison became almost instantly iconic upon the appearance of his most famous published work. The novel's arrival in April 1952 and its subsequent National Book Award signaled a literary watershed, helping to advance the shift from literary modernism to postmodernism and marking a new era of fictional works dealing with issues of race in the United States. Despite the stylistic challenges the novel presents for some readers, most critics and educators would agree that what has caused *Invisible Man* to make almost every "greatest" list is in equal measure its power as a work of literary artistry and the way it engages readers intellectually and emotionally to speak on issues of race and identity—those of the individual, community, and nation—in any given historical context thus far.

As several of the essays in this collection highlight, Ellison's ideas and voice reverberate as we enter the third decade of this century, a period of renewed racial reckoning. The promises of a fully realized participatory democracy remained unfulfilled during those seven years in which Ellison was composing his most famous novel. Voter disenfranchisement and Jim Crow segregation were still the law in the American South, the nation's military branches still observed Jim Crow laws during the war, and de facto segregation ruled housing policy and much of social life in the northern states.[1] While Ellison bristled at the systemic injustices within the culture and his compass reoriented several times toward various ideological allegiances and political projects that he thought might offer remedies, he never gave up on the theoretical potential of the democratic principle—even as its full shortcomings were exposed in the decades after Jim Crow segregation was outlawed.[2] Much has changed in American civic life since the novel's first appearance, but *Invisible Man* still resonates as we acknowledge that "the principle" to which Ellison's unnamed protagonist clings still has not

16    INTRODUCTION

yet been fully enacted—and, sadly, likely will not be for years after the publication of this volume.

Perhaps we see ourselves as a people, in this moment, akin to that protagonist, still coming out of hibernation, poised for action while not yet fully acting, still trying to "affirm the principle on which the country was built" and puzzle out how to embody and pursue that principle—in all of its *e pluribus unum* potential—even as some of our neighbors continue to deny the equality of everyone (Ellison, *Invisible Man* 574). After all, as the protagonist muses, "Weren't we *part of them* [those who "did the violence" historically and more recently] as well as apart from them and subject to die when they died?" (575). We see laughing back at us in the novel the truth that we are still in the midst of a decades-long process, again coming to terms with our failure to cure a cultural sickness, to "figure it out," and really only beginning to awaken to the reality that the narrator speaks: "the fact is that you carry part of your sickness within you" (575).

The question of the national character and its various maladies and embodied contradictions is one that pervades all of Ellison's work. Born in 1913, Ellison came of age in a place that was mediating its own identity as it transitioned from Wild West, semicontrolled federal Indian Territory to just another American locale. Oklahoma had just joined the nation as a state in 1907 and was still a work in progress. The idea of "the Territory" creeps always into Ellison's larger sense of the American mythos. In some ways, Oklahoma's history is a microcosm of US history, a fast-forwarded and condensed replay of pioneering, settler encroachment on indigenous lands, exploitation and then exclusion of Black labor, segregation, and a wave of agricultural populism and socialist activism followed by red-baiting and a wave of conservatism. Ellison's witnessing and keen awareness of this quick unfolding of a place's history seem to have engendered an everlasting interest in what the national character comprises, whether directly, as in the essay "What America Would Be Like without Blacks"; implicitly, as in his essays exploring African American music and the character of American literary fiction; or metaphorically and allegorically, as in his fictional narratives.

Because of Ellison's role as a public intellectual, critical studies and pedagogical approaches to his work that were published before his death in 1994 often take into consideration the critical reception and debates in which he was engaged, such as the famous 1963 Irving Howe essay to which Ellison responded in "The World and the Jug" and the figurative tugs-of-war with the next generation of African American writers and activists, such as Amiri Baraka, James Baldwin, or college students inspired by the nascent Black Power movement. Now, more than twenty-five years since his passing, Ellison as a public figure is less present to a younger generation, while his words and ideas find new purchase outside of the past debates and enjoy new attention in the current set of culture wars in the post-Obama, post-postracial-myth United States.

Ellison is a figure that almost every African American writer after him has had to grapple with in some way, whether directly or indirectly, positively or negatively. He was mentored by Richard Wright and Langston Hughes. He mentored younger writers and critics like James McPherson, Johns S. Wright, Stanley Crouch, and Michael Harper. Toni Morrison communicated with him during her years as an editor at Random House, trying to garner his support for the young Toni Cade Bambara (Morrison, Letter). He butted heads with the likes of Baraka and seemed to steer relatively clear of Baldwin. Colson Whitehead's *The Intuitionist* leans for inspiration on the mysterious elements at work within the plot of *Invisible Man*, while the poet Terrance Hayes grapples with his own disengagement from the Ellison legacy in various versions of the poem "How to Draw an Invisible Man." Ellison's strong presence in African American letters since the mid–twentieth century is indisputable, and, as Matthew Calihman and Gerald Early argue, even Baraka "may be closer than is often thought to Ralph Ellison, who was always alive to the moments in which black lives have gone off-script" (21). Other novelists of color, most notably Chang-rae Lee and Viet Thanh Nguyen, recognize the influence of Ellison's work on their understanding of how invisibility plagues other racialized groups, how histories get erased and recovered through art, and how personal struggles with identities may function as performances within the larger culture. When *The Sympathizer* won the 2016 Pulitzer Prize for fiction, Nguyen frequently mentioned in interviews Ellison's influence on his writing, the elements in *The Sympathizer* that intentionally allude or pay homage to *Invisible Man*, and the fact that he named his own son Ellison because of that influence. Ellison and his work remain perpetually engaged in national and literary conversations, which is why many contributors to this volume discuss how the classroom space works so well for hosting the conversations between Ellison and other authors and filmmakers of various generations.

Those conversations take on a less combative tone today than they did at certain points in Ellison's lifetime. When questioned in a 1973 newspaper interview, "How do you feel about the criticism you sometimes get from black students who feel you haven't been militant enough?" Ellison challenged their root definition by responding, "You be your kind of militant and I'll be my kind of militant" (West). He did firmly believe in the artist as inherently activist and in the novel as not just imaginative entertainment but an immersive means of engaging and moving individuals toward real social change—even in the absence of a prescriptive message. Eddie Glaude, Jr., aptly captures through comparison the gradations of literary activism in the tones of Ellison and a younger contemporary: Ellison "offered a sophisticated treatment of the race problem in the United States that left the ground fertile" for readers to work that space, while Baldwin's overt "anger dripped from the page" and left the "ground scorched" (xxiv). While sometimes personally frustrated and certainly willing to face the truth, Ellison firmly maintained a conceptualization of the fully realized democratic system as a space for both shaping and being shaped by artists. In his younger years, his notion of the role of the writer was more literally militaristic: the artist's social role was one of rendering experience into "a weapon"—but one "more subtle than a machine gun, more effective than a fighter plane!" (letter to Richard

18    INTRODUCTION

Wright, *Selected Letters* 146). Later, the metaphors would become more nuanced as he came to understand the possibilities of metaphor itself as inherently activist. In the social responsibility of the artist, "the interests of art and democracy converge," he would write forty years later, "the development of conscious, articulate citizens being an established goal for a democratic society, and the creation of conscious, articulate characters being indispensable to the creation of resonant compositional centers through which an organic consistency can be achieved in the fashioning of fictional forms" (*Collected Essays* 486). Perhaps his notion of the militant can be understood as a fierce adherence to this belief in the power of art to actualize and a radical expectation that the nation live up to its own promises. In exploring how an art form and its locus might be intertwined, Ellison developed his metaphor of the "raft of hope," alluding to the journey of Huck Finn and Jim in Mark Twain's classic novel (487). He saw a novel—any novel—as itself a kind of vehicle, one that has the potential to move culture rather than physical bodies, not a vehicle sloppily or naively roped together but one carefully crafted of "perception and entertainment that might help keep us afloat as we tried to negotiate the snags and whirlpools that mark our nation's vacillating course toward and away from the democratic ideal" (487). Herein lay the activist potential in metaphor and an artist's deployment of it: a well-crafted, somewhat fun and somewhat risky, not entirely easy to navigate vessel.

While the following sections group the various essays around titles or sets of texts within Ellison's body of work, the contributors to this volume discuss the texts in ways that can be used in a variety of educational settings. In addition to approaches for literature instructors, for example, those teaching writing courses in creative nonfiction will find ways of using Ellison's works as writing models in Clark Barwick's essay on Ellison's letters and Agnieska Tuszynska's essay about teaching a memoir workshop in a prison setting. The contributions that describe teaching Ellison's music essays in the classroom employ a pedagogical lens to add to the already significant multidisciplinary body of criticism on Ellison's music writing, but readers may wonder why there is not a separate section devoted to all of Ellison's essays. Most instructors tend not to teach the essay collections as stand-alone books but use various essays as writing models, as part of the critical apparatus of primary sources for studying the author's fictional works, or as a stepping-off point for creative inspiration or community conversation.[3] Consequently, ideas for using Ellison's essays are peppered throughout this volume, along with ideas for other intertextual dialogues that engage students with both Ellison's contemporaries and relevant twenty-first-century film and literary works. Similarly, while there is one section of this book dedicated to new approaches to *Invisible Man*, "The Invisible One" (as Ellison's wife, Fanny, sometimes called the protagonist) makes cameos throughout this volume. There is only one essay here dedicated specifically to teaching Ellison in the high school classroom, yet teachers will find that many of the strategies discussed in these essays and items in the book's "Materials" section can be adapted for the secondary education setting. This volume's contributors have been generous in sharing their classroom strategies, innovations, assignments, successes, and implicit ideas for do-overs. Readers will find throughout suggestions for preparing students who are new to Ellison to read scenes of racist violence and language as well as suggestions for framing potentially painful discussions about the vulnerability of the Black body in both public and intimate spaces.[4] Instructors will also find many more suggestions for helping students find the power, insight, and imaginative joy in Ellison's writing. Readers are encouraged to engage with these essays in any order, to apply the ideas to their own uses, and to experiment with creative strategies for incorporating Ellison's works in a variety of settings.

The "Approaches" essays are divided into short, focused sections, the first of which returns to the undeniable centerpiece of Ellison's bibliography, *Invisible Man*. With over 750 critical articles and books devoted to the novel, there is no shortage of material resources and critical approaches and perspectives for instructors to turn to in preparing to teach it. The earlier volume in the MLA series Approaches to Teaching World Literature devoted to *Invisible Man* contains multiple ways to think through formalistic, thematic, and contextual approaches that are still applicable today. Yet the increased availability of Ellison's other written work since that volume's publication and the evolution in pedagogical approaches require a new look at the major novel in the context of the author's larger body of work. The essays devoted to the novel here include critical approaches that have gained more traction since that earlier collection and bring the conversation into the context of the third decade of the twenty-first century. Several of the essays in this section explicitly evoke that context, revisiting questions of how Blackness has been elided from much of American history and culture and how civil unrest might provoke a new kind of visibility, how the novel engages these questions in Ellison's own time, and how instructors might engage undergraduates, in particular, with contemporary parallels as they struggle to make sense of an undoubtedly challenging narrative and navigate a challenging world in their daily lives.

This section begins with a personal approach from Ellison's literary executor and friend, the editor of all his posthumous publications, John Callahan, who reflects on coming to understand Ellison's work through his own classroom practices, starting with a first attempt at teaching *Invisible Man* in 1968 and evolving through the decades as he developed a close personal relationship with the author and his work. Callahan's essay includes reflection on the long work of truly understanding Ellison's vision and on moving over time from thinking about the theme of invisibility to more deeply understanding it through increasingly careful consideration of Ellison's linguistic craft. He models how educators benefit from remaining careful students of Ellison's writing themselves and tuning in to each generation of students' understanding of the novel. As the person who helps maintain Ellison's work and bring new posthumous volumes to the public, John Callahan is very likely the first person to ever bring some of Ellison's previously

20    INTRODUCTION

unseen works into a classroom. Calling on his own classroom practice over the years and his deep knowledge of Ellison's personal papers and drafts, Callahan explores how his teaching of Ellison's work pivoted on the author's insistence that for a novel to last from one age to another, its author needs to "tell, retell, and foretell."

The other essays in this section take more specific critical approaches to the novel to affirm its continuing relevancy. Sherry Johnson writes on the challenges of studying and teaching the novel in a culture invested in what she calls "Black lack." While her experiences elucidate the challenges of combating the insistent cultural narrative of Black as "less than," her essay simultaneously makes the case that overtly teaching the value and joy of Black culture is necessary for students' full appreciation of the novel and that the book itself serves as an implicit tool for combating social rhetorics of Black lack.

Kirin Wachter-Grene's work complements Johnson's and moves one step further into joy by focusing specifically on how to create a dialogic space in the classroom that moves from pain to laughter through an intertextual approach to *Invisible Man*'s satire and absurdist humor. She lays out a model for a course with the novel as its centerpiece, teaching it with an eye backward to the folk and early popular culture origins of some of its humor, then bringing it forward to students' own contexts by putting the narrative in conversation with recent films that "heavily riff" on elements of the novel. The overarching focus on how these texts expose "the absurdity of racism" provides her basis for a class that helps students think through multiple registers in response to questions of race.

Although there have been a small handful of critical works on *Invisible Man*'s allusions to queerness, Alvin J. Henry's essay brings the novel into the converging discourses of queer studies and disability studies in ways heretofore neither recognized nor approached in an overtly pedagogical mode.[5] His theory-inflected and intersectional approach helps students to read in ways that make visible the other invisibilities implicit in the cast of characters forming the social fabric of the protagonist's journey, whether because of their implied and pathologized queerness or because of clearly detailed but seldom discussed physical disabilities and mental illnesses.

The section on teaching *Invisible Man* concludes with two more essays that take on specifics within the novel. In tonal counterpoint, both attend to how to teach key portions of the novel in ways that speak to the early-twenty-first-century era of reckoning and social change. J. J. Butts's essay on Ellison and the "urban uprising" considers how to teach the novel's scenes of mass uprising in the light of the specific histories informing the novel's composition in tandem with applications to the uprisings in the movement for Black lives in the present day. Martha Greene Eads takes an intertextual approach to illuminate the strong influence of biblical language on Ellison's narrative and to highlight the novel's motif of love, which is often overshadowed by the chaos, confusion, and frustration that move the protagonist from scene to scene. Pulling the threads of Ellison's biblical syntax and the ongoing motif of love that weaves throughout the novel, she examines how such an approach might enrich students' understanding of Ellison's craft and the protagonist's journey and may even simultaneously "kindle" their own desire "for theologically grounded, socially responsible engagement in the national upheaval we face in this era."

The next section offers wider views of Ellison as a writer and thinker before moving into sections focused on texts from elsewhere in his body of work. Fitting for Ellison, whose intellectual and artistic interests were many, "Broader Contexts" offers a group of essays that, collectively, provide perspectives that demonstrate how Ellison's work implicitly demands engaging it in an interdisciplinary fashion and that doing so moves beyond introducing broad historical contexts or sussing out folk allusions, requiring instead an active conversation with the political, sociological, and musicological. The section begins with the political lens, with an essay from Barbara Foley that draws on her years of teaching various Ellison texts in surveys from introductory to graduate level. Her reflections include practical strategies for selecting and grouping texts by Ellison and others as well as approaches to teaching Ellison as a political thinker by engaging some of the ideological contexts most relevant to the various works. Foley includes brief background information on Ellison's early drafts and introduces a method for teaching with attention to his writing process in which a focus on revision and his carefully crafted patterns of rhetoric and symbol result in an "implied politics." While specifically Marxist in approach, this essay shares a long career of teaching Ellison that provides a model for developing one's own approach to the political and ideological elements within Ellison's work.

The next two essays focus specifically on exploration of the ways in which music undeniably inflects Ellison's fiction and broader worldview. As noted earlier, there is plenty of critical work published on Ellison's relationship with music, but these two essays offer specific frameworks for thinking about and using music in teaching Ellison's works. The essay by Sterling Lecater Bland, Jr., provides practical strategies, listening activities, and assignments that may be applied to classrooms at a variety of levels. Bland argues that spending time helping students learn to listen critically to jazz and understand its "language disruptive of conventional assumptions of form, structure, ideology, and even meaning" will help them better understand not only Ellison's musical allusions but also music as part of his creative compositional "strategy" and a foundational "metaphor for the kind of racialized modernity that Ellison embraces." While Bland's approach is broad and touches on much of Ellison's music writing, the musicologist Jake Johnson takes us into more abstract territory by exploring Ellison's relationship with sound (and even noise), more broadly and theoretically conceptualized. As in Bland's essay, Johnson's contribution offers ideas for how to help students listen critically, but not just to a particular type of music. His focus is on how to help students listen metacognitively in ways that deepen their understanding of the human relationship with sound. Integrating elements of biography and acoustemological theory, Johnson moves beyond allusion and lyrical content within Ellison's work to examine the author's relationship with sound, sound equipment, and

22    INTRODUCTION

listening experiences in order to better understand the invisible influence of the soundscape both on and within Ellison's writing.

From broader contexts, the volume moves to explorations of potential classroom applications for various of Ellison's shorter works: stories, essays, and letters. The short stories especially have received increased attention from teachers since the posthumous release of the previously unpublished stories in *Flying Home*. Before that volume's appearance, the excerpted "battle royal" scene from *Invisible Man* was typically the only short piece anthologized in textbooks. The greater availability of the stories in the past twenty years has expanded the possibilities for including Ellison's work in general literary survey courses and in the secondary-education curriculum. The stories date back to 1937; the genre provided the young writer a form in which to test out his ideas and aesthetic maneuvers as he shifted his energies from the work of critic and editor toward becoming a fiction writer. *Flying Home*'s editor asserts that the early stories chronicle "the discovery of *his* American theme," as he tried out various themes, ideologies, and stylistic experiments (Callahan, Introduction [*Flying Home*] xxiv). Later short pieces, such as "Cadillac Flambé" and a short version of *Juneteenth*, were segments of the second novel-in-progress published in magazines and literary journals as stories, and some of these have continued to find traction in the high school and college classroom as stand-alone pieces, even with the unfinished novel now available in two different forms.[6] The accessibility of the short stories has proven especially useful for high school teachers who want to teach Ellison but have found that the demands of the curriculum and standardized testing regimen, lack of student preparedness for challenging reading, or controversies over some of *Invisible Man*'s more adult content prevent their teaching that novel in the secondary setting.[7]

Keith Byerman's essay provides a helpful overview of the entire collection in *Flying Home* and offers approaches to the stories for educators at any level who are interested in using fiction to teach histories of race. He offers a range of possibilities for bringing historical contexts to bear on Ellison's stories and, conversely, using the stories themselves as a means of teaching such histories as those of the Tuskegee Airmen, the period of racial terror in the early twentieth century,[8] African American folk beliefs, or intersections of race and gender before World War II. In contrast to the wider tour of possibilities in Byerman's essay, Paul Devlin's contribution zeroes in closely on just two titles to model an exercise in using Ellison's stories comparatively, in this case through the theme of intergenerational communication and technology in the stories "Flying Home" and "Cadillac Flambé." The close readings of these two stories illuminate the possibilities for using them comparatively in various types of courses: as a standalone unit or to bookend a study of *Invisible Man*; to explore a range of values and views within African American society during various historical periods; or even to help students reflect on intergenerational tensions in their own experiences. The English language arts education specialist Aimée Myers uses "King of the Bingo Game" to demonstrate how high school teachers can effectively engage Ellison's work through the teaching framework of culturally and historically responsive literacy. In so doing, she advances not just a method for analysis of a story but a model that engages young people meaningfully in an exploration of the real-world notion of resistance to social systems that oppress and deny agency.

Like the short stories, Ellison's essays have enjoyed growing appreciation by readers and have proven useful to educators in a variety of contexts, whether for including shorter pieces in a curriculum with limited room or for broadening the critical apparatus for understanding Ellison's longer works. Agnieska Tuszynska's contribution provides a model for using one of Ellison's essays as the centerpiece of a curriculum that approaches a piece first through analysis and then through stages of research and innovative personal-writing activities. Using the long essay "An Extravagance of Laughter," Tuszynska describes a process for helping students analyze the nuances of social systems and spaces depicted in Ellison's descriptions and expands on his thinking about the concept of freedom by taking the discussion to nontraditional classroom spaces and audiences: the prison classroom or formerly incarcerated student populations. Those who do not teach in such settings will find in her essay a perspective that expands their understanding of the potential in all of Ellison's essays as well as a pedagogical approach applicable to settings focused on invested conversation about the real stakes of our daily movements, on traditional academic analysis, or on memoir writing.

Clark Barwick's contribution to this collection follows with insights into helping students discover more about Ellison as a writer by focusing specifically on his letters, most of which have only recently become more accessible to the public in the critically acclaimed *Selected Letters*. Barwick details how the letters can be used to access autobiographical information or to understand the development of Ellison's writerly voice and how, as does Tuszynska, students can use the letters as models for discovering their own writing voices through the epistolary form. While not exhaustive in covering all of Ellison's nonfiction writing, each of these essays provides a model for using a specific essay or letter in ways applicable to multiple teaching scenarios: undergraduate surveys, Ellison-specific seminars, or nontraditional workshops.

The final section of this book may prove useful for those who have wanted to incorporate the posthumous novel into their teaching or who want to revisit including it after having found the task daunting in past attempts. Unlike many of the previously referenced works, *Juneteenth* has been available to educators for just over twenty years, and the subsequent volume *Three Days before the Shooting . . .* for only about a decade. Realistically, many will choose *Invisible Man* over the unfinished second novel if they cannot fit both within the parameters of a course design. However, a complete study of Ellison requires attention to his entire body of work and the vision he had for the mythic second act of his career as a novelist. To assist in this regard, the section opens with an essay by Keyana Parks that helps readers see how we might place *Juneteenth* within a course dedicated to Ellison's work and help students grapple with the

24   INTRODUCTION

trajectory of Ellison's career and the evolution of his thinking about key intellectual interests. By approaching the second novel through its mysteries—the legendary fire that destroyed part of the manuscript, the conspiracy theories surrounding that episode, and the mystery of its incomplete state decades later—Parks offers critical strategies, companion readings, and assignments for teaching the novel on its own terms, comparatively with *Invisible Man*, or in relation to current events involving the same themes of "individualism, American democracy, and racism." As an alternative to *Juneteenth* in a course's reading list, I propose in the final essay embracing the incompleteness of the novel by teaching *Three Days before the Shooting* . . . . By reading the novel as a work in progress, creative writing and literary studies students can come to empathize with the intellectual and artistic challenges inherent in enacting a vision for a long narrative. Arguing for how *Three Days* may allow them to experience the episodic nature of Ellison's writing process, the essay poses a model for partially mimicking that process by approaching the book through episode-based close reading and writing exercises that encourage students to also pull small pieces together toward a larger thematic vision.

Ellison's work remains an invigorating challenge in the classroom space, and even those who have long read and taught his work know how much remains to be explored. His writing welcomes so many critical approaches, and the growing body of available primary works gives us more to choose from even as *Invisible Man* endures as a powerful and popular classic. While the essays in this volume do not claim to take on every critical approach available or to offer interpretations of each title in Ellison's bibliography, they provide a useful set of case studies for deliberate thinking about how to approach his writings in the classroom. Perhaps this book can inspire new ideas for keeping students engaged with Ellison's work and for participating in the fulfillment of his ideal of the writer's potential contribution to democracy, one reader at a time.

NOTES

1. As Ellison's biographers detail, he refused to risk being drafted into the US military because of its segregation policy and instead enlisted in the US Merchant Marine.

2. For compelling explorations of how Ellison's attitudes about the democratic ideal shifted before and after the *Brown v. Board of Education* decision was enacted, see Ghatage; Warren ("Chaos").

3. In the initial queries fielded for this book, several people reported that they have used Ellison's work for extra- or cocurricular diversity, equity, and inclusion sessions or as starting points for nonacademic community conversations on current events.

4. Ellison's choice to include overtly racist language and violence in his writing was intentional. In keeping with the editorial decision to not replicate offensive terms that appear in quoted material, the n-word is represented as "n____" in quotations.

5. At the time of writing, there are no published works dealing with the novel from a disability studies perspective and only a handful (all from the early 2000s) dealing with

queerness. See Alexander; Ferguson's chapter "The Specter of Woodridge: Canonical Formations and the Anticanonical in *Invisible Man*" (54–81); Hardin; Kim; Steward.

6. "Cadillac Flambé" first appeared in *American Review*, vol. 16, 1973, pp. 249–69; "Juneteenth" was initially published in *The Quarterly Review of Literature*, vol. 4, 1965, pp. 262–76.

7. One of the most recent, widely publicized bans occurred in September 2013 in Randolph County, North Carolina, when the novel was purged from high school library shelves after controversy about its inclusion in a summer reading program for juniors. Some parents lodged complaints that its content was "vulgar," but a national outcry in defense of the novel resulted in an arrangement for the county's high school students to receive free copies on request. The ban was reversed and the book was reshelved in school libraries nine days later.

8. The phrase "racial terror" is used by the Equal Justice Initiative (eji.org) to describe the over four thousand socially sanctioned lynchings that took place in the United States between 1880 and 1940.

# *INVISIBLE MAN* IN THE TWENTY-FIRST CENTURY

# Layers of Identity:
## Learning to Teach *Invisible Man*

*John F. Callahan*

Late in his life, Ralph Ellison answered a letter from a recent immigrant from France, a young woman writing to thank him for revealing so much about the mystery and possibility of her new nation in *Invisible Man*. In his letter Ellison speculates on the "willing collaboration" the novel form generates between a novelist and an individual reader, a collaboration he had amplified forty years before in the style, substance, and shape of *Invisible Man*. Readers, Ellison believed, provoke a novel into life "by bringing to it emotions and insights gained from their own unique experiences" (*Selected Letters* 961). He went even further, asserting that "each reader recreates a different book by playing his or her own variations on the writer's all too limited picture of reality" (962).

Ellison's implication that each student brings a different *Invisible Man* to the classroom would not seem to bode well for the prospects of those daring to teach it. Yet even though I was not fully aware of these extravagant claims during most of the five decades in which I taught the novel, I sensed that *Invisible Man* encouraged a radical fluidity on the part of both teacher and students. The more I taught the book, the more I felt something of an impostor in the sense that I was a learner more than a teacher.

Perhaps I had been an impostor well before I was a teacher, beginning at the cusp of the 1960s, when as an undergraduate I stayed up all night reading *Invisible Man* and the next morning cut a Tacitus class in which I was clinging to a D. I refused to desert Invisible Man. I did not know that his journey (and mine) would not end after the novel was over. That May was also an unforeseen time of sit-ins at Southern lunch counters. Organized and carried out by Black students with a few white recruits, the sit-ins awakened many sleepwalking Americans, old as well as young.

But I did not go south. I stayed in school. There, I answered the question Invisible Man posed in his last sentence: "Who knows but that, on the lower frequencies, I speak for you?" "Who knows?" I whispered with pursed lips . . . "I know."

I knew I would reread *Invisible Man*. I had no idea—none—I would ever teach the novel, let alone teach it over and over, year after year, with fear and trembling each time as one generation of students yielded to the next from the fall of 1968 to the spring of 2015.

I first taught (or, better, wrestled with) *Invisible Man* in my mid twenties, starting out where I would stay, and end up, at Lewis and Clark, a liberal arts college in Portland, Oregon. I had gone there to write in absentia my dissertation on F. Scott Fitzgerald and American history. I wanted to learn how to teach on my own rather than as the sequestered teaching assistant I'd been at the University of Illinois, Urbana-Champaign.

In the chaotic fall of 1968, I met the poet Michael S. Harper. Harper had published a few poems (the remarkable "Dear John, Dear Coltrane" comes to mind) but not yet a collection. As for me, I was trying to learn and practice the discipline required to research and write a thesis worthy of becoming a real book.

In the middle of a warm Indian summer afternoon, Harper and I struck up a first conversation that did not end until dusk. (Not even then, in fact, because for the next forty-eight years we had many talks in what now seem like long passages in a friendship book unfinished when he passed away out of season in 2016.) Michael befriended me that afternoon; he took me under his cold eye and swift wing, brandishing the archangel's fiery sword above my head when it was necessary. He did so partly because F. Scott Fitzgerald intrigued him and partly because I was struggling over how to teach *Invisible Man*. When I nudged him shyly to tell how *he* taught *Invisible Man*, he refused. Instead, he read to me the first poem in the collection he was about to peddle to any publishers willing to read the manuscript—and there were not many of those in 1968. He said nothing more, but, listening to him read "Brother John" out loud, I gaped.

> Black man:
> I'm a black man;
> I'm black; I am—
> A black man; black—
> I'm a black man;
> I'm a black man;
> I'm a man; black—
> I am—

## 28 LAYERS OF IDENTITY

As he read his stuff, Harper's voice became a tenor saxophone. The last stanza was an intricate set of variations on the first. When he put down the manuscript and his eyes caught my face, he looked away, a little embarrassed. After I stammered incoherent words of praise, he stood up.

"Man, I got to go. My old lady's waiting dinner."

He grabbed a characteristic armful of books and headed out. Then he turned back in my direction, a magnificent grin commanding his face.

"Having trouble with *Invisible Man*?" he mocked. "I say, look, man. You're not the only one. Look what it did to me—and I'm a blood."

I tried. But I did not teach *Invisible Man* in a true sense of the word that fall. Nor did I *do Invisible Man* in the vainglorious erotic boast of the time. Fortunately, I knew enough to start with invisibility, but for some reason Michael's incomparable riff on Ellison's "I am an invisible man" did not soar from my jumbled underground. If he had already written the amazing later line "Soul and race are private dominions," and I had read it, I might have dared to enter Ellison's novel through the eyes of Michael Harper and his poem ("Here Where Coltrane Is"). Even better, if I had understood that his refusal to answer my question about how he taught *Invisible Man* was his attempt to teach me that a "very stern discipline" is required to understand and confront your own "private dominions" of "soul and race," I might have entered the novel through my truest eye. But I did not yet understand.

Instead, I traipsed around the makeshift basement classroom lighting cigarette after cigarette (in those days smoking was permitted if none of your students objected). Soon I couldn't help but notice their expressions turning from amused indulgence toward their young instructor to impatience at my self-protective propriety toward Ellison's game-changing metaphor of invisibility. Hindsight soon told me that if I had done an honest deep dive into what I thought qualified as invisibility or visibility in things and persons, with no holds barred, I might have reached them "on the lower frequencies."

When asked if Ellison had "layers of identity" in mind, I did not grasp the student's arm and pull myself up on the raft. Rather, I retreated to where I started and merely underlined the word I'd written on the blackboard: *invisible*. I was determined to push ahead to some *right* definition of invisibility. It did not occur to me to let the students in on the secret I was only beginning to grasp and wouldn't have dared utter for fear of turning the class upside down. It was nothing more or less than the merciless fact that, confined in desks that were chairs and chairs that were desks, the individual young men and women in my class were more invisible to me, their teacher, than I, their teacher, was to them.

"Them's years," Invisible Man's grandfather told his grandson in a dream (Ellison, *Invisible Man* 33), and like that invisible young man it took me years to heed Yeats and forsake "embroideries" in favor of walking "naked" (Yeats 127). In my early years as a teacher, I chose the new critical "embroideries" that had been used and misused in graduate school. I keyed on a few passages

*John F. Callahan* 29

(characters, speeches, places, objects, names) treating the novel's particulars as if they were images and lines in poems to be explicated rather than restless excursions into the picaresque, vernacular forms and language Ellison so clearly intended. Fortunately, the students unfolded their arms and scratched what itched *them*. They followed their nagging, irrepressible different hunches that the condition Ellison and his invisible man declared as invisibility might be theirs, too, in a guise that belonged to them.

My first time teaching *Invisible Man*, and also in subsequent years, young women often took the lead, coming to my rescue as well as Invisible Man's and even Ralph Ellison's. Somehow they were able to see and testify how the predicament explored in *Invisible Man* began as a racial condition and predicament in Jim Crow America. However, far from becoming resolved and solved on racial grounds, Ellison's novel soon radiates out to human relations everywhere in different human contexts all over the earth. Neither were the young men wallflowers. They joined the women to chime in with comments like "I'm not Black . . ." (or "I haven't had Invisible Man's *actual* experiences"), "but that doesn't mean people see who I am inside."

Such assertions carried the ball down the field, and I recovered enough of my balance to guide our scrutiny of how and why the narrator is still an invisible man in the epilogue after he's told the story of his invisibility. In short, my first efforts teaching *Invisible Man* were not a total loss. The students were wary, willing, and ready, provided that they and I learned that discussion was needed to put our readers' lives into the mix of the life of the guy whose memoir is Ellison's novel. Though I hadn't yet read nor had Ellison written his letter about "willing collaboration," these first students began to teach me that what they brought from "their own unique experiences" made *Invisible Man* a "different book," as Ellison would write to the last student he wrote in the distant future of 1989 (*Selected Letters* 961–62).

In the meantime, year after year, I followed Invisible Man's vernacular, picaresque journey through its labyrinth of places ("border area" on the edge of Harlem [Ellison, *Invisible Man* 5]; Black college in the Deep South; Men's House and Mary Rambo's room in Harlem; a bigger apartment than he needs rented by the Brotherhood "on the upper East Side . . . in a mixed Spanish-Irish neighborhood" [331]; underground hole, again); unforgettable characters (his grandfather; Bostonian trustee Mr. Norton; Jim Trueblood, incestuous father and natural-born bluesman; Black college president Dr. Bledsoe; Miss Susie Gresham, "guardian of hot young women" [114]; the vet, locked up because of wise ravings considered insane; Liberty Paints boiler man Lucius Brockway; Mary Rambo; Tod Clifton; Brother Jack, the "great white father" of the Brotherhood; Brother Tarp; Ras the Exhorter/Destroyer; Sybil—"'YOU WERE RAPED BY SANTA CLAUS—SURPRISE'" [522]; and the shape-shifter Rinehart, to name a few); wild episodes (reefer-inspired meditation, "the end is in the beginning" [6]; the "battle royal" ritual of white power and dominion; Invisible Man's speech while swallowing blood; a treacherous showdown with Bledsoe; the vet's "be your own

30     LAYERS OF IDENTITY

father" warning; Invisible Man's mixed-message protest speech at a Harlem eviction; the yam man's advice; and on and on to the riot in Harlem at the narrative's but not the novel's end; the epilogue, the beginning in the end); and, above all, as Ellison wrote in his address on receiving the National Book Award in 1953, idiom, idiom, and more idiom: "an alive language swirling with over three hundred years of American living, a mixture of the folk, the Biblical, the scientific and the political. Slangy in one stance, academic in another, loaded poetically with imagery at one moment, mathematically bare of imagery in the next" (*Collected Essays* 152).

With all those riches, it is little wonder that teaching *Invisible Man* led me to different ways of shaping its complexity. In the mid-1970s, when issues of aesthetics and identity threw into relief Ellison's striking choices regarding time, I stressed how the novel flows in *B*, *A*, *C* currents of time. The prologue is a kind of present past—call it *B*. In it, Invisible Man broods about invisibility and prepares to write his story in his underground lair where Ellison unspools all the chapters Invisible Man narrates. They are *A*, the past he's lived before he escapes the Harlem riot in a coal cellar underground. In the epilogue that follows, he writes, also from underground, in the immediate present that hovers between past and future, *C*. On the last page, he declares that he "must come out. I must emerge . . . since there's a possibility that even an invisible man has a socially responsible role to play" (438–39). Year after year, in a belated, obvious bit of commonsense pedagogy, I devoted the first class session to the prologue, the last to the epilogue, and in between my students and I followed Invisible Man's picaresque journey from South to North in Jim Crow America from the 1920s to the early 1950s, before the *Brown v. Board of Education* decision of 1954.

Paraphrasing Ellison's remarks about chaos and form in the epilogue, I must admit that the foregoing was a pattern that also informed other scholarly work I was doing. The first was an essay I wrote in 1977 called "Chaos, Complexity, and Possibility: The Historical Frequencies of Ralph Waldo Ellison."

Reenter Michael S. Harper. You'll recall that he had been the big-brotherly guardian archangel keeping me on a more-or-less disciplined course toward finishing my dissertation; one of his outsized gestures had been showing up at my office with the great gift of bluish, blurred, mimeographed copies of two Ralph Ellison essays. He thought they might awaken the weary pores in my mind and spark me to come up with something original on what I'd been insisting all too vaguely was F. Scott Fitzgerald's preoccupation with the Civil War in *Tender Is the Night*. The essays were "Society, Morality, and the Novel," from 1956, and "Tell It Like It Is, Baby," also started in Rome the same year but abandoned, not to be picked up and finished until 1965. Since then, they have become essays inspiring to many, and certainly they bestowed an amazing grace that enabled me to do much more than I thought I could in unraveling how history worked in Fitzgerald.

Out of gratitude and appreciation as well as curiosity, I sought for almost ten years to write about Ellison's essays. However, if this had been the shadow, the act was a long time coming. Like the notes for their own novels that English professors tuck away in an otherwise-undisturbed desk drawer, I scribbled things each year from 1969 on when I was teaching *Invisible Man* along with these two essays. My mantra was still "history, history, and more history." I was the proverbial academic flash in the pan, a young writer who falls back on talking about a second book rather than writing it. Yet, as life went along, I wrote about other Black writers, though Ellison never left my mind, and my slowly emerging book had to do with the oral tradition.

Lightning struck in 1977 while I was in Chicago for a yearlong National Endowment for the Humanities institute and came across a call for papers on the theme of the uses and meaning of history in modern Black American fiction for the *Negro American Literature Forum* (which was about to become the *Black American Literature Forum*). Noticing that papers needed to be postmarked by the following day, I crumpled the flyer and was about to toss it into the round file with a mock jump shot when I heard a taunting voice.

"Fool," the gremlin said, "seven or eight years you've been telling yourself and other people, too, you've got big things to say about Ralph Ellison and history. You try your students' patience by filling every vacuum in class by shouting at them, 'history, history, history.'"

The gnarled little bastard left me standing in the Regenstein Library, a blank stare on my face until the words on a small sign on the wall seemed to grow larger as I focused on them. "Those with faculty status at the University are entitled to 24-hour access to the library." I'd seen it before and mocked it in reverse snobbery along with a couple of other fellows at the Institute on Culture and Technology fond of masquerading as "regular guys" in the hothouse demesne of Hyde Park.

In a jiffy, I went home and asked my wife to do bedtime duties with our three-year-old, which we loved doing together. I gathered up my portable typewriter along with a few books and a bottle of Wite-Out, said good night to my family, and at dusk headed back to the library. I found an unreserved carrel on the third floor and took a silent blood oath not to emerge until I batted out a draft. To my surprise, I did just that, and as first light was breaking I arrived back home, where I grabbed two or three hours of agitated sleep and, with the help of black coffee, edited and corrected the double-digit pages, slapped my "Historical Frequencies" title on the first page, and sent it off to the editor of the journal.

Writing this reminds me that over the many years I taught *Invisible Man*, I kept in mind Reverend Alonzo Hickman's exhortations to his African American congregation in the "Juneteenth" episode Ellison published from his novel-in-progress. "Keep to the rhythm," Hickman urges members over the generations before *Brown v. Board of Education*, "keep to the way" (Ellison, *Juneteenth* [Vintage] 131).

Lately, unspooling my many years teaching *Invisible Man*, I realized that for a half dozen years before I took the plunge and wrote "The Historical Frequencies of Ralph Waldo Ellison," I was digging down to deepen and widen the theme of history in my *Invisible Man* classes. As it does when we least expect it, time stretched out, elongated over the years while my students and I wrestled with *Invisible Man*, glad that its genie, once out of the bottle, continued to release fresh drafts of air into the world.

In that 1977 essay, I contended that the "historical frequencies" Ellison explored in his essays provided a way to read the classics of American literature as well as *Invisible Man*. For Ellison, the "moral predicament of the nation" was present at its founding and has continued to be at the center of its still-precarious experiment. What I did as a teacher led to what I did as a scholar, and, once out in the world, what I'd written boomeranged back at me in my classes. "Historical frequencies" is a phrase that germinated slowly from my attempts to teach *Invisible Man*. The theme led to the idea that Ellison's essays were a way to read past and future classics of American literature with *Invisible Man* as the exemplar. And I would be withholding important evidence if I did not note that the published essay had the additional unforeseen, unintended consequence of my meeting Ralph Ellison and soon becoming his close friend, and he mine.

Time does not stand still. The events I've described were not the last or only confluence between *Invisible Man* and other seemingly unrelated preoccupations in my teaching and writing.

Gradually during the 1970s and 1980s I became fascinated by the spoken in the written word. I was familiar, I thought, with the tradition of call-and-response and was finding its pattern in the fictions of many African American writers, not least among them Ellison's *Invisible Man*. Yet I fell into the same trap I'd had with history, reducing multifaceted reality to a single word—in this case, *voice*. As usual, my students were patient while I became insistent, so much so that one day a young woman put up her hand and said, "Professor Callahan, I know I should know the answer, but what do you mean by *voice*?"

I paused, stammering with increasing sheepishness before I realized that I didn't know, *really* know, what I meant.

Back in the classroom I did my best to finesse the question and promised a full answer the next day. The hour before the next class it came to me with stunning clarity that what I needed to sort out if I were to write a worthy book was call-and-response. Once more, a student's courage about what she knew and what she didn't know had rubbed off on me. For example, I did not understand yet that what Ralph Ellison was playing with in Invisible Man's several speeches was not something vague like voice but was complex and particular. He was adapting the pattern of call-and-response to the changing rhetorical frequencies and contradictory purposes of his narrator's contingent voice. Invisible Man's move from speaker to writer as he tells his story and tries for eloquence on the written page embodies Ellison's commitment to show how "every serious novel is, beyond its immediate thematic preoccupations, *a discussion of the craft*," and also how Ellison intended his own novel to be very much a novel "bound up with the notion of nationhood" (Ellison, "Society" 699–700; emphasis mine). As they had before and would again, my students beckoned me toward theory and form in ways Ellison might well have called "somewhat 'mammy-made' or eclectic" (*Selected Letters* 739).

*In the African-American Grain: The Pursuit of Voice in Twentieth-Century Black Fiction* published in 1988, but when the University of Illinois published a paperback edition, I insisted the subtitle be changed to "Call-and-Response in Twentieth-Century Black Fiction." In both editions, the climactic chapter is called "Frequencies of Eloquence: The Performance and Composition of *Invisible Man*."

Since 1982, the Random House paperback edition of *Invisible Man* has included Ellison's lengthy autobiographical introduction. By then, my students knew that Ellison and I were friends. After a particularly good class, I might reward them with a tale or two about a dinner I'd enjoyed recently with him and Fanny at 730 Riverside Drive. For several years, I devoted a class to exploring how "Brave Words for a Startling Occasion," the address Ellison gave on *Invisible Man*'s gestation when receiving the National Book Award in 1953, was instructive about the published novel (*Collected Essays* 151–54). Coincidentally, a close friend, Reed College microbiologist Stephen Arch, who loved reading novels in his spare time, urged me to read Thomas Kuhn's *The Structure of Scientific Revolutions*. I did, and I was struck by the similarity of Kuhn's argument that scientists who ended up creating revolutionary paradigms began by trying over and over again to solve the problem using the prevailing paradigm. Only when they failed and failed, and, failing, moved outside it did they solve their particular problem. And they did so by concluding that the specific circumstances of the problem required a new paradigm.

In the case of *Invisible Man*, Ellison, thinking through questions of novelistic style and form in the mid and late 1940s, considered the two dominant forms of the contemporary American novel. He found the "tight, well-made Jamesian" novel "too concerned with 'good taste' and stable areas. Nor," he added, "could I safely use the forms of the 'hard-boiled' novel, with its dedication to physical violence, social cynicism and understatement," not to mention "its monosyllabic utterance." He concluded that for his story of invisibility, a "novel whose range was both broader and deeper was needed" (*Collected Essays* 152). For what he had to write, the language had to be the vernacular; its form, a picaresque rendering of the rhythms and riffing improvisations of jazz. Soon I was making the case that Ellison created something of a new paradigm for the novel in ways similar to what Kuhn's scientists did for their branches of science. In short, Ellison melded qualities that are essential to unfolding discoveries in science and necessary to keep the novel a resilient, evolving form: qualities of both the traditionalist and the iconoclast.

I'll close with the confession that although I retired several years ago, I have not resisted invitations to teach a *Zoom* class or two on *Invisible Man* and, now, *Juneteenth*, in the chaotic years of 2020, 2021, and 2022. Rethinking and teaching

34  LAYERS OF IDENTITY

*Juneteenth* twenty years after its initial publication in 1999, I looked for an angle whose urgent importance I had not dared explore. Leafing through *Trading Twelves*, the Ellison-Murray correspondence I edited with Al Murray in 2000, I discovered, as if I'd never seen it before, Murray's vivid memory of Ellison telling him, when the two men ran into each other in 1945 "on Seventh Avenue near 135th Street" in Harlem, that "stories endure not only from generation to generation but also from age to age because literary truth amounts to prophecy." In that same conversation, Ellison added emphatically, "Telling is not only a matter of retelling but also of foretelling" (Murray, Preface xxiii).

As I prepare to teach and write something new on each of these novels, I intend to attempt a medley, and then some, of what I've done as teacher and writer on Ralph Ellison. The tease I'll give the reader is that I'd like to see what there is of foretelling and prophecy in the last pages of the classic *Invisible Man* and the ever-provisional *Juneteenth*, from the unfinished, epic second novel.

NOTE

I am warmly, keenly grateful to Paige Talbot of the English faculty at South Seattle College for providing her memories, as well as those of friends, of studying *Invisible Man* at Lewis and Clark College. She also wrote an invaluable critique and made many wise suggestions, which vastly improved the initial draft of this essay.

# Resisting Black-Lack Readings of *Invisible Man*

## *Sherry Johnson*

It was a period in my undergraduate critical approaches course. We were using Ralph Ellison's *Invisible Man* as a principal text; in this class period we'd continue our discussion of the text and literary theory with a focus on African American literary theory. My objective was that students would walk away understanding the ways that this theory helped them *see* ways of analysis that before had been *invisible* in their reading. We'd just reread Trueblood's tale, and the amused way in which I tried to animate his voice was met with silence. The students didn't get it. One even asked, "What's so funny?" Good question. My plan this class period was to introduce the long tale and blues humor. We discussed Ole John and Ole Massa in the folktales; I pointed out the humorous manner in which one could address serious matters. We talked about the trickster character and how he wasn't above telling tall tales to reach his desired ends. We returned to Trueblood and the story he told Mr. Norton. In groups, the students analyzed the tale for clues of trickster elements. It was a bit challenging getting the students to speak, as is wont to occur at times—certainly in the midwestern, predominantly white classroom in which race was an overt part of the discussion. At just about the end of the class period, one young woman raised her hand: "I don't believe this is a tale, Dr. Johnson. I believe that this man raped his daughter and now he's using her to get money for it."

Let me provide a little more context for the course. I've already noted that we use Ellison's *Invisible Man* as the principal text. Over the course of the semester, we study *Invisible Man* through a survey of literary theories. Using one main novel along with a number of secondary resources is a pedagogical strategy that helps students meet the principal learning objectives: to understand theory as providing a lens through which to analyze a text and that each theory offers perspectives that make various topics and themes in a text evident; finally, after going through a variety of theories, students walk away understanding that even within a particular theory there is variety. Said another way, there is not a static way of reading any text.

Over the course of the semester, I repeatedly emphasize the course learning objectives. Typically, students approach the various theories with confusion and disorientation. Many are new to theory; moreover, they walk into the classroom believing that there is one way to read a text. Consequently, as they begin to see things anew, I typically answer questions for clarification; as we begin to compare how one theory opens analysis in one way but closes off analysis in another, we discuss the ramifications. And, to shore up students' understanding, I provide multiple opportunities for practicing analysis both individually and in group settings.

36 RESISTING BLACK-LACK READINGS

Given the work we'd accomplished over the course of the semester, and in this particular unit covering parts of the African American Vernacular Tradition (AAVT), I was stunned—not just by the student's bold declaration but also by her tone, which was resolute. She might as well have proclaimed that she already knew all that she needed to know about this dirty old Black man; literary theory and the AAVT be damned—nothing would alter what she knew. Of course, she *could* be right. One most certainly could read the Trueblood episode in the primary way that the text invites; moreover, one can read it at face value and still analyze it effectively through the African American rhetorical strategy of signifying or through blues humor that highlights life's absurdities. But the student could not state, based on what she knew, the analysis I'd provided to be wrong. She simply *knew*.

It was time to go. I quickly reminded students of what was needed for the next period and dismissed the class. But I couldn't get the incident out of my mind. What was it about the other theories that had allowed her to trust what I'd presented? What was it about this one that made her resist the reading of the Trueblood scene as a tall tale told so that he may continue to receive white philanthropy? Of course, I don't mean to suggest that there is any singular reading of the text; I'm most interested here in what informed the student's response.

It's not the first time I have received hostile student responses aloud; silence, too, is a commonplace demonstration of hostility. Teaching Ellison's *Invisible Man* presents challenges because of its richness and complexity. Still, before we can even get to discussions about what *Invisible Man* offers readers concerning what it means to be an American in the United States, we must face the challenge of students who see Blackness and Black literature as pathological or inferior, as solely for Black people, or as an educational opportunity for racists. Like the student discussed above, the vast majority of students come to the reading of Black American literature woefully unprepared, having never read any before. Many are often resistant, if not openly hostile. The anecdote I relay at the beginning of the essay serves to emphasize the ease with which a student accepted textual interpretations from other literary theories but resisted a reading of the provocative Trueblood scene that viewed the character as a trickster playing upon white philanthropists' preconceived notions of Black pathology in order to take their donations. I do not mean to suggest that any student new to Black literature or to literary theory who provides an alternate reading is anti-Black; rather, I mean to suggest that her *resistance*—based on something she could not name— is anti-Black. My goals in writing this essay are multifold. First, I am interested in providing a way for educators to think about how the roots of anti-Blackness in the United States inform students' responses to the text, and second, I want to give strategies for addressing these responses.

There are two perspectives that inform the methodology I propose for educators in thinking about and responding to students' responses to the text. First is my perspective as a Black student reader in a predominantly white classroom at a predominantly white institution (PWI). The second perspective is that of a Black woman professor reader, again in a predominantly white classroom at a PWI. As such, the suggestions I make for teaching *Invisible Man* come from a Black perspective. I also consider how my Black perspective impacts learning and teaching Black texts in an anti-Black culture.

Educational development on principles of Black lack makes discussions of race difficult for many students—regardless of their race.[1] Yet seeing race is critical to the reading of Ralph Ellison's *Invisible Man*. How, then, to read it? The theory for critical reading that Toni Morrison offers in the essay "Black Matters" opens an opportunity for approaching the reading and teaching:

> There seems to be a more or less tacit agreement among literary scholars that, because American literature has been clearly the preserve of white male views, genius, and power, those views, genius, and power are without relationship to and removed from the overwhelming presence of black people in the United States. This agreement is made about a population that preceded every American writer of renown and was, I have come to believe, one of the most furtively radical impinging forces on the country's literature. The contemplation of this black presence is central to any understanding of our national literature and should not be permitted to hover at the margins of the literary imagination.　　　(*Playing in the Dark* 5)

While Morrison speaks of the ways in which the (in)visible presence of Black people is critical to the stories largely told by white writers in American literature, the concept is useful, too, for questions of how the culture of that Black population impacts mainstream American culture—particularly, as I posit, that consideration of the centrality of anti-Black culture to American culture is critical to the ways in which students approach the text. Finally, while Morrison's call is for literary critics and scholars to see Black figures in American literature and investigate the ways that these figures inform white notions of self, it is also interesting to consider how the cultural norm of ignoring or not speaking about race impacts white readings of Black texts in the classroom. Reading Black texts is related to the same practice of willful ignorance—or what James Baldwin might have called innocence (*Fire* 292). Or, if it is not willful, then certainly a deliberately developed sense, throughout United States cultural history, that there is little value in that which one might see as Black—so much so that students enter the classroom seeing Black in what can be summed up in two ways: Black as "wrong" and Black as "not (for) me." Both result in a discomfort in reading and discussing the text that shows that white readers see Black as outside of and beyond themselves. It's an interesting quandary when reading Black texts in largely white spaces because one thing that "Black Matters" makes clear is that, in spite of the absence of discussions of them in white American literature, the Black figure has everything to do with the way that Americans have historically identified as white.

## Reading as a Student

I first encountered Ralph Ellison's *Invisible Man* in graduate school. I was troubled from the start. I don't mean from the prologue; I mean from the moment the Invisible Man turns off the beaten path to take Mr. Norton to Trueblood's place. My marginal notes in that first copy indicate my disbelief: "No way . . . ," "Seriously??," and simply "????" appear frequently. I couldn't understand why Invisible Man would bring Mr. Norton to see Trueblood, a man who was an embarrassment to the well-to-do Black people about town—and certainly on the campus. I couldn't understand why he wouldn't find *some* mask to don for this elderly white man to prevent a deeper foray into trouble at the Golden Day. The protagonist's discomfort indicates his knowing, on some level, that this is not the direction in which he should go. It was difficult for me to believe that a Black character, born to and raced/raised in the United States by Black people so as to survive, could be so foolish with a white person. What was this narrator *doing?* I kept reading to see what I'd find, although I didn't understand what the point was because I didn't believe that it was possible to be so daft.

In classroom discussions, my contributions centered largely on the question, But what is Ellison doing? I meant a number of things by that question. I wanted to know what Ellison meant to show by writing a character who not only presented as invisible but who was also blind.[2] What was it that *I* was supposed to take away? Looking back, I realize that how one is raced/raised in an anti-Black culture informs the reading of Ellison's *Invisible Man.* It is one reason the book disoriented me; it countered how I had been raced/raised in my Black community to interact with white people in authority.

Eventually, I came to realize that in the protagonist, Ellison was showing what happens to a young person who is wholly disconnected from Black folk culture, one who sees Black Americans as complex and multidimensional—as human beings. Coming from predominantly Black spaces, Invisible Man was lost because he didn't understand the value of his culture for survival. Ultimately, we see him "get it" when he comes to use a cultural strategy for survival—masking—as he readies himself to return aboveground. "Oh! *Now* I get it!" I thought to myself. But my relief at understanding something of what Ellison was doing was swiftly replaced by another realization: this book was not written for me.

In looking back, I learned my own preparation for survival as a Black person in a predominantly white culture informed my befuddlement. I was raised in Black Canadian Caribbean communities, where I enjoyed folklore as a part of my everyday family life. Adults shared memories from "back home," jokes, stories of how they bested authorities in the new land with their wit. Listening to adult stories of white supremacy in the workplace where Black people (or their ideas) were often openly devalued or panned (only to reappear under their white colleagues' names), and *how they survived*, was commonplace. In other words, I learned blues humor intimately. Critical to survival was a space where one could be with others who understood what Black life in the white mainstream is like.

By the time I went off to college, I already knew that there were two rules when it came to surviving white institutions: one, I had to produce one hundred percent more than a white person did to even be in the same room, and two, let them know your words but not your mind. There were many times when this was said to me explicitly as I matriculated from kindergarten through twelfth grade, but the lessons were always reinforced in the moments when I remained quietly listening to these adult stories. Around white people, masking was the principal means of surviving; one simply could not trust them—no matter how nicely they presented.

At the time, believing that Ellison had written the novel for an unknowing— that is, white—audience helped me contextualize what the author was doing in the story: showing the impact on Black people of walking through society in the United States, highlighting the ways in which the white American identity required Black Americans, emphasizing the danger in which one must live when those in the mainstream don't see them. Still, that raised another question for Black-student me: Why would Ellison share with a predominantly white audience that masking is a necessary survival strategy for Black Americans? After all, as often the only Black person, or maybe one of two or three, in a white classroom (most often with a white teacher), I certainly masked to make it until I could return to some safe space.

Consider what I've outlined above as a template for one way that Black students at PWIs enter the classroom that reads Ralph Ellison's *Invisible Man*. Excitement at seeing a Black protagonist is replaced by disorientation as one must discuss masking with white students or discuss characters like Trueblood with peers whose cultural identity as normal or good is wholly based on identifying Black Americans as pathological or bad. Even though as a student I wanted desperately to discuss what was going on with one of the first multidimensional Black characters I'd read, I simply could not do so in mixed company—and that's precisely where Black students are in a classroom at a PWI. I felt more than uncomfortable; I felt vulnerable.

## Reading as a Teacher

White students, too, find it difficult to see Ellison's *Invisible Man* as *for them*. It is ironic, of course, since the Invisible Man that Ellison writes in the beginning of the text more resembles a student who does not think very much about his culture and how it impacts the way he moves through the world—a white student. Still, I reiterate that the centrality of anti-Black culture to mainstream American culture is critical to the ways in which students approach the text. While some Black students may not see themselves as the text's target audience, white students may not see the book as for them because the principal subject is a Black man. Societal institutions are replete with the praxes of anti-Blackness, but I want to focus on its praxis in the United States education system. And, most particularly, I want to highlight a landmark decision around education in the

40  RESISTING BLACK-LACK READINGS

United States as a point where one might begin to see that anti-Blackness is part of how fair education is defined, the 1954 decision in *Brown v. Board of Education*. It seems ironic, indeed, that I might point to the decision to integrate schools as a root of anti-Blackness in schools. However, the narrative that now surrounds the court decision (that it was a good thing) ignores the perspective of Black cultural critics and writers who took issue with the decision—including Ralph Ellison.

To begin, I turn to a part of the Supreme Court's decision that cites another, earlier verdict in the Kansas courts about the integration of schools. The excerpt reads:

> Segregation of white and colored children in public schools has a detrimental effect upon the colored children. The impact is greater when it has the sanction of the law, for the policy of separating the races is usually interpreted as denoting the inferiority of the negro group. A sense of inferiority affects the motivation of a child to learn. Segregation with the sanction of law, therefore, has a tendency to [retard] the educational and mental development of negro children and to deprive them of some of the benefits they would receive in a racial[ly] integrated school system.
> (qtd. in United States, Supreme Court; bracketed text in source)

There are a few important observations here. First, there is an assumption that the only group negatively impacted by segregation is Black children. There is no discussion of the impact of such separation on white students.[3] Second—and more to my point here—the statement that segregated schools have the effect of delaying the development of Black students completely demeans and dismisses the value of Black teachers—the majority of whom were women—not to mention dismissing the value of Black culture in the schools. To be most explicit, the decision for desegregation essentially implies that there is nothing valuable to be found in Black schools—not the students, not the teachers, and certainly not any culture that dwelled therein. These "Black things" bring nothing to the table and ought to be discarded. It is to this that I point when I note that *Brown v. Board of Education* is a critical step in the foundation of anti-Blackness in the United States education system. Notions of Black inferiority are explicitly expressed; that Black culture has nothing to offer mainstream—predominantly white—American schools is certainly implied. And it's a stance at which Ellison balked.

Any suggestion that Black culture was inferior to any other was going down the wrong path for Ellison. He fell more in line with the framework W. E. B. Du Bois set for each chapter in *The Souls of Black Folk*. In fact, he used spirituals as one example of Black genius: "One ironic witness to the beauty and universality of this art is the fact that the descendants of the very men who enslaved us can now sing the spirituals and find in the singing an exaltation of their own humanity" (Ellison, *Shadow and Act* 172). Mainstream American culture was a *métissage*, and all contributions were worthy of acknowledgment. Invisible Man's positionality in the basement in the prologue and epilogue symbolizes where the mainstream United States sees African Americans. I also help students to see the basement as a place that gives him "a critical perspective on its [white culture's] shortcomings" (Walker 55). Black culture, for sure, a sort of counterculture to white America, was of "great value" and had much "richness"; it had much to offer (*Shadow and Act* 316). Anders Walker, author of *Burning House*, offers an interpretation of Ellison's "The Art of Fiction" interview that I find useful here. Walker emphasizes the author's centering of Black Americans, their culture and experiences of what it means to be an American, quoting from Ellison's interview:

> "The history of the American Negro," argued Ellison, is a most intimate part of American history," not only because it reflected a "courageous expression" of the will to defy oppression, itself a core American ideal, but also because it boasted a transformative quality, a capacity to change the very lives of those responsible for that oppression. Ellison made a case both for recognition of the African American experience as an otherwise marginal chapter in the American drama and a repositioning of that experience at the center of that drama. (Walker 57)

Counter to the suggestion that Blackness was inferior and had nothing to offer white American classrooms, in *Invisible Man* Ellison repositions Blackness at the center of how the nation defines itself writ large. This repositioning shows that the novel is for both Black and white readers: it reinforces his view that there is nothing inferior about Blackness and shows in brilliant scenes like the paint factory that definitions of whiteness require Blackness.

And so we return to the analytical framework that Morrison offers for reading American literature. While my argument here is about ways in which students approach Ralph Ellison's *Invisible Man*, the framework that Morrison suggests is also useful for an argument about the centrality of anti-Black culture to white culture in the United States. Furthermore, it is useful to see the ways that Black American writers signify on any notion of Blackness as inferior (or invisible) to whiteness in the American imaginary. Ellison says as much:

> For despite the impact of the American idea upon the world, the "American" himself had not . . . been finally defined. So that far from being socially undesirable this struggle between Americans as to what the American is to be is part of that democratic process through which the nation works to achieve itself. Out of this conflict the ideal American character—a type truly great enough to possess the greatness of the land, a delicately posed unity of divergencies—is slowly being born. (*Shadow and Act* 26)

In *Invisible Man*, Ellison demonstrates that the possibilities for Morrison's assertion go beyond Black characters in the American fiction by white authors;

42     RESISTING BLACK-LACK READINGS

Morrison's framework applies to consideration of interrelationship between Blackness and whiteness in the United States. Furthermore, Ellison provides a corrective to any notion of Black as inferior implied in *Brown v. Board of Education*.

Understanding that students are more likely than not walking into my classroom with a conscious or unconscious idea of Black lack—not just in the literature but in the teacher, too—I walk into the classroom prepared to teach Ralph Ellison's *Invisible Man*. My principal objective is to have students talk about Black culture and how it is central for a young Black American man—likely the same age as they, my students, are—finding and understanding his Americanness. I also want them to know that Black culture is critical to any definition of *American* culture; it's critical to how even they come to understand themselves in this nation.

In a course at a PWI on literatures of minority groups in the United States, I begin by highlighting a lineage of essays wherein the authors emphasize the importance of Black Americans to American culture. I've already gestured to *Shadow and Act*, essays by Ellison, and *Playing in the Dark*, by Toni Morrison. Albert Murray's "The Omni Americans" is a solid standby—particularly in a time wherein there are questions about what it means to be patriotic versus anti-American. Finally, in establishing a history of Black authors consistently asserting the importance of Black culture to the larger national culture, I really enjoy using "The Forethought" from Du Bois's *Souls*, wherein the author gently admonishes the "Gentle Reader"—presumably white—that the matter of the color line is of interest to them (3). Moreover, today's readers see that the color line remains a problem at the turn of the twenty-first century, as it was at the turn of the twentieth century. But I love to share and have students consider what Du Bois says in the way that he frames each chapter with both a "Sorrow Song" and excerpts of European poetry. It helps students to see that defining what it means to be an American in the United States explicitly leans on African Americans, and their cultural contribution to the nation is not a novel idea. Thus, they see that Ellison works in a legacy of establishing "Black" as critical to understanding what it means to be American; it also establishes a legacy resisting notions of Black lack.

Reading Ellison in the vein of resisting Black lack offers the opportunity to analyze contemporary Black authors as writing in that African American legacy of "Black being." Coupling Claudia Rankine's *Citizen* with Ralph Ellison's *Invisible Man* comes easily, particularly as one considers the question of what it means to be an American when one is Black. Rankine's short vignettes pack a power punch—especially in contrast to Ellison's writing in the form of the epic. Still, in both texts, that which is unsaid or invisible resounds. There is a scene that helps students see how Morrison's notion of the importance of the Black figure can be applied to white Americans' understanding of their own identity:

> A woman you do not know wants to join you for lunch. You are visiting her campus. In the café you both order the Caesar salad. This overlap is not

> the beginning of anything because she immediately points out that she, her father, her grandfather, and you, all attended the same college. She wanted her son to go there as well, but because of affirmative action or minority something—she is not sure what they are calling it these days and weren't they supposed to get rid of it?—her son wasn't accepted. You are not sure if you are meant to apologize for this failure of your alma mater's legacy program; instead you ask where he ended up. The prestigious school she mentions doesn't seem to assuage her irritation. This exchange, in effect, ends your lunch. The salads arrive.  (Rankine 13)

One imagines that lunch being very long—no matter how short in time—since the woman spits out her reason for joining the narrator for lunch before the salads arrive: to blame the protagonist and perhaps to have her soothe (agree with?) her. Space for Black people disrupts her legacy; in order for her legacy to continue uninterrupted, Black people needed to get (and stay) out. The protagonist doesn't say much, yet her silence is resounding.

Rankine's use of the pronoun "you" raises the question of who this text is written for, too. Here, the "you" can be white or Black. This time, the Black reader is not alone in their vulnerability. This time, the secret isn't a strategy for survival in a nation that needs you to be a noncitizen so that they can be citizens. It's that such aggression as displayed by the woman who joins the narrator for lunch is as quotidian as ordering lunch. Reading the episode confirms yet another instance in which a white person who mourns Black people's access to spaces once reserved for white people seeks solace in a Black person's bosom. Today, you still remain invisible. And it still hurts.

The underlying goal I have in teaching *Invisible Man* is to do the work of resisting Black lack. In this way, I follow Ellison's legacy, particularly as I try to highlight for students elements of Black culture. Returning to the story with which I opened: to be told "I don't believe you" or "You're wrong" is still jarring, because based on what knowledge would this student know? American culture is replete with Blackness. Of course, all of this coming from my Black self means that some students walk away thinking I'm biased or that I engage in reverse racism—the go-to terms when one highlights the centrality of Black culture to American culture. But the majority walk away conscious of the gaps in their own understanding of what American literature is and the importance of Black figures to its development.

NOTES

1. I define the term *Black lack* as naming how the majority culture perceives Blackness—whether racially, culturally, or both—as "less than," inferior or deficient.

2. I refer here to an inability to see his position relative to Mr. Norton—a white, male donor to the university—and thus to know what he ought to let Norton see and not see.

3. In her interview with Larry Ferlazzo, Gloria Ladson-Billings reflects on the impact of Black teachers on her preparedness for success in desegregated environments and on the importance of white students' having Black teachers: "It is important for White students to encounter Black people who are knowledgeable and hold some level of authority over them. Black students ALREADY know that Black people have a wide range of capabilities. They see them in their homes, their neighborhoods, and their churches. They are the Sunday School teachers, their Scout Leaders, their coaches, and family members. But what opportunities do White students have to see and experience Black competence?"

# Can the Joke "Slip the Yoke"?
## *Invisible Man* and the Knot of Black Humor

### *Kirin Wachter-Grene*

Ralph Ellison's only novel completed during his lifetime remains as vital as it was in the mid–twentieth century. And his voice? Just as fierce and formidable. Returning to Ellison's work and reconceptualizing how we teach it amid a collective reckoning with increasingly public instances of violent anti-Black racism is imperative. Situating *Invisible Man* within an anti-racist genealogy is perhaps the most urgent and judicious context in which to teach the novel to today's college students, many of whom are a vital part of the Movement for Black Lives. And while I certainly do contextualize the novel with primary and secondary texts from the Black radical tradition, I remain committed to also teaching students to read and think critically about satire and dark humor—risky and complicated tactics Ellison used liberally in the novel as an additional tool, dating back to slavery, in Black peoples' arsenal of subversion, resistance, and critique to reject "the image created to usurp [Black] identity" (Ellison, *Shadow and Act* 55). Despite, or because of, the fact that many critics and readers have continuously overlooked *Invisible Man*'s humor, we must not forget that Ellison's narrator is, as the author states, giving us "one long, loud rant, howl and *laugh*" (57; emphasis added).

The first half of the semester in my upper-level undergraduate seminar Masterworks: Ralph Ellison's *Invisible Man* is spent reading Ellison's novel alongside historical and canonical primary and secondary materials from the archives of Black studies. Reading in conversation with canonical cultural figures such as Booker T. Washington, W. E. B. Du Bois, Marcus Garvey, and Richard Wright and critics including Larry Neal, Claudia Tate, and Erica Edwards aids in mining the novel's expansive sociopolitical depth and reach.[1] The class interrogates how these texts and their ideas implicitly and explicitly build upon one another so as to pay sustained attention not only to the many political and ideological stances in the novel but also to multitudinous iterations of Blackness—one of the novel's core truths.

The term's second half is spent reflecting on *Invisible Man* by narrowing the focus to humor—a uniquely difficult genre largely because it is challenging to teach students to read for tone, particularly incongruity. Nevertheless, I commit to this approach for several reasons: humor is a core component of the narrator's tonal register, his ironic worldview has deep cultural resonance outside of the novel, and there is a need, always, and especially during flashpoints of crisis and racial reckoning, for multiple critical frameworks. I structure the semester in this specific order because "to discuss satire effectively requires extensive discussion of the cultural and historical discourses in which it is embedded, since those discourses are most often the 'targets' of the satire itself" (Maus xviii).

46    BLACK HUMOR

I invite a bridge between these two approaches to the novel by introducing satire, and specifically Black satire, through an initial opening lecture. I explain to students Ellison's theory of masking from his famous 1958 *Partisan Review* essay "Change the Joke and Slip the Yoke," putting it in conversation with Louis Chude-Sokei's theory of Black minstrelsy (which, in part, theorizes Ellison's stance) and Paul Beatty's and Derek C. Maus and James J. Donahue's histories of African American humor and post-soul satire.[2] I then ask students to reflect in writing on the following prompt before opening the discussion: How do we get to contemporary African American satire from *Invisible Man*? What specific satirical instances come to mind for you from the novel? What was being satirized, and for what purpose? These prompts, particularly the latter two questions, invite an exploratory discussion of the novel in a new light, initiating a deeper engagement with scenes that, due to their seemingly inappropriate bouts of—or suppression of—hysterical laughter, are confusing at first (the manic silliness of the Golden Day or the explosion at the paint factory and subsequent surreal hospital scene, for instance).

As the second half of the semester progresses, the class reengages with *Invisible Man*'s trickster characters (Peetie Wheatstraw and my favorite persona, Bliss Proteus Rinehart) and darkly subversive strategies (what I interpret as Jim Trueblood's grotesque performance of depravity and Brother Tod Clifton's Sambo-doll puppeteer minstrelsy). While we have first attempted to comprehend these characters within their own sociohistorical context, I contextualize our reencounter with them by analyzing contemporary texts and films that heavily riff on the novel, including Beatty's *The Sellout* and Boots Riley's *Sorry to Bother You*. Beatty's satirical novel—winner of numerous prestigious literary awards—is about a Black protagonist named "Me" who tries to reintroduce segregation in modern-day Los Angeles and who enslaves a man named Hominy Jenkins on his farm, where he grows marijuana and watermelon. These actions lead to a Supreme Court case, *Me v. the United States of America*. Boots Riley's surrealist film concerns Cassius "Cash" Green—a young, Black, broke telemarketer who adopts a "white voice" to rise in the ranks of his company. In so doing he uncovers a vast conspiracy and is forced to choose between his own personal success and organizing in solidarity with fellow labor activists to accelerate the company's demise. These latter texts create (often absurdist) variations on some of *Invisible Man*'s core themes that have much to say about the state of Black American life in the twenty-first century, depending on how one glances at it. These texts, by the sheer nature of their wild excessiveness, help throw *Invisible Man* and its more challenging characters into stark relief. We consider how Beatty's and Riley's work might be read as continuations or extensions of Ellison's novel.

My students overwhelmingly resonate with and embrace the first, historicist approach in the semester's opening weeks. Unsurprisingly, the contemporary texts and their particular brand of Black humor (confounding and "tricky/uncomfortable" for many students, according to course evaluations) prove far harder to teach than the more straightforward historical and theoretical contextualizing of the novel that I begin the semester with.[3] And teaching contemporary representations of Black satire proves to be more challenging than our initial encounters with, again, what we might read (and what I do read) as Ellison's trickster and minstrel characters, despite the fact that they are no less ambiguous or confounding.

I propose that the challenge of the latter work and pedagogy is likely a result of our contemporary politics and students' increasing sensitivity to, and demand for, the urgency of anti-racist and decolonial pedagogy and curriculum. In other words, subversive black humor (and here I mean both the tradition of African American satire and the broad genre of dark, or gallows, humor) does not *feel* like it necessarily has a place in this climate, despite the fact that such aesthetics and practices are deep, well-established, and celebrated vernacular traditions in Black literature, art, and culture going back centuries.[4] Therefore, while I share and make available some of my curriculum and pedagogy in this essay, I do so while self-consciously thinking through the discomforting trajectory of my class that asks students to attend to the strategies Ellison and those he influenced used, not only to satirize the absurdity of racism but "for the sheer joy of the joke" (Ellison, *Shadow and Act* 55). This latter use—"sheer joy"—is, in my experience, the most difficult for students to analyze and discuss. However, what is, for many, a struggle, to consider joy and pleasure as sharing the same space with, if not drawing from the deep well of, pain and trauma, is the subject for another essay.

What I offer here is this: the tension I am beginning to describe is what I am referring to as "the knot of Black humor." Consider the *Oxford English Dictionary* definition of *satire*: "A poem or (in later use) a novel, film, or other work of art which uses humor, irony, exaggeration, or ridicule to expose and criticize prevailing immorality or foolishness, esp. as a form of social or political commentary" ("Satire, *N*."). To get the joke means to recognize how the humor is wrapped up in often racist and offensive ideas and stereotypes that many people, certainly most of my sensitive and conscientious students, want to reject. And to get the joke means to lay bare (expose) and therefore criticize those of us who laugh at it. The joke brings us face-to-face with our complicated (foolish and immoral) considerations of race. To begin to pull at the threads of this tangled knot in the classroom means to confront artistic strategies—including strategic minstrelsy, masking, and the trickster's many guises—on their own unapologetic terms (including "for the sheer joy of the joke") and forces a recognition in how we choose to meet such tactics head on. Or how we attempt to sidestep.

The urgency of our political moment makes unfurling the knot an exercise in messiness. To be clear, to refer to the Movement for Black Lives as a moment is ahistorical and anemic—we have breathed, and struggled to breathe, this anti-Black air for centuries. Ellison's novel makes this point plainly, and painfully. Nevertheless, the historic specificity of #BlackLivesMatter is being emphasized as a distinctive tipping point in twenty-first-century American history. Black humor (particularly as it moves and is rendered visible through the "political ambiguity and ambivalence" of the minstrel or the trickster) might feel, now, antithetical, counterrevolutionary, or anti-liberationist (Chude-Sokei 78). Feelings of confusion in the classroom can abound when attempting to balance a confrontation with satirical material that, while perennially challenging, feels particularly so in this political climate in which many of us are deeply invested in a public performance of moral and political purity. What we might come to realize in grappling with these complexities (what I *hope* we will come to realize) is that the knot can never be untangled and that there *is* no moral or political purity, as Ellison's satirizing of political ideology—the Brotherhood—makes plain. The mask, as Ellison argues, is indigenous to American culture—"America is a land of masking jokers"—and our motives for masking "are as numerous as the ambiguities the mask conceals" (Ellison, *Shadow and Act* 55). Ambiguity, like humor, is another difficult representation to teach (one reason why Beatty's hyperbolic Uncle Tom character in *The Sellout*, Hominy Jenkins, presents a maddening puzzle for students).

If my commitment to teaching the knot reveals anything, it is that discomfort can be a productive space from which to learn not only how to read culture but how to read one's affective relationship to it. However, such productive discomfort can only be generative if care is taken to first develop trust and vulnerability in the classroom. I begin my class on day one by establishing the groundwork to help my students openly engage with or relearn American historical constructions of Blackness and racism. I initiate the first day of class with two approaches toward this end.

First, I give a brief lecture on racial formation theory and positionality by drawing on the foundational work of Michael Omi and Howard Winant and using myself, as a white scholar and professor of Black literature, as an example. My purpose is to provide the class with some initial shared language with which to discuss race, racial formation, and power dynamics within American society so that students might critically consider their own positionality and how it informs how they approach texts. During the semester I invite students to draw upon their positionality and racial formation to consciously bring it to bear in their reading, writing, and discussion of Ellison's novel and the framing texts. I use daily, low-stakes in-class writing activities as a form of thinking to prompt introspection, analysis, and discussion. One such prompt that I provide to students midway through the semester at the completion of the novel is as follows:

> *Invisible Man* begins with the word "I" and ends with "you," forcing readers to contemplate how connected they are to the stories of others, and (as the narrator claims) on a deeper level than readers might realize. Thinking about your own positionality, how do you relate to this novel? Or, if you feel you do not or cannot relate on a personal level to this novel, explore in writing why it is you think that. Aim to write with specificity.

Through this increased attention, I ask students to begin to interrogate how they know what they know (or claim to know) about race and power, specifically. These are, of course, the very same questions Ellison's narrator grapples with throughout *Invisible Man*.

Second, I invite students to develop community agreements or guidelines for how they want the classroom to be structured and to run, and, in so doing, I ask them to consider how they will adhere to personal and communal accountability.[5] Beginning from the simple premise that we are all members of the class who will be spending a great deal of time writing, thinking, discussing, and creating together, I explain that it is important for us to communicate our needs and wants as collaborative learners so as to make our seminar responsive to issues that arise. Or, as one student explained it, we are attempting to determine from the onset how to "create a safe and respectful environment that encourages discussion and even disagreement in productive ways." We develop these agreements or guidelines in several collaborative steps, and when the exercise is finished I emphasize that that we will reflect upon and revise our community agreements and guidelines document as the semester progresses. To this end, I provide a midsemester check-in that asks students to provide reflective feedback on how they are upholding and abiding by these agreements or guidelines and what, if anything, needs to be changed or added.

Students have noted in their course evaluations that both my opening lecture and the community-building exercise help to construct a "code of respect" conducive to developing a "welcoming and inclusive class" and a "safe space for everyone to enter the discussion." However, the concept of a "safe space" is complicated, as all teachers know. Before we begin our reflection on Ellison through the lens of contemporary Black satire, I acknowledge that the second half of the semester will likely be difficult for many, and I explicitly remind students of community agreements or guidelines that are particularly relevant to help us collectively navigate these choppy waters. In fall 2019, these agreements and guidelines were "treat everyone, and the texts, with respect" and "be prepared to be challenged, and let challenging things open up your discussion."

The concept of a "safe space" is fraught. Many of the satirical texts we read and watch, including, of course, *Invisible Man*, are painful, and a pedagogical commitment and consensual agreement to facing challenging texts with "respect," "patience," and a lack of assumptions does not minimize the pain—painfully funny at times, yes, but tender, agonizing, and potentially traumatic, nonetheless. And facing and interrogating pain, particularly pain in relationship to humor, is among the most difficult entanglements to teach, despite the fact that it is a defining feature of Black humor, as Ellison's commitment to the blues aesthetic makes plain. *Invisible Man*'s narrator describes such an entanglement in the epilogue as "funny and dangerous and sad" (Ellison, *Invisible Man* 564). All these affective responses are wrapped up in one another in teaching Black satire and Black humor. It feels risky to read the humor welling up from the depths of sorrow; it feels profane to laugh.

Perhaps nothing emphasizes the challenge of teaching the knot more than a day during the second half of the semester when I screen *Richard Pryor: Live*

50     BLACK HUMOR

*in Concert*, a legendary stand-up performance from 1979. After cackling uproariously in the darkness for the better part of an hour, students proceed, once the lights are flipped on, to interrogate themselves and their responses as they pick apart the "problematic" nature of Pryor's jokes. Essentially, they spend the next portion of class analyzing why Pryor is, in fact, *not* funny, despite having just laughed long, deep, and loud. When we start to untangle the stand-up, suddenly the joke is no longer comical because we come face-to-face with ourselves (which, of course, was one of Pryor's aims, as is the case for satirists in general). I try to frame this moment as one useful for attending to positionality. I prompt students to engage in private, reflective writing: Pay attention to your visceral response to Pryor's stand-up from your own positionality. When are you pulled in? When are you pushed out? And why?

The stickiness here illustrates why discomfort can be productive in the classroom; it invites an in-depth analysis of laughter's many gradients across distinct genres (What works more effectively in stand-up comedy versus fiction, and why?). I pivot the conversation in this direction by, again, using private, prompted writing about students' experience as viewers rather than as readers. I then use Pryor's stand-up as a way back into Ellison's novel by pointing out to students that in his introduction to *Hokum: An Anthology of African-American Humor*, Beatty writes, "I see laughter as a learned response and not a reflexive one" (4). Next, I share with students Ellison's oft-quoted commitment to the blues aesthetic as inherently wrapped up in humor: "The blues is an impulse to keep the painful details and episodes of a brutal experience alive in one's aching consciousness, to finger its jagged grain, to transcend it, not by the consolation of philosophy but by squeezing from it a near-tragic, near-comic lyricism" (Ellison, *Collected Essays* 121). I ask students to think, through writing, about what both Beatty and Ellison might mean. Inevitably, we come to an interpretation about the importance of laughter as a honed, crafted, and purposeful response to external, often painful stimuli—an act Pryor performed with unparalleled brio.

With Beatty's and Ellison's claims fresh in our minds, I break students into small groups to close read specific scenes of laughter in *Invisible Man* that illustrate the narrator's learned responses (these scenes include the battle royal, chapter 11's hospital scene, chapter 13's yam eating, and the epilogue's recollection of the narrator's confrontation with Mr. Norton on the subway). Through our close readings, we discuss the lessons learned that the narrator's laughter speaks back to, and we analyze the quality of his laughter in different scenes (bitterly ironic; relieved or as a mitigation of discomfort; self-shattering; punning; punishing; as a fugitive, sidling gesture). Part of what we reaffirm through this analysis is the narrator's use of laughter and humor as an expansive articulation of expression that helps him counter his invisibility. At the end of the three-hour class period, having practiced attending more closely to laughter as studied and supple, I invite a reflection back to Pryor and to what was, for some, an uneasy relationship to his performance. I contextualize Pryor's irrefutable brilliance using Mel Watkins's analysis,[6] and I invite the class to move from shame, shaming, or denial of our supposed reflexes to a private analysis of the lessons each of us have learned from our respective positionality that contributed to our laughter in the first place. And I should be clear: just because these are private writing prompts does not foreclose public sharing. Students self-select where, when, and how they make themselves vulnerable to the class.

Teaching the knot of Black humor is delicate work that takes bravery and willingness on the part of the students and an intrepid commitment on the part of the teacher. Many students do and will struggle with it—particularly with the figure of the trickster and his off-kilter gestures that *seem* antithetical to Black liberation because this mode of "artistic discourse" might seem flippant in the context of the anti-Black racism we are still collectively grappling with and grieving (Maus xiii). But the knot of Black humor is with us always, even as we push forward toward an anti-racist world. As Chude-Sokei reminds us, "every local articulation of race is itself shot through with its own parodic undoing, its own masquerade" (125). Pryor and Ellison, Beatty and Riley were and are, of course, deeply ensconced in the contextually specific anti-Black racism and movements for Black liberation of their historical moments and chose such subversive gestures and tactics in the full knowledge of and commitment to their messiness. Ellison knew that "archetypes seem doomed to be with us always" (*Shadow and Act* 46). The question therefore became, How does one engage with such home-grown stereotypes, especially from the vantage point and positionality of a Black artist in America?

Prescient writers such as Ellison have always found ways to attest to and imagine the multiplicity of Black lives—including profane representations—within the ever-present violence of American culture and the urgency of Black liberation struggles. Such a representation of multiplicity is a testament to the novel's expansive celebration and indictment of humanity's contradictions and an homage to the uncontainability of Blackness, Black people, and Black thought and imagination. When considered from this perspective, the fact that some students who are committed to social justice struggle with historical and contemporary iterations of Black humor is therefore especially curious and, if I am honest, frustrating to those of us who spend our careers in the classroom struggling against political and ideological stances from both the right *and* the left of the political spectrum that seek to contain African American art and literature in narrowly specified ways. Who says the Black radical tradition does not, or should not, consider humor as a strategy of struggle or joy in the face of seemingly perpetual violence and pain?

The complications that grow over the course of the semester as students encounter texts and concepts that confront their expectations and platitudes speak, I believe, to the difficult necessity of figuring out the *many* ways to position ourselves fluidly in response to work that confounds us with its artistic discourse amid the urgency of our times. But "if we're to survive and get on with

## 52   BLACK HUMOR

the task of making sense of American experience," Ellison reminds us, we would be wise to "view it," in part—even, perhaps, the absolute worst of it—"through the wry perspective of sanity-saving comedy" (*Collected Essays* 859).

NOTES

1. More specifically, these texts include Washington; selections from Du Bois; Garvey; *Marcus Garvey: Look for Me in the Whirlwind*; R. Wright, "Ethics" and *Twelve Million Black Voices*; Neal; Tate; and selections from Edwards.

2. See Chude-Sokei; Beatty, *Hokum*; and Maus and Donahue.

3. Throughout this essay I quote directly from student feedback provided on my fall 2019 Masterworks: *Invisible Man* course evaluations so as to reflect upon the benefits and challenges of the course in students' own words. One student wrote, "The readings Kirin chose to share with us are timeless and still relevant in today's sociopolitical sphere."

4. See Beatty's *Hokum*, an archival collection of blues and hip-hop lyrics, poetry, political speeches, prose, and more testifying to African American humor and satire from the nineteenth through the twenty-first centuries, as well as Watkins.

5. My thanks to Robin Tremblay-McGaw for the idea and inspiration behind this exercise.

6. See Watkins, especially the chapter "Pryor and Thereafter" (526–70).

# "Punking" *Invisible Man*:
# Reading Race, Queerness, and Disability

## *Alvin J. Henry*

This essay provides a set of lessons for teaching Ralph Ellison's *Invisible Man* to undergraduate students to guide them to explore, discuss, and analyze representations of race, sexuality, and disability in the novel. It is not typical that students read this text through the lens of queerness or disability; the standard pedagogical approach is to identify themes of race, racism, and masculinity—intersections that are indeed central to the novel.[1] Yet Ellison goes much further, as he crafts nearly every major and minor Black character with bodily impairments and disabilities. In fact, such impairments abound in the text. Primary examples include the Founder, with nonfunctional genitals; a man with advanced syphilis, who begs for money; Lucius Brockway and Brother Jack, who both use prosthetics; Reverend Homer Barbee and the prizefighter Sam Langford, who are both blind; Jim Trueblood and the veterans, who have various cognitive disabilities and neurodiversities; and Brockway, Brother Tarp, and Mary, who suffer from infirmities due to old age. Finally, Ellison constructs the protagonist, Invisible Man himself, as a gay punk at a time when homosexuality was regarded as a mental "handicap."[2] When Ellison penned the novel in the 1940s, it was widely known in New York City that "punks" were young men seeking relationships with older men who were often more financially secure or, in some cases, with other punks close to their age.

The disabilities so closely associated with characters in the novel are ignored for at least two reasons. The first involves changing social codes and discourses of disability and queerness since Ellison's publication of the novel in 1952. Ellison lived in an epoch when race and disability were defined, policed, and experienced in radically different ways than in the generations since. Today still, structural forces such as anti-Black racism, homophobia, and ableism shape reading practices, and some students assume a heteronormative worldview in which all characters are straight, cisgender, and able-bodied, unless, of course, obvious contradictory evidence is presented. Even when they do think about disabilities, students might assume that characters with disabilities do not possess and contribute key knowledge to understanding the novel in terms of its characters and worldbuilding.

Two examples help illustrate these points for students who are not versed in the discourses of disability and queer studies. Students tend to classify queer people as either gay or lesbian, yet in recent years they have begun to acknowledge more often the lives and histories of genderqueer, gender nonconforming, nonbinary, and trans people. When Ellison penned the novel, however, a variety of gay male identities in circulation in queer communities remained elusive to mainstream groups: punk, trade, wolf, normal, and husband—not to mention

54   RACE, QUEERNESS, AND DISABILITY

a lost third sex, fairies—expressed a range of queer identities. A second lost framework is that the medical establishment classified homosexuality as a mental "handicap" until 1973. Thus, the queer characters in *Invisible Man* represent a range of queer disabilities.

When teaching *Invisible Man*, I want students to appreciate and grapple with Ellison's project to illuminate the invisibility of Black cultures in which disability plays a role. The idea is to teach students how Ellison represents and celebrates the varied experiences of Black people with a disability—and that community's knowledge and cultural productions—as well as how Black characters with disabilities subvert and critique people and systems that dismiss and oppress them. I do this by creating lessons that reveal the overlapping histories (whether lost or forgotten) of race, disability, and sexuality. These lessons provide resources from disability studies, queer studies, and Black studies as well as sample readings and activities. In undergraduate seminars, I assign my intersectional reading of disability, race, and sexuality in *Invisible Man* from my book *Black Queer Flesh* (Henry 105–57). It is imperative to tell students that Blackness was imagined by the medical industry and general public as a disability as a way to demean African Americans. Ellison refuses this definition and proposes a rich alternative. Since African Americans with disabilities were rarely given the opportunity to publish stories about Black life or the lives of African Americans with disabilities, Ralph Ellison stepped in and created *Invisible Man* to convey and celebrate their perspectives, insights, and cultures.

## *Lesson 1: Terminology*

The learning outcomes for this lesson are to comprehend the historically contingent aspects of key terminology in Black disability studies and Black queer studies and to analyze how power operates through language (terms and categories) to oppress people.

When introducing students to historical terminology, it is important to provide adequate warnings in advance of using the terms—for example, give sensitivity warnings to the class days before students are to read and discuss the materials. When students are to encounter potentially emotionally challenging course materials, it is best to prepare them to manage these materials. In this way, students learn how language and categories were used to oppress and group people while also having an opportunity to practice self-care. Instructors would do well to remind students that the past does contain instances of violence and oppression that will be uncomfortable to read about, view (in terms of images), discuss, and write about. It is essential to also frame the history of the term *punk*, for instance, which moved from queer cultures to the mainstream (as a negative category and identity) and then into music and other subcultures. The term is becoming again more popular in queer communities; we can thus point out to students that, while queer communities continued using the term *punk* and embodying punk identity since the early part of the twentieth century, it was less prominent in the public imagination (though it still existed in the margins). In describing people with disabilities, many offensive and crude terms and categories have been deployed. I use the term *handicap* in this article because it was used across medical, philanthropic, literary, and vernacular discourses during the period when Ellison wrote the novel. When speaking, however, I prefer to replace historically offensive terms such as *handicap* with *disability* or *person with a disability*. I convey to students that this correction of historical inaccuracy is required to honor people as full persons rather than reinforcing negative and oppressive language. Students should also be aware of continued debates within African American studies as to how African Americans self-identify. The two most prominent terms are *African American* and *Black people*, although there are ongoing debates, and each term has its own historical lineage and meanings. A full lesson on the terms used in this chapter could be integrated into the lessons or delivered before engaging the materials; lesson 3 ("Ableism and the Medical Model of Disability") could be a helpful resource for additional terms to cover.

## Lesson 2: Reclaiming Punk Sexuality and Disability

The learning outcomes for this lesson are to trace the history of queer identities as framed as a form of disability by the medical establishment and mass culture, to analyze Invisible Man's punk sexuality as it intersects with race and gender identity, and to comprehend *Invisible Man* as a Black queer coming-of-age novel as well as a gay love story.

Mass culture and the medical establishment regarded homosexuality as a cognitive disability (handicap), and the American Psychiatric Association itself only delisted homosexuality as a mental disability in 1973 (*Diagnostic and Statistical Manual*). It is crucial to understand that Ralph Ellison came of age in a culture that deemed queer people mentally disabled or "crippled." (Remind students that *handicap* and *cripple* are historically accurate—yet derogatory and offensive—terms but that they should use *disability* or *person with a disability* to break the isomorphic relationship between terms and people that made Black and gay people "problems.") In constructing the Emerson character, Ellison imagines him as "a psychologically crippled white man . . . grappling with his personal flaw—which can be homosexuality" (qtd. in Foley, *Wrestling* 206). At the same time, Ellison was intimately familiar with gay culture and understood its rich subcultures from living in the two centers of gay culture in New York City: the West Village and Harlem. Ellison shared an apartment with gay sculptor Richmond Barthé and received mentorship from Langston Hughes. He initially penned Bledsoe to be a homosexual, too (Foley, *Wrestling* 166). During his college education at the Tuskegee Institute, Ellison, according to his biographers, was sexually harassed by his dean, who was the model for Bledsoe (Rampersad

## 56 RACE, QUEERNESS, AND DISABILITY

61; Jackson, *Ralph Ellison* 135). The "ugly laws" viewed gay people as infected with sexually transmitted disease or mental illnesses—and thus under their purview. Some of the laws included the regulation of "improper dress" such as "wearing clothing of [the] opposite sex" as reasons to be deemed unsightly and disabled and thus removable from the public sphere (Schweik, *Ugly Laws* 144). Ellison also captured a fairy, a third sex that has all but disappeared from the American mainstream landscape, in his photo collaboration with Roy DeCarava (Ellison, "Harlem" 56). This fairy would have been removed from the streets for wearing clothes from the "wrong" gender. By learning about queerness as a disability and less-known forms of queerness—that is, beyond the homosexual-heterosexual divide—students can access how *Invisible Man* is a text not only about disability but also about Black queer identity.

Historian George Chauncey reminds scholars that many gay identities thrived in the first half of the century but were later eclipsed under the rubric of "gay." The fairy or invert was considered an intermediate sex (a third sex) between male and female. These people usually enacted a conventional feminine identity and typically assumed the receptive sexual role with men known as trade and wolves, who performed conventional masculine identities. Trades would have sex with fairies and cisgender women, while wolves, also known as husbands and normals, were attracted to fairies and punks. In Ellison's work, Invisible Man is a punk. George Chauncey describes a punk as "often neither homosexually interested nor effeminate, but [who] was sometimes equated with women because of his youth and his subordination to the older man (wolf)." Wolves often provided financial support and life advice to punks (Chauncey 88). The modern reader might not register the nuances and variety of these gay identities that prominently circulated in 1930s and 1940s New York City, when Ellison began writing the novel and when he himself was immersed in Black queer culture.

Besides the reader losing sight of these gay identities, Ellison removed additional scenes (in his revisions of 1948–52) where Invisible Man's queer sexuality was represented more transparently. In an excised chapter for the novel, Cleo, a boarder at Mary's, "calls out Invisible Man as potentially gay" (Henry 141). In a much longer and complex draft of the Woodridge episode, the narrator asks for help from a fairy mentor. Woodridge, a literature professor at the fictional Tuskegee Institute, appeared in a working draft of *Invisible Man*. In his revisions, Ellison cut nearly all mentions of Woodridge's queer influences, and in the published text the character is briefly mentioned twice but without context that would show he is queer (*Invisible Man* 40, 354). In the draft episode, however, Woodridge instructs Invisible Man to drop his straight life: "All you need to deny it [normative sexuality] is humanity, self-acceptance, which is what you need more than self-reliance" (Henry 142). The fairy (or invert, as Ellison refers to Woodridge in his notes) instructs Invisible Man to accept his punk sexuality. This quoted line is scratched out in the draft, while the entire exchange is deleted from the published novel. In the original hospital episode, Invisible Man tries to explain why he ended up in the hospital. He tells Mary, now an orderly, that he injured

Alvin J. Henry    57

himself trying to escape from a wolf who propositioned him for sex. Ellison cues the reader into the coded language gay people who were "in the life" exchanged to safely greet one another. A key sentence Invisible Man recounts is the white wolf who asks him, "What kind of man am I?," to which Invisible Man replies, "A white man." The wolf reattempts to initiate the sexual encounter by asking, "But what other kind of man am I?" and a few lines later, "So I'm a white man, and what are you?" (Ellison, "Out" 254). The wolf even gives Invisible Man money for sex, but Mary remains clueless that our hero is a punk and is being propositioned for sex. The "correct" answer would have been for Invisible Man to say that he was a punk and that the man wasn't a man but a wolf.

The coded language that gay people used to identify each other resurfaces when Invisible Man meets Young Emerson. Emerson offers Invisible Man financial stability in the form of employment as well as sexual fun: he is a gay wolf. And Invisible Man, too, recognizes and plays into the sexually charged exchange, ultimately taking the job Emerson arranges at Liberty Paint. Other clues about Emerson include references to Club Calamus (Walt Whitman's title for the section on queer love in *Leaves of Grass*), Freud's treatise on homosexuality (*Totem and Taboo*), and phrases that gay men exchanged to know it was safe to come out. Invisible Man—and not Emerson—asks, "What kind of man are you, anyway?" (*Invisible Man* 189). These questions directly echo the white wolf propositioning Invisible Man for sex. Students should be attuned that Invisible Man is asking this question and that Emerson responds by freely acting as a gay wolf. The two men are able to come out in this sly exchange. Students should note that even with the alternative hospital scene with the gay white wolf, Ellison remained committed to having Invisible Man be seduced by a white man. While Invisible Man accepts a wolf's offer for financial help in the novel, he rejects Emerson's sexual advances because he desires the love and bodies of other Black men.

Punk sexuality emerges in the Golden Day fiasco. Invisible Man fixates on the muscular body of Supercargo—and his erection. As Supercargo rushes out of a room where he was having sex with a prostitute, he wears only skimpy boxer shorts. Again, Invisible Man draws attention to the body and erection—but he thinly conceals his desires (147–51). When Supercargo is pushed down the stairs, Invisible Man describes the beautiful body as rigid or hard. Everything is erect on Supercargo's body, and, for students who have read Freud, this scene is filled with desire leaking out in each description of Supercargo's body. In analyzing this scene, students quickly identify Invisible Man's erotic gaze and appreciation of Supercargo's muscles and erect body parts. Punk desire, triggered by further erections, will be discussed later in the section on the "battle royal" lesson.

Almost one-fifth of the novel explores Invisible Man's punk love for Tod Clifton, another younger Black leader of the Brotherhood. This section of the novel, which is longer than some other novels in their entirety, showcases Invisible Man as he fully embraces his punk disability and finally thrives. A love story emerges between the two men—and whether the feelings are returned by Tod or the relationship consummated is left to the reader's imagination. Invisible Man

# 58    RACE, QUEERNESS, AND DISABILITY

introduces Tod as another gay punk. I ask students to closely read Invisible Man's first encounter with Tod. His descriptions of Tod are a confluence of feminine and masculine metaphors that represent punk identity. The terms used to describe him vacillate between a feminine and masculine binary of soft and hard objects in the section from "I saw that he was very black and very handsome [. . .] leaning tall and relaxed" to "velvet-over-stone, granite-over-bone, Afro-Anglo-Saxon contour of his cheek" (363). Students might be tempted to view the list as opposites, in tension, or as layers; rather, we can instruct students that this is a unity from the point of view of punk sexuality and that the narrator is openly expressing his sexual attraction for another punk. This knowledge recalibrates the reading of the two men running around Harlem together not just as friends but as potential lovers—or, in the worst-case scenario, unrequited lovers. More importantly, comprehending Invisible Man's queer desires helps students read the novel as a love story.

This love story frame further contextualizes Invisible Man's herculean efforts to organize Tod's funeral. Invisible Man's eulogy is key to unpacking his feelings for Tod and his outing himself to the Black community. In the eulogy, he protests discrimination against punks. With vim and vigor, Invisible Man claims that Tod "forgot his history" and that this led to his death because "he thought he was a man" (457). This phrase raises a number of questions regarding Black masculinity and African American men as legitimate persons or positive forms of manhood, but students should understand its lineage within the scope of queerness. The latter phrase is coded language to determine gay identity. Woodridge, Emerson, Invisible Man, and the white wolf from the hospital scene all recycle this language of figuring out different types of manhood—gay men are never "men" but rather punks, normals, wolves, trades, and husbands, or a third sex, fairies and inverts. Tod could never be a man—heteronormative white or Black—but rather belonged to one of these queer identity categories. Invisible Man's open pronouncement to the crowd of his and Tod's queer identities and love radically transforms Invisible Man's identity from his own perspective. This open pronouncement and acceptance of Black punk disability along with his retreat from society partially account for Invisible Man's burning of his identity materials: he has sloughed off an able bodymind in favor of a new identity grounded in Black queer disability. As students read the epilogue, they can begin to question Invisible Man's emergence: what community might he join as he emerges from the underground?

## Lesson 3: Ableism and the Medical Model of Disability

The learning outcomes for this lesson are to assess the role of ableism in society and how it shapes worldviews, to define the limits of the medical model of disability, and to analyze how people with disabilities have resisted the medical model.

Students should be introduced to and versed in how race and disability have been used to police African American identities and people. Ableism is the practice of discriminating against people with perceived or actual disabilities. Those enforcing ableism assume that people with "typically" or "normally" functioning bodyminds are superior and those with neurodiverse bodyminds, mental disorders, and intellectual or physical disabilities are inferior. The bias holds that bodies without impairments or disabilities are privileged and superior and thus can define and enforce normality. This also works in tandem with anti-Black racism to keep those living with disabilities invisible in the public sphere. Beyond the problematic of individual actors enforcing ableism, institutional ableism remains a major challenge. For example, sidewalk corners were built without ramps because people using mobility aids were not the average pedestrian; to help students relate, I ask them to analyze the college campus for impediments to access for neurodiversity and mobility diversity. While many structural access issues have been addressed by the Rehabilitation Action of 1973, Voting Accessibility for the Elderly and Handicapped Act of 1984, Fair Housing Amendments Act of 1998, Americans with Disabilities Act (ADA) of 1990, and Individuals with Disabilities Education Act (last revised in 1990), these issues continue to demonstrate for students how people and institutions assume able bodyminds as the norm and thus legitimize discrimination against bodyminds with neurodiversity and neurocognitive issues and people with mental disorders or intellectual disabilities. If instructors assign a reading of sections of the 1990 ADA, I recommend the text and associated resources on the ADA website ("Americans"). Students should also search online for the differences between neurodiverse bodyminds, mental disorders, and intellectual disability. These categories remain in flux, and instructors should consult contemporary debates for the most recent discussions in critical thought—especially the framing of categories and bodyminds.

Many understandings of disability draw exclusively upon a medical model. According to this approach, bodyminds classified as disabled should seek a cure or fix to eliminate the disability. Students can often recall medical TV dramas where a patient "needs" a prosthetic to be fully human or a cutting-edge surgery to "restore" vision or hearing.[3] These cures aim to make the body "whole" and assume that disability is a negative and inferior condition of human life. On the flip side, these shows can present a "Supercrip" character who thrives in spite of their disability. This tokenism is harmful also, as it continues to represent disability from an ableist and medical standpoint.

An exercise to help illustrate ableism and the medical model of disability involves reflecting upon the veteran characters. Ask students to make a table with four columns and to imagine they are medical professionals. Column 1 contains a list of veterans and their medical conditions (posttraumatic stress disorder, traumatic brain injury, psychosis, and amputations [and homosexuality in the drafts]; "Vet," Henry 138). In column 2, students will list previous medical treatments for the conditions listed in column 1. By returning to the past, students can historicize treatments to reflect Ellison's understandings and learn how the medical industry made assumptions about mental health.[4] In column 3, students will

60  RACE, QUEERNESS, AND DISABILITY

reflect on the goal of the treatments. Sample questions for column 3 include the following: Do the treatments aim to restore normal functioning? And if so, what is normal and why? Do the disabilities make us view the characters as inferior? And finally, do any of the characters thrive without medical interventions? Finally, column 4 records how Ellison celebrates the lives and knowledge of veterans. Burnside can serve as a focal point for these discussions because Invisible Man will acknowledge his perspectives and worldviews as correct later in the novel. Students can read closely how veterans resist their institutionalization, seek out pleasure, and come to view themselves as a community. This exercise will illustrate for students the trend to fix or to cure disabilities as the first option when considering the lives of people with disabilities. Column 4 also asks students to recognize the rich experiences of veterans with disabilities.

## Lesson 4: The Intersection of Race and Disability from Antebellum America to 1970

The learning outcomes for this lesson are to comprehend why African Americans, as a group, were imagined, through the forces of anti-Black racism and ableism, to be disabled in the nineteenth century; to grasp the ways that racial formation can overlap or be reinforced with the making of disability, or vice versa; and to understand that the categories of race and disability are constantly evolving and multiple.

In discussing the relationship between race and disability, I provide students with an overview of how the making of race and the making of disability have proceeded, historically, along similar if not overlapping paths. Pioneering Black disability studies scholar Christopher Bell argues that race and disability are mutually constitutive. To complicate this model of identity formation, Therí Pickens cautions that models of "mutual constitution [attend] to the fiction of fixity often ascribed to race and disability writ large" (25). Pickens instructs that neither race nor disability should be imagined as fixed or cohesive. This follows Rosemarie Garland-Thomson's research on the construction of the category of disability. She notes that "a blind person, an epileptic, a paraplegic, a deaf person, an amputee, for example, have no shared cultural heritage, traditional activities, or common physical experience. Only the shared experience of stigmatization creates commonality" (Garland-Thomson 15). I teach students that when we use the terms *disability*, *race*, and *sexuality*, such terms are evolving and not static.

I provide students three key readings and a powerful image to explain how African Americans were classified as disabled in the nineteenth century. In searching through archival records, Douglas Baynton found that "the most common disability argument for slavery was simply that African Americans lacked sufficient intelligence to participate or compete on an equal basis in society with white Americans" (20). Baynton's overview article as well as Dea Boster's research on antebellum racialization in her chapter "Sources of 'Unsoundness' in African American Slaves" can provide a robust introductory lesson on race and disability (see Boster 34–35). I assign students the reading of a short 1863 article from *Harper's Weekly* to illustrate how a body made infirm and "disabled" by enslavement could be transformed into an able body through joining the military ("Typical Negro"). The main photograph from this article can be found in the online archives of the Library Company of Philadelphia (McPherson and Oliver). These two historical sources reveal the visual politics of disability and race. Note that when teaching historical documents instructors should preface the lesson with a caveat about how academics cite and read offensive terms for African Americans and why academics show students disturbing and offensive images from the past. Remind students they should not read aloud words that are designed to demean and oppress African Americans.

The most salient piece of historical evidence to indicate how race was shaped by disability is found in the "ugly laws." Susan Schweik uncovered how city governments in the nineteenth and early twentieth centuries channeled anti-Black racism into fears of contagion to police African Americans into the category of disability. The ugly laws sought to physically remove "unsightly" people from public spaces—that is, from streets and parks to businesses. The city of Chicago, in its version of this law, sought to remove "any person who is diseased, maimed, mutilated, or in any way deformed, so as to be an unsightly or disgusting object, or an improper person to be allowed in or on the streets [. . .] or public places in this city," saying "[he] shall not thereon expose himself to public views" (Jamieson and Adams 325). This broad definition confused and muddled the definition of disability—visual and invisible, differently abled bodies and neurodiversity—such that people who beg, disabled or not, became enfolded into disability. Their imagined contamination of the public sphere, the ugly laws demanded, made them disabled (Schweik, "Begging" 59). African Americans began migrating to northern cities after slavery, and often employers and unions refused to employ Black people. As some African Americans turned to mendicancy, they were once again deemed unsightly and disabled. I assign a brief excerpt from the Chicago municipal code along with chapter 8, "Race, Segregation, and the Ugly Laws," in Schweik's monograph to acquaint students with the mechanics of how the ugly laws circumscribed African Americans (*Ugly Laws* 184–205). Schweik also provides images that can be shown to students. The *Wikipedia* page on the ugly laws can also provide a quick summary.

The ugly laws partially account for why characters with disabilities in *Invisible Man* are unwanted in public spaces and attempts are made to remove them. Brockway is banished to the basement, the man with syphilis whom Invisible Man encounters during his speech at the arena begs and lives in an alley (Ellison, *Invisible Man* 337), Tod Clifton is shot and killed on the streets, the Provos must get out of the streets even during their eviction, and Invisible Man himself lives out of sight in a basement. The ugly laws also anticipate the hypervisibility of disability. In the battle royal episode, the Black "disabled-person-as-spectacle"

## 62  RACE, QUEERNESS, AND DISABILITY

conveys how ableist culture and practices sometimes highlighted Black disability to further debase African Americans as a group (Adelman).

## Lesson 5: The Social Model of Disability and the Battle Royal Episode

The learning outcomes for this lesson are to analyze how Ellison moves from the medical to the social model of disability in chapter 1 of the novel and to learn to closely read the novel for the knowledges, cultures, and experiences of characters with disabilities.

The frequently anthologized battle royal chapter provides the most robust concentration of how to misread the intersection of race and disability. It also portrays how Invisible Man moves from the medical model to the social model of disability. The young narrator, striving for success as defined in white culture, tends to portray the events in the episode through an ableist and internalized anti-Black perspective. As the author, Ellison dramatizes Invisible Man's misreadings as originating from his adoption of the ableist medical model of disability. The battle royal asks the reader to see the world differently by exaggerating how race is seen as an expression of disability from the perspective of anti-Black racism. The scene then transitions to a social model of disability. During this transition period, Invisible Man explores his Black queer disability through his (queer) desires. Pivoting to the social model of disability allows Invisible Man to celebrate Black cultures that were historically read as disabled.

The scene opens with a group of young Black men, blindfolded, joining a boxing match for the white leaders of the town. While the Black men decide in advance the winner of this absurd display of Black disability, Invisible Man misrecognizes the other Black men's subversion of this forced linkage of race and disability. During the fight, Invisible Man evokes the medical model of disability when, within his temporary loss of sight, he proclaims, "I wanted to see, to see more desperately than ever before." Only when his blindfold becomes askew and his sight is partially restored—when he "cures" his disability and restores able-bodiedness—does he feel better, as normal: "with my eye partly opened now there was not so much terror" (Ellison, *Invisible Man* 23). This moment can be misread as Ellison playing into the stigma of Blackness as disability. However, the savvier working-class and non-college-bound Black men approach the situation by taking ownership of disability-as-spectacle; they know that they are playing a role for the racist white men. The boxers' rebuffs of Invisible Man's reactions to a loss of vision and insistence on seriously competing in the ring provide a critique of the ableist ideologies espoused by the young narrator. In this way, Ellison relies on characters with metaphorical disabilities to advocate an awareness of ableism within Blackness, as well as to literally knock sense into Invisible Man.

As the Black men later beg for what they believe is real money that is tossed onto an electrified rug, Invisible Man begins to critique how African Americans are viewed as disabled by white culture. The shock of the men anticipates the electric lobotomy episode by showing "unsightly, disabled" Black men who beg to receive electroshock therapy. Now questioning the social construction of race as disability, Invisible Man attempts to throw a white spectator onto the electric rug. This exposes that the Black men are not in fact disabled but forced into that position.

In these two scenes, Ellison represents how disability can police and demean African Americans. In the battle royal, Ellison then asks what it might mean to actually be disabled and Black: What do Black people with disabilities experience, and what knowledges do they produce? Ellison's response is to craft an entire novel that explores the first-person experiences of an African American character with a disability. At the same time, Ellison introduces the social model of disability, which crip scholar Alison Kafer argues approaches disability, debility, and impairment as "site[s] of questions rather than a set of firm definition" and which locate disability as a socially produced category and center first-person experiences of disability (11). This includes asking questions, such as the following: What "makes" people be perceived as disabled? What common cultures have disabled people created? What are the experiences of the group? And finally, what are the first-person perspectives of embodiment and experience of disabled bodyminds? The social model seeks to understand how the category of disability is constructed and maintained to police and discipline certain bodyminds. It also asks us to center the perspectives, histories, and experiences of characters with disabilities so we can learn how disability is lived and celebrated.

In the battle royal, Ellison sets the stage for the reader to distinguish between the medical model of disability and the social model. The temporary and imagined disabilities in this chapter accentuate the medical model and the unquestioned assumption for intervention. At the same time, Ellison asks the reader to interrogate how race and disability converge and render people with disabilities as deficient, particularly because they are placed under a medical model that seeks to cure them since disabilities are imagined as bad or harmful. Rather, Ellison crafts a model of social disability by showcasing the firsthand experiences of a Black character with a disability. As the naked, blonde dancer captivates most of the men's gazes, Invisible Man, surrounded by bare-chested Black men, focuses on the erections of the Black men. He describes his desires as he takes in an attractive peer, Tatlock, who is "wearing dark red fighting trunks much too small to conceal the erection which projects from him" (Ellison, *Invisible Man* 20). The descriptions of the white men in the scene are quite unflattering, yet Invisible Man evokes highly eroticized language to describe his Black peers and their erections, openly revealing his attraction to other Black men. Ellison not only challenges how Blackness and Black bodies are socially constructed as people with disabilities but also centers the experiences of a Black queer and disabled hero. It is this lived reality of queerness and disability that Ellison celebrates in the novel.

64     RACE, QUEERNESS, AND DISABILITY

## Lesson 6: *Metaphorical Disability and the Arena Speech*

The learning outcome for this lesson is to comprehend how Ellison deploys a metaphorical understanding of disability to critique anti-Black racism.

In the Harlem arena scene, Ellison brings Invisible Man to the cusp of avowing his queer disability. In this episode, a diseased and disabled Black man who begs is ripped from the history pages of the ugly laws (*Invisible Man* 337). As Invisible Man awaits his turn at the arena podium, he reflects on how an African American boxer lost his sight in that arena due to a fixed fight. Ellison creates this context of two disabled Black characters as the foundation for Invisible Man's transformative speech. Before encountering these men, Invisible Man planned to talk about racial uplift through communism. Instead of being an able-bodied race warrior, Ellison advocates for a new type of subjectivity for Invisible Man and the Black audience: Black disability.

On the stage of the arena, Invisible Man critiques racial uplift ideology as a form of blinding because it removes the ability to attend to structural issues shaping Black experiences. Invisible Man moves from an actual bodymind experience of disability—a temporary impairment via a loss of vision—to a metaphorical understanding of disability. A purely metaphorical approach to disability can be troubling, as it reduces the lived experience of people with disabilities to a metaphor. Black disability studies scholar Sami Schalk explains that African American authors have used metaphors of disability to implement subversive political projects. In her analysis of Black literature, Schalk argues that ableism and anti-Black racism work in concert to oppress African Americans—disabled and not—and African American authors call attention to this relationship by evoking disability metaphors. In this scene, Ellison dovetails with Schalk's findings. Invisible Man also imagines himself as infirm. He feels "very young and inexperienced and yet strangely old, with an oldness that watched and waited quietly within" (*Invisible Man* 337). This oldness evokes the lessons from the infirm African American characters he has encountered: Brockway, Brother Tarp, Mary and a blind old man (from the drafts of the novel), and the Provos (a couple being evicted in Harlem). Onstage, Invisible Man experiences temporary metaphorical blindness because "the light was so strong that I could no longer see the audience" (341). At the same time as he metaphorically experiences old age and blindness, Invisible Man also embodies and lives as a disabled gay punk. By centering Black disabilities in the arena speech, Invisible Man changes his subjectivity by embracing a shared culture of disability among many different kinds of disability. In doing so, he enacts a different strategy to critique political and social projects—the Brotherhood and uplift—that ultimately oppress African Americans.

In analyzing the arena speech, I focus on why Invisible Man frames Black people as blind. He claims that "we're so un-common [. . .] they've dispossessed us each of one eye from the day we're born [. . .] we're a nation of one-eyed mice" (343). Ellison does not evoke the medical model of disability with this metaphor. Instead, he embraces the lack of vision and sight because it yields a new sense of understanding among African Americans. As the speech progresses, Invisible Man advocates that African Americans take note of the amazing kinship that develops within Black disability: "Did you ever notice [. . .] how two totally blind men can get together and help one another along? [. . .] Let's get together, uncommon people" (344). Ellison centers Black disability for the crowd to activate a new way of seeing and experiencing the world as blind people. Invisible Man further drives home the fact that people lacking complete vision can still analyze and participate in the world if they come together to celebrate Black disability. He wants African Americans, as a collective, to "take back our pillaged eyes! Let's reclaim our sight," but not in a curative fashion (344). Invisible Man emphasizes that the new sociality created by African Americans coming together allows for additional perspectives. It is thus within blind cultures among Black people that he advocates the ability to "see [that] there's only one enemy" (344). By occupying Black disability as a lived experience and metaphor on the arena stage, Invisible Man learns from the disavowed knowledges created and circulated in communities of Black people with disabilities. And on the stage, he shares this knowledge with the entire African American community, to the shock and horror of the white members of the Brotherhood—the "one enemy."

## Essay Prompts

An essay prompt or an in-class writing assignment would ask students to reframe a character with a disability from the medical model to the social model to analyze what key knowledge and bearing of witness to bodily and cognitive existence occurs within the arc of the novel. You can also ask students to analyze the representation of disability in the novel in relation to the theme of invisibility. How are "invisible" disabilities such as mental illnesses or queerness represented differently from more "visible" disabilities in the novel? Students can be asked to further consider the effects of "visible" and "invisible" illnesses and disabilities on how the reader empathizes with the character.

A paper on affect and disability is another direction you can ask students to explore. For instance, students might analyze whether characters with "visible" disabilities and illnesses are treated differently from characters with "invisible" disabilities and illnesses. Ask students to support *how* empathy is created in the novel—or how it is not created; if it is not, ask students what emotions are evoked and why. Advanced undergraduates might be asked to analyze how a group or a character offers a crip-of-color critique. The latter approach seeks to actively reject ableism and compulsory bodymindedness by calling attention to forms of power, for instance. Another essay prompt could ask the following: How does a character contribute to reshaping the reader's understanding of one

## RACE, QUEERNESS, AND DISABILITY

culture of Black disability? How has that character given us knowledge of how they celebrate their Black disability? You might also ask students to analyze the ways in which the novel explores the intersection of race, sexuality, and disability: How do the characters in the novel navigate the complexities of race, sexuality, and disability through an intersectional identity? And, depending on which identity is most salient for Invisible Man or for those interacting with him, what themes emerge? For an upper-division course, students could be asked to analyze how Invisible Man frames his experiences of race through the lived and metaphorical experiences of disability.

Another essay prompt might ask students to closely read Ellison's use of language to understand how friendships and sociality form and maintain within a group (or how characters invite Invisible Man into their group). Finally, with the emergence of artificial intelligence programs such as *ChatGPT*, you might ask students, in the early phases of *ChatGPT*, to analyze a character in the novel for their disabilities or queerness and then compare how the program assesses historical identities. Students can also work with *ChatGPT* to design a lesson plan on how to teach about specific disabilities or sexualities within *Invisible Man*, or you can ask students to ask *ChatGPT* for medical cures for specific disabilities in specific years and compare it for accuracy with the suggested essays.

### NOTES

1. Students are not the only readers to overlook sexual and disability identities. The critical scholarship includes one reference to disability and two related to Black queer desire.

2. We should recall that the term *disability* replaced the offensive term *handicap* in academic and medical discourse.

3. For an example article to teach on the medical model of disability and race, see Orem's analysis of the medical drama *Grey's Anatomy.*

4. For information on past treatments, have students consult Stein and Rothbaum; Cifu et al.; Spielman et al.; A. Wilson; Spandler and Carr; Blakemore.

# *Invisible Man* and the Urban Uprising

## *J. J. Butts*

The Ferguson uprising of 2014 in Missouri catapulted the Black Lives Matter movement into students' consciousnesses nationwide, arguably giving them more exposure to race and equity issues, explanatory theoretical and historical frameworks, and modes of resistance than at any time since the peak of the civil rights movement. Many students spent the long pandemic summer of 2020 engaged in protests in solidarity with Black communities after videos of the police killing of George Floyd in Minneapolis circulated on social media.[1] This context of elevated awareness and mass action around racial equity has profound implications for teaching African American literature and, in particular, Ralph Ellison's *Invisible Man*, which reaches its narrative climax in an uprising in Harlem. For students in the twenty-first-century classroom, understanding *Invisible Man*'s engagement with some of the most pressing political developments of Ellison's time and our own is crucial. The novel echoes the insurgent culture of the "indignant generation" of African American intellectuals to which Ellison belonged while anticipating later uprisings in the 1960s and the present.[2] This essay examines *Invisible Man*'s uprising scene and the symbolic characters of Black political action connected with it as a complex exploration of the possibilities of mass protest, while also highlighting several useful intertexts for teaching this part of Ellison's novel. The uprising scene offers a window into discussion of several issues salient to current situations including causal conditions, political dynamics, and effectiveness. Ultimately, by refocusing on African American political insurgency, Ellison's novel refuses the closure that journalistic accounts and riot commission reports often seek to impose on uprisings. Recognizing this focus helps students understand Ellison's excitement and ambivalence at the possibilities of action marked by the urban uprising's emergence.

As for many African Americans, Ellison's exposure to urban racial violence came at a young age. The Oklahoma City community in which he lived was shaken by a 1920 lynching that drove Ellison's mother to temporarily relocate her family. Ellison also witnessed the 1921 Tulsa Race Massacre's aftermath. He recalled the thriving Greenwood community where his cousin lived as "devastated and all but destroyed by bomb and fire," an image he revisited in his planned second novel in the form of a charred piano, a symbol of class aspiration and attainment in ruins (*Collected Essays* 455). During the early twentieth century, Oklahoma City's *The Black Dispatch* and other Black-press newspapers reported on similar attacks extending the scale of lynching by making Black citizens interchangeably and jointly accountable to white mobs, in Atlanta, East St. Louis, Omaha, and Wilmington, North Carolina, among other cities. During the Red Summer of 1919, after a series of mob attacks on Black communities across the United States, African Americans in Chicago and Washington, DC, fought white Americans in the streets.

68    URBAN UPRISING

In the 1930s, fighting back took a new form in New York. Ellison had not yet moved to the city when the 1935 Harlem uprising occurred, but it was discussed widely in the Black press, and its effects still lingered in 1937 when he arrived in the city. The uprising began on 19 March 1935. Its proximal cause: a rumor that Lino Rivera, a Puerto Rican teenager, had been beaten and killed in the basement of the white-owned Kress Five and Ten after being accused of shoplifting. Over the next two days, three African Americans died from injuries, over one hundred were arrested, and shops along 125th Street sustained losses due to closures, break-ins, and theft while crowds battled the police. A riot commission appointed by New York City mayor Fiorello La Guardia sought to manage the events by discerning their causes and offering recommendations for addressing the conditions that led to them.[3] While these recommendations helped ameliorate some issues, Harlem, like many other Black districts, became identified in the press and in literature with poverty and simmering rage. Ellison was in New York in 1943 when Harlem exploded again during one of several racial conflicts in American cities that summer.[4] These conflicts were inflamed by the inequitable treatment of African American soldiers and war industries workers, which added an acute form to existing grievances. On 1 August, a policeman detained Marjorie Polite at Harlem's Hotel Braddock. Robert Bandy, a soldier home from the front, was shot when he attempted to help Polite. Although Bandy was taken to the hospital and lived, rumors of a soldier's killing while trying to defend a woman from police harassment precipitated two nights of unrest. This uprising led to six deaths, hundreds of injuries, significant property damages, and yet another riot commission report.

Students would benefit from comparing how today's politicized media sphere defines and positions the Black Lives Matter protests with the varying interpretations the Harlem uprisings spurred. In their focus on commercial sites, the "commodity riots," as Marilynn S. Johnson terms these events, reflected a salient change in African American political responses to injustice: "This new form of rioting reflected the increasing isolation of the post-war ghetto as well as the changing dynamics of American racism, a racism that became more subtle, impersonal, and bureaucratic. Moreover, the rioter's hostility toward police and other municipal authorities suggested the state itself was now directly implicated in the problem of racism" (270).[5] While some media outlets sought to dismiss the uprisings as the result of a few individuals causing trouble—what historians term *riffraff theory*, still typical in commentary on uprisings—the systematic targeting of white-owned businesses made the uprisings' protest element clear. Black activists sought to counter redlining, restrictive covenants, inadequate housing and public health conditions, high costs of goods and services, discriminatory policing, and a dearth of work opportunities. The campaigns they organized helped define these injustices and raise public opposition, creating the conditions for insurgency. The focus on stores in the 1935 uprising reflected recent "Don't Buy Where You Can't Work" campaigns focusing on discriminatory hiring in the Harlem retail landscape, even while the spectacle of the uprising often eclipsed those campaigns in the broader public view. Many observers saw it as a new form of social unrest, leading to discussions in mainstream and Black press venues over its general meaning and what to call it.[6] The Federal Writers' Project (FWP) New York City guidebooks, on which Ellison worked, figured the 1935 Harlem uprising as a warning, suggesting governmental inaction would lead to more unrest while simultaneously making a case for state-led interventions like public housing and social insurance.

Ellison provided an eyewitness account of the 1943 uprising for the *New York Post* in "All of Harlem Was Awake," a useful intertext for students. Ellison leaves a Harlem subway station at 3:00 a.m. "to the sound of gunfire and shouting as of a great celebration," signaling the uprising's affective confusion (49). On the street he learns the uprising is in response to the killing of Bandy, confirmed by a passerby but later recognized by Ellison as rumor. Ellison's account illuminates the chaotic sensory environment but also the participants' purposiveness, stating, "Instructions were shouted among the mob as to what stores to attack. As in the uprising of 1935, no Negro store was knowingly molested" (50). Ellison notes the selective targeting of grocery stores and pawnshops, direct contact points of monetary transfer from Black citizens to white-owned businesses. At the same time, he highlights the way the uprising takes on a life independent of elite direction. He notes the inefficacy of the attempts of a local organization, the Negro Neighborhood Victory Committee, to calm the crowd with assurances of La Guardia's attention to their concerns. In the end, Ellison states that although "the crowds had thinned [. . .] the situation has not ended" (51). Echoing a common rhetorical positioning in other African American studies of urban social dynamics of the era, he asserts that municipal responsiveness would likely determine future peace or unrest, an open ending that foreshadows the uprising of his novel.

*Invisible Man* presents the unfolding events of the uprising in a chaotic series of images and rumors filtered through the narrator's consciousness as he rushes across the Harlem landscape. It moves away from the diagnostic framing of riot commission reports designed to assess causes, provide potential methods of redress, and restore a sense of ease to the public. Instead, the subjective framing shows how the uprisings in Harlem and elsewhere offered a new approach to political action. Effective political organizing was a central concern for Ellison, as it was for many other intellectuals of his generation, and the Harlem uprisings occasioned both hopes and concerns.[7] Ellison's friend and mentor Richard Wright spoke of the need for mass movements to simultaneously resist racial and class exploitation in his 1941 photodocumentary book *Twelve Million Black Voices*, which pairs well with Ellison's novel. Viewed by Wright as spontaneous outbursts against inequity, injustice, and neglect by "inarticulate black men and women, filled with a naive, peasant anger," the uprisings were strikingly different from the organized, class-conscious movement Wright's photobook envisions emerging in urban industrial contexts (*Twelve Million Black Voices* 145). Letters from Ellison to Wright after the publication of *Twelve Million Black Voices*

70    URBAN UPRISING

show that he largely approved of Wright's analysis, and Ellison's depiction of the 1943 uprising as a "naïve, peasant-like act of revenge" directly echoes Wright's division between class-conscious, organized action and folk reaction (Ellison, "All" 50).[8] Similarly, Ellison's 1948 essay about the Lafargue Clinic, "Harlem Is Nowhere"—another intertext on which students could draw—builds on Wright's ideas about psychology, culture, and organized action to portray the uprising as a collective lashing out linked to the failure of both governmental remedies and effective organizing. Ellison hoped the clinic would offer Harlemites "an insight into the relation between [their] problems and [their] environment, and out of this understanding to reforge the will to endure in a hostile world" (*Collected Essays* 327). Like Wright, Ellison saw healing from trauma and mental reframing as necessary precursors to effective political action. This accounts for much of his ambivalence in the novel.

These depictions of the Harlem uprisings as largely reactive elide a deeper focus on Black political organizing. Claude McKay's "Harlem Runs Wild," a 1940 essay for *The Nation*, provides for students an excellent contrast with Ellison's 1943 eyewitness account as well as an introduction to the complex dynamics of African American activism. McKay argues the backdrop of the 1935 uprising was a web of collaborating and competing groups, including communist Young Liberators, the Negro Industrial and Clerical Alliance of Sufi Abdul Hamid, and the Citizens' League for Fair Play of Adam Clayton Powell, Jr. McKay shows how the defeat of these groups and subsequent rollback of their achievements left Black Harlemites frustrated and bereft of good political options as entrenched white interests undercut organizing efforts. Cheryl Greenberg affirms McKay, detailing how both the 1935 and 1943 Harlem uprisings were spurred by the collapse of political efforts that had helped Harlemites articulate grievances (397). Ellison, too, would have been aware of these dynamics, as he worked for the Greater New York Coordinating Committee for Employment, Powell's successor coalition to the Citizens' League. Following the 1943 uprisings in Los Angeles and Detroit, Ellison presciently lamented his disappointed hopes to Sanora Babb: "my people want action so desperately and attended the meeting not because so and so sponsored it, but came because some action would be forthcoming. Instead the riot came. And more will follow" (*Selected Letters* 160).[9]

Political disinvestment does figure as a cause of *Invisible Man*'s uprising, but the narrator perceives that disinvestment as the result of a Brotherhood calculation that fragments Harlem's political leadership. In his interview with Brother Hambro, the narrator learns the Brotherhood is sacrificing Harlem to advance their cause elsewhere. A proponent of the need to tie international anti-fascism to struggles against Jim Crow during World War II, Ellison saw the American Communist Party (CPUSA) as having committed an unforgivable strategic error in deprioritizing homefront justice.[10] Placing blame on the Brotherhood for the uprising threatens to subsume the novel's political exploration of uprisings into Cold War conspiracy fantasy and evacuate the narrative of Black agency.

However, Ellison's narrator is notably mistaken in his judgments on several occasions, and an account giving the Brotherhood that much agency would undercut the novel's critique of rational planning. This should give readers pause in confirming the Brotherhood as the primary agent of the uprising. So, too, should the novel's slippage between figuring the Brotherhood as an avatar for the CPUSA and its role in an allegory of American whiteness. In lieu of McKay's field account of neighborhood organizing, *Invisible Man* offers a critique of causal certainty while mediating its account of African American political agency through symbolic figures connected to the uprising.

As a causal counterpoint to the Brotherhood conspiracy, the narrator encounters several rumors about the cause and course of events, including police shootings of various people, attacks on women and children, political agitation, even the weather. Studies of race riots have pointed out how rumors and interpretations of events tap into deep-seated anxieties and senses of injustice, even encouraging theories of conspiracies.[11] For students comparing Ellison's representation of uprisings with the present, one crucial development has been the increased availability of amateur video evidence and social media networks allowing distribution of documented abuses. Ellison's focus on rumor seems to contrast with the seeming certainties of video documentation; juxtaposition in the classroom could highlight the framing and distribution of documentary artifacts and also how their accompanying narratives facilitate insurgency. The novel's focus on uncertainty points toward Ellison's attempt to grapple with this new dynamics of protest that was neither fully planned nor immediate. While not fully conscious, in Wright's sense, and certainly risking media and political appropriation, these mass uprisings nevertheless presented a degree of efficacy, making injustices visible and present in ways that were difficult to efface.

Ellison's exploration and evolving views of the social and cultural phenomena shaping Black politics throughout the 1940s also informed his understanding of the uprisings' significance. "Harlem Is Nowhere" suggests much of urban Black culture was held over from a Southern agrarian past and thus poorly adapted to urban political environments. However, in his FWP work, Ellison encountered folklore theories by Sterling Brown and Benjamin Botkin that viewed urban vernacular culture as a continuously creative and present-engaged mode of expression.[12] The modernity of vernacular culture in this framing also made its expressions more available as a basis for political action. In 1943, clashes between armed services personnel and zoot-suited Mexican American, Filipino American, and African American sharpies—members of a jazz-and-blues subculture—flared in Los Angeles, Philadelphia, and Detroit. Sharpies' fashion, lingo, and behavior all struck back at the citizenship ethos of the war, flouting somber evocations of patriotic duty and consumer goods rationing. Ellison became fascinated by the inventive vernacular dynamics of this expression of resistance.[13]

Understanding these vernacular political contexts can help students make better sense of Rinehart, who, among many identities, appears as a sharpie and catalyzes the narrator's exploration of the political possibilities of Black urban

72    URBAN UPRISING

vernacular culture. Rinehartism expands the covert operation of the narrator's grandfather into a shifting, multifront war of position, one about which the narrator remains ambivalent. Rinehart's chameleon act is politically promising insofar as it allows him to operate across multiple contexts. But Rinehart also occasions questions that reflect Ellison's concerns about the uprisings. When one of the narrator's Brotherhood comrades, failing to recognize the narrator in his Rinehart disguise, challenges him to draw his switchblade, the comrade invokes stereotypes promoted in the media of young Black men as prone to knife violence. As the narrator encounters others who know Rinehart, he recognizes that Rinehart seems to have few priorities other than himself, and the narrator starts to equate "Rinehartism—cynicism" (*Invisible Man* 504). For Ellison, this cynicism might be enough to generate action but not enough to support an organized politics. It might even lead to serious mistakes: the narrator figures his susceptibility to the Brotherhood's plan as being a result of his willingness to pretend to go along with them.

The wealth of critical discussion on the phantomlike Rinehart contrasts with the comparative dearth of commentary on Dupre and his men, whom the narrator encounters during the uprising. Bringing together Ellison's interests in the psychology of Harlem, vernacular culture, and political possibilities, Dupre symbolically represents an alternate, more collective, and more violent response to disinvestment in Harlem, if again one about which Ellison remains somewhat ambivalent. Linking Dupre to Mary Rambo and Rinehart as symbolic folk figures, George E. Kent notes how Dupre extends the book's focus on the politics of the vernacular: "The dramatic and symbolic function of Dupre and his followers is to reflect the folk ability to move with poise amidst chaos and in contradiction to the flat rational assumptions of the Brotherhood concerning its mission as planners for others. The rioters move with a plan that directly confronts Reality" (54). Their plan follows the pattern of the Harlem uprisings, linking the historical response to community disinvestment to Ellison's symbolic one. The narrator joins Dupre's group as they systematically appropriate consumer goods from stores, symbolically highlighting their exclusion from labor and consumer goods. Then they pivot to set fire to another symbol of their exclusion, the tenements where they have suffered. Dupre notes, "My kid died from the T-bees in that deathtrap, but I bet a man ain't no more go'n be *born* in there" (Ellison, *Invisible Man* 546). His willingness to destroy his own home speaks to the feeling of being "nowhere" that Ellison chronicled in his essay on Harlem psychology.

Like Rinehart, Dupre raises questions about what kinds of action are possible and most effective in changing deeply entrenched structures of oppression. Ellison's answers are both complex and ambivalent. The narrator is awed by the purposiveness and follow-through of Dupre. He exclaims, "They did it themselves . . . planned it, organized it, applied the flame" (549). The admiration here speaks to the narrator's hunger for effective action and his frustration with dependency on white resources and agendas that have undercut many of the other political strategies explored in the novel. Symbolically, setting fire to the tenements is a powerful statement of the desperate defiance captured in McKay's poem "If We Must Die" and Langston Hughes's meditation on a dream deferred in "Harlem." It highlights the Harlemites' refusal to put up with secondary citizenship status that consigns them to precarity. Politically, it is more of a gamble. Dupre's wager is that eliminating the substandard housing will force change; the state or some other actor will have to acknowledge the problem and remedy the irreversible damage. The revision of public housing policy in New York to include targeted housing for Black neighborhoods after the 1935 uprising suggests that this gamble may indeed pay off.[14]

At the same time, the narrative questions whether Dupre's actions are ultimately helpful or harmful. Unlike the taking of goods from white-owned stores, which yields a material surplus for little risk, the burning of the tenements may potentially hurt Dupre's men and their families as much as their landlords, who have likely insured their property. Ellison figures his concern in the confrontation between Dupre and Lottie, his pregnant spouse, who pleads, "Please Dupre [. . .] *please*. You know my time's almost here . . . *you know it is*. If you do it now, where am I going to go?" (546). Her concern is warranted. Slum-reform policies often focused as heavily on destroying substandard housing stock as they did on replacement, while other measures systematically excluded African Americans from the explosion of suburban housing that New Deal housing acts helped to engineer.

The novel's ambivalent take on the uprising prefigures Ellison's notable reserve as the slow pace of reform in the 1960s flared into more urban uprisings.[15] At the same time, Ellison continued to see the value in moving people to the point that they would see themselves as capable of taking action. In "If the Twain Shall Meet," his 1964 review of Howard Zinn's *The Southern Mystique*, Ellison highlights the way that African Americans were preparing for a more democratic society by engaging in acts of protest (*Collected Essays* 578–80). Ellison told a 1966 Senate subcommittee investigating the uprisings that war and civil unrest had often benefitted Black claims of citizenship, stating, "When there is a breakdown of the structure, democracy spreads" (qtd. in Rampersad 428). *Invisible Man* provides a critical rejoinder to the diagnostic and preventive pattern of the riot commission report, the sensationalized simplification of journalism, and the heroic telos of revolutionary accounts. Refocusing the uprising narrative on questions of Black political agency, Ellison's novel refuses to see mass uprising as an endpoint. Instead it becomes part of a broader politics of critical engagement, hovering between the consciously planned and the spontaneous, and driven by experiences that require processing through multiple cognitive, affective, and historical frames as the narrator does when he moves underground. In this way, the uprising scene anticipates the narrator's attention to the value of vernacular "chaos" as counterpoint to "pattern" in *Invisible Man*'s epilogue (Ellison 580–81). At a time

74    URBAN UPRISING

when African American grievances have again flared into open mass protest, Ellison's attention to causal overdetermination of mass protest, exploration of its political dynamics, and insistence on complexity and creative engagement may well offer the novel's most important lessons. Whether students are trying to understand why uprisings occur or seeking to understand their effectiveness, the uprising scene in *Invisible Man* offers a complex and engaged account of an emergent midcentury insurgency.

NOTES

1. A conflated, politically valenced lexicon attends these moments of upheaval. In this essay, I use the term *uprising* to describe mass urban actions led by members of minority groups because it offers a balance of intentionality, spontaneity, and confrontation while indicating the dynamics of power. The commonly used term *riot* problematically cuts off considerations of agency, directionality of violence, and connection to organized politics, and historically it has been used to shield insurance companies from damage claims by Black policyholders. I have limited its usage to references to riot commissions, the term *commodity riot*, common names of specific uprisings such as the Zoot Suit Riots, and the catch-all phrase *race riot*.

2. See Jackson, *Indignant Generation*, for an expansive account of the culture and politics of African American writers between the 1930s and the 1960s.

3. See Lupo's *Flak-Catchers* for an account of the role of riot commissions in managing public anxieties over uprisings. She notes, "Essentially, [the riot commissions'] charge is to prevent further violence. In doing so, riot commissions process the violence into politics as usual" (10).

4. Sites of other racial conflicts that summer included Beaumont, Texas; Detroit; Los Angeles; and Mobile, Alabama.

5. Johnson's article focuses on the 1943 Harlem uprising as the origin of the commodity riot, but primary sources show the 1935 uprising was seen as its launching point.

6. See Lupo 54 on riffraff theory in riot commission and media accounts. On concerns about terminology, see, for example, Claude McKay's essay on the 1935 Harlem uprising "Harlem Runs Wild" or, by Adam Clayton Powell, Sr., "The Harlem Riot of 1943," both of which are available in Sundquist's *Cultural Contexts for Ralph Ellison's* Invisible Man.

7. For a range of critical accounts tracing Ellison's interest in Black leadership, see Jackson, *Indignant Generation*; O'Meally, *Craft*; Rice; McSweeney; and Waligora-Davis.

8. See also Ellison's 3 Nov. 1941 letter to Wright in *Selected Letters* 143–47.

9. Ellison most likely refers to the Negro Freedom Rally in Madison Square Garden on 7 June 1943.

10. See Ellison, "Negro," for his views on wartime political strategy.

11. See Marilynn S. Johnson for discussion of the role of rumors in the 1943 uprisings and Waligora-Davis for how Ellison handles these in *Invisible Man*.

12. See Hirsch 61 for a discussion of Ellison's participation in the FWP folklore projects and their influence on *Invisible Man*.

13. In a 4 July 1943 letter to Sanora Babb, Ellison notes an unpublished attempt to grapple with the zoot suit phenomenon intended for *Negro Quarterly* (*Selected Letters*

160). See also Jackson, "Ralph Ellison, Sharpies" for a discussion of the evolution of Ellison's thought on the political potential of the zoot suit and Black vernacular culture.

14. While seeing Ellison prior to their marriage, Fanny Buford worked for the Urban League from 1943 to 1945 and then the New York City Housing Authority from 1945 to 1946 and would have been deeply familiar with the issues of inadequate housing.

15. See Rampersad 413–61 for an account of Ellison's political activities and the reaction against him during the 1960s. Ironically, sociologists deployed Ellison's concept of invisibility to explore the origins of the 1965 Los Angeles uprising. See Johnson et al.

# Claiming the Lens of Love:
# Reading *Invisible Man* through 1 Corinthians 13

*Martha Greene Eads*

Having taught *Invisible Man* for over two decades, I recognize the near absurdity of trying to do so in anything less than a semester-long, upper-level graduate seminar. As Whitman wrote of himself, the lengthy novel contains multitudes. Even so, I persist in inviting undergraduate students, usually in survey courses, at least to sip from the many wells Ellison taps: music, trickster traditions, foodways, political movements, and literary precedents. Although I inevitably fret over rushing too quickly to do the novel justice, I remind myself that Ellison would surely urge me to practice laughing in the face of absurdity. With that outcome in mind, I devote considerable time to acquainting students with yet another source that feeds the novel: the Christian scriptures, especially 1 Corinthians 13.[1] What could be more absurdly hopeful than embracing that passage's challenge to "[rejoice] in the truth; [bear] all things, [believe] all things, [hope] all things, [endure] all things"—even in the frustration of having to hurry through a masterpiece of world literature?

Taking time to foster students' understanding of trauma and resilience at the beginning of the unit packs the schedule even tighter but proves worthwhile. Among the materials I introduce from my university's Center for Justice and Peacebuilding (CJP) is John Paul Lederach's "meeting place" model for transcending harms. In this imaginative exercise, Lederach, a cofounder of the center, challenges peace-builders to bring truth and righteousness as well as mercy and peace into any effort to respond to wrongs. He bases his model on a sentence from Psalm 85.10: "Mercy and truth are met together; righteousness and peace have kissed each other." Lederach has demonstrated through years of mediating seemingly intractable conflicts that applying all four virtues to an injustice can sometimes enable those affected to reach understanding, empathy, and even reconciliation. Although Ellison does not draw directly from Psalm 85, he clearly depicts Invisible Man's exercises in truth seeking and telling. That Invisible Man also pursues righteousness, rendered in many English translations of the Hebrew scriptures as "justice," as well as mercy and peace eventually becomes evident in our considerations, as well.

Students and I also discuss the CJP's Strategies for Trauma Awareness and Resilience (STAR) program's Cycles of Violence (fig. 1) and Breaking Cycles of Violence (fig. 2) diagrams, which help us contend with the novel's painful content and envision social and political change. The Cycles of Violence diagram helps us see how Invisible Man, for example, "acts in" before trying on "acting-out" behaviors modeled by such characters as Bledsoe. Breaking Cycles offers a hopeful trajectory in which Invisible Man's acceptance of losses might be only a first step. Students need not come from any faith tradition to find these CJP resources intriguing. Many report that they are personally as well as academically helpful.

Certainly, the novel's ultimate if tentatively hopeful vision transcends religion, and to overemphasize its religious aspects will confuse and even alienate some readers.[2] Nevertheless, introducing students to biblical resources that have informed conflict and trauma studies as well as *Invisible Man* itself enriches their understanding and may kindle their own hope for theologically grounded, socially responsible engagement during the national upheaval they face today. Invisible Man's rejection of forms of Christianity that have accommodated and even exacerbated injustice in the United States, his awakening to compassionate solidarity through encounters with erotic love, and his longings for deep connection and authentic spirituality are experiences to which students still relate, over half a century after the book's publication.

Invisible Man's engagement, disengagement, and tentative reengagement with Christianity fit within the book's broader dialectical trajectory. That trajectory becomes apparent through his repeated allusions to another work of Christian spirituality, T. S. Eliot's *Four Quartets*, whose repeated line "in my beginning is my end" (123) echoes throughout Ellison's text. First, in the prologue, when he pulls himself back from recounting incidents that occurred well after his arrival in New York, Invisible Man says, "But that's getting too far ahead of the story, almost to the end, although the end is in the beginning and lies far ahead" (Ellison, *Invisible Man* 6). At Tod Clifton's funeral, Invisible Man alludes again to the *Four Quartets*: "That's the end in the beginning and there's no encore" (454). Finally, when he retreats underground to reflect on his experience, he utters another variation on the phrase, a sort of verbal talisman: "The end was in the beginning" (571). Having reached the limits of history and science as presented to him, Invisible Man retrieves religion—or at least one aspect of it: the understanding of love the apostle Paul outlines in his first letter to the early Christian community at Corinth. Retrieving also the metaphor of a boomerang he has employed previously (15, 476), Invisible Man says, "Thus I have come a long way and returned and boomeranged a long way from the point in society toward which I originally aspired" (573). As he comes to terms with not only his shattered illusions but also his complicity, he explains:

> The very act of trying to put it all down has confused me and negated some of the anger and some of the bitterness. So it is that now I denounce and defend, or feel prepared to defend. I condemn and affirm, say no and say yes, say yes and say no. I denounce because though implicated and partially responsible, I have been hurt to the point of abysmal pain, hurt to the point of invisibility. And I defend because in spite of all I find that I love. In order to get some of it down I *have* to love. I sell you no phony forgiveness. I'm a desperate man—but too much of your life will be lost, its meaning lost, unless you approach it as much through love as through

hate. So I approach it through division. So I denounce and I defend and I hate and I love. (580)

While the forms of Christianity Invisible Man has previously encountered feature phony forgiveness (indeed, phony everything), the love Paul extols requires, even rejoices in, truth telling (1 Cor. 13.6).

As he announces the birth of a love that includes denouncing wrongs, Invisible Man also proclaims his intention to emerge from hibernation, shedding his "old skin" to embrace a form of social responsibility quite different from that about which he tries to speak in the "battle royal" scene (Ellison, *Invisible Man* 580, 581; 30–31). The hibernation image, like that of the boomerang, has appeared first in the prologue, where Invisible Man notes its dialectical nature as a form of retreat, providing "covert preparation for a more overt action" (13). Moreover, while his use of skin imagery deepens his identification with hibernating creatures, it also sounds an echo among readers familiar with Jesus's teaching about not putting new wine in old, brittle wineskins incapable of stretching to accommodate fermentation (Matt. 9.17; Mark 2.2; Luke 5.37–39). Reentering society is going to stretch Invisible Man in all kinds of ways; the love compelling him to try again must be willing to "[suffer] long" (1 Cor. 13.4).

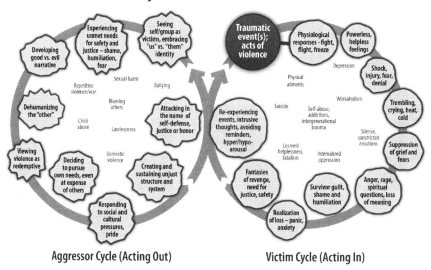

Figure 1. Cycles of Violence diagram. © Carolyn Yoder and Strategies for Trauma Awareness and Resilience (STAR), Center for Justice and Peacebuilding, Eastern Mennonite University. Based in part on the writings of Olga Botcharova, Peter Levine, Vamik Volkan, and Walter Wink. Reprinted with permission.

Although Invisible Man has surely often heard and read Paul's hymn to love (rendered "charity" in the King James Version of the Bible to which the character alludes), many if not all of those he has heard preach it have failed to embody it. The Church Ellison depicts serves as a stage on which even the white characters who enact benevolence cannot completely conceal the "blood-froth sparkling their chins like their familiar tobacco juice, and upon their lips the curdled milk of black slave mammies' withered dugs, a treacherous and fluid knowledge of our being, imbibed at our source and now regurgitated foul upon us" (Ellison, *Invisible Man* 112). While encouraging Black people to aspire, these white Christians simultaneously "described to us the limitations of our lives [. . .] the staggering folly of our impatience to rise even higher" (112). In such a confusing and corrupt social context, "[e]ven one of the more fashionable pastors" can join the leering, jeering crowd at the battle royal, a community ritual both racist and misogynistic (18).

This form of white Christianity functions as a container for the Black Christianity of Invisible Man's youth, markers of which emerge in the prologue. His reefer-induced reverie features not only an African American spiritual but also

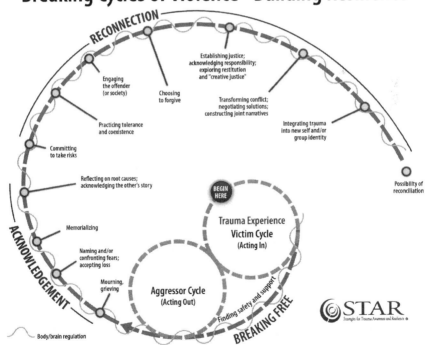

Figure 2. Breaking Cycles of Violence and Building Resilience diagram. © Strategies for Trauma Awareness and Resilience (STAR), Center for Justice and Peacebuilding, Eastern Mennonite University. Adapted from Botcharova, p. 288. Reprinted with permission.

80     LENS OF LOVE

a call-and-response sermon, echoes of those he has undoubtedly heard since early childhood. Juxtaposed against song and sermon are the sounds of a slave auction, and the singer describes her complicated and tortured relationship with the man who both owned her and fathered her children. Later in the novel, Invisible Man describes in religious terms his college, based on the Tuskegee Institute. Invisible Man may have initially conceived of the college as "Eden," but its founders and funders are white people whose charitable acts are characterized "by a benign and impersonal indifference" and whose "most innocent words were acts of violence" (110). These deep-pocketed donors demand that he and his fellow students "accept and love and accept even if we did not love" (112). As he reluctantly departs from that faux Eden on his way to New York, Invisible Man glimpses a snake reminiscent of the one in the book of Genesis, the serpent tempter (156).

Invisible Man eventually learns that Black as well as white Christians can succumb to the temptations of deceit, greed, and manipulation. Although his memories of the campus swirl around a lovely steepled building from which the sounds of bells, trombones, organ, and voices ring, the college chapel, like that in Eliot's *Waste Land*, is a site of peril and desolation (36–37).[3] The praise there rises not willingly to God but dutifully to Horatio Alger philanthropists; the body and blood appear not symbolically in Eucharistic bread and wine but literally in the presence of formerly enslaved and still-abused Black people; the mood is not one of worship but one of judgment (111, 109). The institution's president, Dr. Bledsoe, sits at the campus's center, spinning lies for Black students as well as for white donors. Looking to Bledsoe as a role model, Invisible Man fails to understand how disposable he is to the older man, even after hearing him speak in the bluntest possible terms of gaming the system at other Black people's expense (143).

Although Invisible Man is initially unaware of the problems associated with both white and Black Christianity, my students are not. They are therefore unsurprised when he sloughs off his formational religious practices upon going North. While his impulse in times of stress has been to pray (107), thinking about praying now makes him homesick. Picking up a Gideon Bible in his room at the Men's House, he finds that he cannot even read its familiar words. "I put the Bible aside," he says. "This was New York. I had to get a job and earn money" (162). After all, Mr. Norton, the donor whose regard Bledsoe wanted to preserve at all costs, has told Invisible Man "[s]elf-reliance is a most worthy virtue" (108). With this counsel in mind, Invisible Man sheds conventional religion. In its place, he dons various alternatives: trade unionism, communism, Pan-Africanism, Rastafarianism, and a yet another predatory form of Christian expression, exemplified by Rinehart, whose name—as Bledsoe's does—suggests much about his character.[4]

Even as Ellison searingly depicts some of the abuses American Christianities have perpetrated, he nevertheless endows Invisible Man with a wistfulness about religion that suggests longing for faith in a purer form. The young man's

Martha Greene Eads    81

relationship to his landlady Mary, whose name is also significant and whose loving hospitality is surely rooted in faith, exemplifies this ambivalence. Ellison's essay "Harlem Is Nowhere" illuminates the disorientation experienced by many African-Americans who migrated, as Invisible Man does, for economic and social opportunities:

> Not that a Negro is worse off in the North than in the South, but that in the North he surrenders and does not replace certain supports to his personality. [. . .] *[H]e leaves a still authoritative religion which gives his life a semblance of metaphysical wholeness*, a family structure which is relatively stable, and a body of folklore [. . .] that serves him as a guide to action. [. . .] [W]ithout institutions to give him direction—*the religious ones being inadequate*, and those offered by political and labor leaders obviously incomplete and opportunistic—the individual feels that his world and his personality are out of key.    (57; italics mine)

Mary's modest way of life will not accommodate Invisible Man's ambitions, yet he cannot entirely escape its hold. While he senses that he cannot remain with her and achieve his dream, he nevertheless longs to return to the haven she has made of even a roach-ridden apartment.

As memories of Mary haunt him, scriptural passages also continue to surface unexpectedly in his thinking. He may have suspended regular Bible reading, but the Word has permeated his consciousness. He alludes directly to 1 Corinthians 13.1–2 in his speech after the eviction, declaring that the "theory and practice" of those in power is "break him! Deprive him of his wages! It's use his protest as a *sounding brass* to frighten him into silence; it's beat his ideas and his hopes and homely aspirations into a *tinkling cymbal*! A small, cracked cymbal to tinkle on the Fourth of July! Only muffle it! Don't let it sound too loud!" (342, italics mine).[5] Reflecting in the prologue on his impulse "to put invisibility down in black and white" and the possibility of resuming his work as an orator and rabble-rouser, he concludes, "Who knows? All sickness is not unto death, neither is invisibility" (14). The phrase "sickness unto death" comes from the Gospel of John, in which Jesus, upon hearing of his friend Lazarus's illness, observes, "This sickness is not unto death, but for the glory of God, that the Son of God might be glorified thereby" (11.4). Lazarus subsequently dies but emerges. Invisible Man is, by the book's conclusion, entombed in a sense, too, preparing for his own form of resurrection.

What, then, summons him forth? Love—akin to that described by the apostle Paul, who experienced being blinded by a brilliant light that illuminated his spiritual darkness. In his Damascus-road experience, described in the New Testament book of Acts, Paul (then called Saul) heard the resurrected Jesus ask, "Saul, Saul, why persecutest thou Me?" From that point, Paul joined the followers of Jesus he had formerly helped strike down. A prolific correspondent, he instructed converts from various backgrounds in doctrine and practice. Even

82     LENS OF LOVE

today, the thirteenth chapter of 1 Corinthians is among the Bible passages most familiar to Americans, including college students who may have little other acquaintance with the Bible.[6] Often read in wedding ceremonies, Paul's "love chapter" to which Invisible Man so often alludes challenges Christians to relate generously to others.

Invisible Man, of course, ventures nowhere near the marriage altar, and his interactions with women are hardly exemplary.[7] I invite students to consider, however, how Invisible Man's encounter with the young woman at the battle royal, bordering on the pornographic in its treatment of both sex and violence, serves as the startling starting point for his growth in love. The "magnificent blonde" procured to dance for the event's white hosts is as nameless to Invisible Man as he and his fellow fighters are to them (18). Indeed, if the language he first uses to describe her is any indication, Invisible Man despises and objectifies her as surely as the white men despise and objectify him.

Reviewing the STAR Cycles of Violence diagram at this point in class discussions illuminates how dehumanizing language emerges and recurs in cycles of interpersonal and systemic violence (fig. 1). This review helps free us to acknowledge our emotional responses to the scene and others like it even as we examine critically how demeaning language and behaviors function. We note that even without any awareness of Lederach's "meeting place" practice, Ellison depicts in the battle royal how empathic identification can emerge. As he observes the dancer in distress, Invisible Man moves from lusting after her to empathizing with her, recognizing "terror and disgust in her eyes, almost like my own terror and that which I saw in some of the other boys" (20). Although he is insufficiently prepared yet to process the incident's significance, Invisible Man is beginning to recognize his kinship with a fellow American also objectified and used by the powerful.

Later, in his own bid for power, Invisible Man resolves that he, too, will use women and thus illustrates the STAR model's illustration of how victims of injustice sometimes subsequently oppress others. Determining to seduce the "tipsy and wistful" Sybil, Invisible Man initially accepts the role of lover-predator in her interracial sexual fantasy. Although he seems at first to be emulating Bledsoe, who has earlier acknowledged that he "had to wait and plan and lick around . . . Yes, [. . .] to act the n____" to achieve his goals, Invisible Man does not follow through (143).[8] Instead, he engages in self-examination: "What had I done to her, allowed her to do? Had all of it filtered down to me? [. . .] All of it? I'm invisible" (525–26). Invisible Man remains largely invisible to Sybil, but she was never invisible and now is no longer a pawn to him.

While Sybil is sufficiently perceptive to the sense that the two of them are "kind of alike," her awareness stops there (520). Invisible Man, in contrast, considers the likely roots of her rape fantasy, concluding, "[W]hy be surprised, when that's what they hear all their lives. When it's made into a great power and they're taught to worship all kinds of power?" (520). Such reflection demonstrates his capacity to "acknowledge multiple stories," an important growth point on the STAR Breaking Cycles of Violence diagram (fig. 2). Furthermore, his self-knowledge has enabled him to move beyond using Sybil to empathizing with her, a process not unlike one Paul describes in 1 Corinthians 13.11–12: "When I was a child, I spake as a child, I understood as a child, I thought as a child: but when I became a man, I put away childish things. For now we see through a glass, darkly; but then face to face: now I know in part; but then shall I know even as also I am known." Within the novel's own world, Invisible Man's understanding of Sybil's plight harkens back to his earlier identification with the blonde dancer. Using imagery straight from the fight, Invisible Man says that Sybil "had [him] on the ropes" (520, 21). To reinforce the connection between these scenes, Ellison also has Invisible Man compare the specks of dust on his briefcase to his memories of the battle royal (527).

These memories rise unbidden, he says, like a "remembered prayer" that surfaces for Invisible Man when he is in bed with Sybil. "I must have dozed," he says, waking to "the tinkling of ice in a glass, the shrill of bells" (526). Realizing that the phone is ringing, he says, "[F]or no reason at all, the words of a childhood prayer spilled through my mind like swift water" (526).[9] When the call, a warning from someone in the Brotherhood, is cut short and Invisible Man tries to return it, the rhythmic sound of the busy signal reminds him of a repeated "Amen-Amen-Ah man" (527). Ellison does not reveal what Invisible Man's prayer has been, but it is likely the Lord's Prayer, in which Jesus teaches His followers to ask, "Forgive us our trespasses, as we forgive those who trespass against us" (Matt. 6.9–15 and Luke 11.2–4).

Strikingly, the prayer and Invisible Man's mention of it a page later each follow Sybil's having twice called him "Boo'ful" (526, 527). He has earlier asked her for her name, even though he already knew it—a question she never asks him. He addresses or thinks of her by name repeatedly, sometimes even calling her "Syb," "Sybil, dear," and even once "Sybil, my too-late-too-early love" (523, 521, 528). In contrast, even after they spend an evening in bed together, she observes dismissively, "Poor boo-ful. [. . .] Don't know his name." As he, however, directs a cab driver to get Sybil safely home, Invisible Man tells the man, "She's precious, a great lady" (532). After they part, he thinks, "Sybil, forgive me" (532). Disabused of the brief vision he has entertained of meaningful connection with her, he nevertheless declines to hold Sybil's treatment of him against her. Drawing on mercy and peace, he has already forgiven her "her trespasses."

Invisible Man's erotic experiences, first with the unnamed blonde dancer and then with Sybil, thus serve as bookends in a novel about loving citizenship. The two women are not "merely" women; they are, like Invisible Man, American, as the dancer's United States flag tattoo and the seduction-rape scene's American Beauty roses remind us (19, 516). Indeed, Invisible Man even asks Sybil, in reference to her fantasy, "What's happening here [. . .] a new birth of a nation?" (522). While he is, of course, alluding to the 1915 D. W. Griffith film in which white women face the constant threat of rape by Black men, Ellison's word choices are always purposeful. A nation in which white women fantasize about being raped by Black men in order to get close to power *needs* renewal. The same

84     LENS OF LOVE

nation, in which Black men subject themselves to being mouthpiece-pawns in white men's colleges and social movements, needs to be born again.

Bledsoe, Invisible Man's early role model, has already acknowledged the systemic nature of these abuses, illustrating one stop on the STAR diagram's "acting out" cycle of violence. Expressing pride in the way he has managed to make the system work for him, he explains, "The only [white folk] I even pretend to please are the *big* white folk, and even those I control more than they control me. This is a power set-up son, and I'm at the controls. You think about that. When you buck up against me, you're bucking against power, rich white folk's power, the nation's power—which means government power!" In a perverse hymn to power, Bledsoe declares, "Power doesn't have to show off. Power is confident, self-assuring, self-starting, and self-stopping, self-warming and self-justifying" (142). Readers familiar with 1 Corinthians 13 may recognize the kind of sequencing Paul offers in verses 4 and 5: "Charity suffereth long, and is kind; charity envieth not; charity vaunteth not itself, is not puffed up, / Doth not behave itself unseemly, seeketh not her own, is not easily provoked, thinketh no evil." Bledsoe has, in effect, turned those verses inside out. Much later, even having listened to this perverse teacher and tasted the bitter fruit of his misguided gospel, Invisible Man remains sufficiently great-hearted to wonder whether politics can "ever be an expression of love" (452). Bledsoe may have sent Invisible Man on a poor-Robin chase for power, but the young man finds love, instead, and with it a kind of absurd hope.

Although Invisible Man comes to an awareness of what to negate and what to affirm through his encounters with fellow Black people such as Bledsoe and with sexually desirable or desiring white women, the ways in which the women become linked in his mind to American identity help him finally to identify and empathize with even white-men oppressors, past and present. Reflecting on advice his grandfather gave him long ago, Invisible Man realizes that

> he *must* have meant the principle, that we were to affirm the principle on which the country was built and not the men, or at least not the men who did the violence. [. . .] Was it that we of all, we, most of all, had to affirm the principle, the plan in whose name we had been brutalized and sacrificed—not because we would always be weak nor because we were afraid or opportunistic, but because we were older than they, in the sense of what it took to live in the world with others and because they had exhausted in us, some—not much, but some—of the human greed and smallness, yes, and the fear and superstition that had kept them running. (Oh, yes, they're running, too, running all over themselves.)     (574)

Invisible Man's realization affords my students and me an occasion to read "Manners" from *Notes on the State of Virginia*, in which Thomas Jefferson himself confesses, "Indeed I tremble for my country when I reflect that God is just: that his justice cannot sleep for ever: that considering numbers, nature and natural

*Martha Greene Eads* 85

means only, a revolution of the wheel of fortune, an exchange of situation, is among possible events: that it may become probable by supernatural interference! The Almighty has no attribute which can take side with us in such a contest." That Invisible Man can affirm and not merely negate our country, empathize and identify with as well as denounce those who wield power in it, seems so remarkable to some of us as to be the work of grace. Such a feat takes us back to Lederach's "meeting place," in which "mercy and truth are met together; righteousness and peace have kissed each other."

This final section of the novel, too, compels my students and me to consider *Invisible Man*'s epigraph from Melville's *Benito Cereno*, in which the hapless and naive American sea captain Amasa Delano unwittingly rescues the title character, a Spanish captain, from the enslaved Africans who have overtaken his ship. When the tragic and terrifying episode ends, Delano cannot understand the Spaniard's inability to move beyond it. In response to Delano's question, "[W]hat has cast such a shadow upon you?," the traumatized man declares, "The negro." That Ellison has provided Delano's question as a point of entry into *Invisible Man* helps us understand even better how the novel shows that forgetting our past—or attempting to—carries a high price. Remembering has brought Invisible Man to love's door; love may yet empower Invisible Man to forgive, as he has forgiven Sybil, those who would oppress them both.

*Invisible Man*'s conclusion drives us back to the Bible yet again. In preparation for his discussion of love, the apostle Paul writes about the way in which Jesus' followers are bound to and dependent upon one another: "For by one Spirit we were all baptized into one body—whether Jews or Greeks, whether slaves or free—and have all been made to drink in one Spirit. For in fact the body is not one member but many. [. . .] And if one member suffers, all the members suffer with it" (1 Cor. 12.13–14, 26a). As the passage continues, Paul reflects on the variety of skills these members employ in service to the body, including the kind of rhetorical skill Invisible Man employs, leading into the declaration beginning, "Though I speak with the tongues of men and angels and have not love . . ." (1 Cor. 13.1). Echoing Paul's idea, Invisible Man asks of his fellow Americans, including those who oppress, "Weren't we part of them as well as apart from them and subject to die when they die?" (Ellison, *Invisible Man* 575). This question is the novel's point—or one of them, as Ellison himself divulges in the introduction he added in 1981, writing,

> [M]y task was one of revealing the human universals hidden within the plight of one who was both black and American, and not only as a means of conveying my personal vision of possibility, but as a way of dealing with the sheer rhetorical challenge involved in communicating across our barriers of race and religion, class, color and region—barriers which consist of the many strategies of division that were designed, and still function, to prevent what would otherwise have been a more or less natural recognition of the reality of black and white fraternity. (xxii)

86 LENS OF LOVE

While the foundation for Ellison's vision of interdependence originates not in religious faith but in our founding principles and in the hope that we might do better than our forebears by them, reading *Invisible Man* through the lens of 1 Corinthians 13 helps us see how this is so.

Before our final class period on the novel, I distribute a handout that provides the King James Version's rendering of 1 Corinthians 13, along with selected passages from the novel in which I have italicized allusions to it. I ask students to prepare for discussion by drafting answers to these questions: What does Ellison seem to mean by "love"? Why does he allude to 1 Corinthians 13? Does Invisible Man love? If so, whom and what? Resulting conversation is invariably rich. Among the many discussions I've savored with students over the years, one of the most memorable took place in April 2010, when a perceptive student named Yana, the daughter of Kazakh Baptist immigrants, observed, "Love is not allowing others to become invisible." Claude Atcho illuminates this point in detail in the first chapter of his book *Reading Black Books: How African American Literature Can Make Our Faith More Whole and Just*. Noting that *Invisible Man*'s first word is "I" and its last is "you," Atcho contends that the novel's central challenges are to identify, empathize, and seek solidarity with others:

> The first word of the novel, then, is like a preached word, an indicative truth: I am an invisible man. And the last word, like the conclusion of a well-crafted sermon, drives the audience toward self-reflection: Does this narrative, in any way, speak for you? In this manner, the novel's framing—epilogue and prologue, opening salvo and final word—invites us to consider our shared human association, how we see each other and live together. (23)

Such considerations surely demand of readers the truth, mercy, justice, and peace lauded in Psalm 85; just maybe, our pursuit and practice of them will yield the love described in 1 Corinthians 13.

Atcho's insights, Yana's assessment, and peace-building and trauma-awareness tools thus continue to deepen my understanding of and gratitude for opportunities to teach *Invisible Man*. As Confederate statues come down and school boards debate whether to change building names and ban books, the novel's lessons feel as fresh as this morning's headlines. In the wake of the #MeToo movement and revelations about the Southern Baptist Convention's sexual abuse cover-up, Invisible Man's ability to empathize with the traumatized dancer and later with Sybil offers hope. As we remember George Floyd, Breonna Taylor, Tyre Nichols, and the charge to say their names, Invisible Man's unrelenting repetition of Tod Clifton's name at the funeral makes a new kind of sense to us. As we watch footage from gatherings of angry fellow citizens, whether on the left or on the right, we aspire to see, as Invisible Man manages to recognize in the gathered funeral mourners, "not a crowd but the set faces of individual men and women" (459). In giving us a hero who learns to see in their distinctiveness and dignity individuals who often go unseen or whom we ourselves might prefer not to see, Ellison provides us with a primer in loving our neighbors, whatever our religions, genders, and races may be.

## NOTES

1. Harriss has written insightfully in *Ralph Ellison's Invisible Theology* about the novelist's engagement with the Christian scriptures; Harriss does not, however, address Ellison's use of 1 Corinthians 13. Quotations of Bible verses in this essay are from the King James Version (see *Bible*).

2. In "*Invisible Man* and the Politics of Love," an exploration of what he believes to be an unfair and under-informed critical and political dismissal of Ellison and his work, Robert Butler contends that the novel celebrates the Christian love that animated Martin Luther King, Jr.'s civil rights efforts (44).

3. Strikingly, the song from which the reverend Barbee quotes in his college-chapel sermon, a song that he reports Bledsoe led, extols, among several virtues, hope and faith but not love, from 1 Cor. 13 (Ellison, *Invisible Man* 125).

4. After being mistaken for Rinehart, Invisible Man reflects on "the merging fluidity of forms seen through the lenses. Could this be the way the world appeared to Rinehart? All the dark-glass boys? 'For now we *see as through a glass darkly but then*—but then—' I couldn't remember the rest" (Ellison, *Invisible Man* 491; italics mine). The text I have italicized quotes 1 Cor. 13.12.

5. Ellison is also probably alluding to 1 Cor. 13.1 in Invisible Man's account of the echoed "tinkling" words before the Faulknerian address to Miss Susie Gresham in chapter 5. That reverie describes inauthentic preaching that functions much as "sounding brass or a clanging cymbal" (1 Cor. 13.2).

6. Invisible Man himself is familiar with Paul's conversion story; he says his grandfather had frequently told him, "You start Saul and end up Paul. [. . .] When you're a young'un, you Saul, but let life whup your head a bit and you starts trying to be Paul—though you still Sauls around on the side" (Ellison, *Invisible Man* 381).

7. My students sometimes opine that the novel advances a Madonna-whore dichotomy, with saintly Mary representing the former and the sexually predatory Emma and Sybil, the latter. Invisible Man's honoring of the latter's dignity problematizes that categorization, at least to some degree.

8. Ellison provides another Pauline allusion as Invisible Man reflects on Sybil's expectations that he enact male Blackness as represented by such figures as Joe Louis and Paul Robeson. Employing a phrase Paul uses to describe Christ in his letter to the church at Philippi, Invisible Man refers to himself as "Brother-Taboo-with-whom-all-things-are-possible" (Ellison, *Invisible Man* 517; Phil. 4.13).

9. Students usually catch this further use of the word "tinkling" and link the auditory images to the sounding brass and tinkling cymbal of 1 Cor. 13.1.

## BROADER CONTEXTS

# Historicizing Ellison:
# Politics and Pedagogy

*Barbara Foley*

In order to historicize Ralph Ellison, I need, first, to historicize my own engagement—as a reader, a scholar, and above all a teacher—with his oeuvre. This engagement has involved a number of moving parts: changes in my own political outlook and scholarly practice, the expanding access to Ellison's papers at the Library of Congress after his death in 1994, and evidence that Ellison's views altered quite dramatically over the course of his life. In this essay, I aim to tease out some of the pedagogical challenges posed by this ever-shifting historical terrain. I close with the proposition that Ellison's earliest writings may be of greatest relevance to the questions and challenges students face in the third decade of the twenty-first century: the end may be in the beginning.

I first encountered *Invisible Man* in the spring of 1970, when I was just beginning graduate school in literary study. I had been assigned exactly one literary work by an African American author during all my undergraduate years, James Baldwin's *The Fire Next Time*; *Invisible Man* was the only Black-authored text I would be assigned during my entire time in graduate school. When I opted for a special field examination in African American literature, I was among the very first students in my department to do so. Even though my academic studies were leaving me somewhat culturally deprived, however, I was coming into contact with the leftist anti-war movement, where anti-racism, anti-imperialism, and internationalism were stressed as central to the project of radical social transformation. Fights for African American and Chicano studies were just beginning; expanding the literary canon was still a project for the future. But what I was learning in the streets would put me on a collision course with much of what I was absorbing in the groves of academe.

This was the context—political, intellectual, and cultural—shaping my initial response to *Invisible Man* in a seminar room at the University of Chicago. I had such an incomplete understanding of African American history that I barely grasped the novel's allegorical representation of twentieth-century Black experience from South to North, or from Booker T. Washington's accommodationism to Marcus Garvey's Black nationalism. I was so ignorant of left and labor movement history that I knew nothing of Depression-era class struggles in either Harlem or Alabama, nor did I recognize the Brotherhood as a stand-in for the American Communist Party (CPUSA). But if I didn't know much about history, I was being thoroughly trained in New Critical and neo-Aristotelian formal analysis. The professor in my course on the modern American novel impressed upon me Ellison's skill in establishing an accreting series of symbols delineating the forces depriving the novel's unnamed protagonist of individual selfhood: tropes signifying blindness and invisibility, pieces of paper supplying the hero with new names, strategic appearances of white women in scenes where Black men are symbolically castrated. As an anti-war radical suspicious of patriotism, I was disturbed by the American nationalist note I heard in the grandfather's closing words about the need to "affirm the principle on which the country was built" (Ellison, *Invisible Man* 574). As a young white person largely unaware of the causes and effects of racism, however, I was deeply moved by Invisible Man's devastating experiences with being seen and not-seen. Given how negatively white people were portrayed throughout the novel, moreover, I felt honored to be accepted, however provisionally, into the broadcast audience for whom, in the epilogue, Invisible Man proposes to speak "on the lower frequencies" (581). This hope for inclusion was facilitated by my schooling in humanist universalism, which had taught me that the greatest works of literature are those that transcend the particularities of time and place and speak to a shared human condition.

Now let's fast-forward some twenty-five years. The novel was the same, but I had changed—or at least had continued along that leftward trajectory begun in 1970. I was now teaching American literature at the university level and, having made serious efforts to overcome my previous miseducation, was regularly asking my students to read texts by a racially diverse range of writers, as well as many associated with the proletarian literary movement. In teaching *Invisible Man*, I still found pleasure in drawing my students' attention to Ellison's consummate skill in constructing such a formally well-wrought urn. In the intervening years, however, I had learned a good deal about African American and United States working-class history. I was thus in a position to not only recognize Ellison's political-historical allegory but also subject it to critique. I noted that, despite the torturous cruelty exhibited in the opening "battle royal" chapter—which ends with Invisible Man making his Booker T. Washington–esque speech with a bloody rope of saliva hanging from his mouth—Ellison had refrained from portraying the full murderous violence of the Jim Crow South exhibited in Richard Wright's *Uncle Tom's*

90    HISTORICIZING ELLISON

*Children* or, later, in Baldwin's "Going to Meet the Man." I increasingly wondered, too, why Ellison had chosen to portray the Brotherhood in such an unremittingly hostile light, when Communists, I had learned, had in fact led much of the multiracial movement against racism in the United States during the Depression years. I was all the more confused by Ellison's harsh treatment of the left because I knew that, in the late 1930s and early 1940s, he had published in *New Masses* and in other organs of the left nearly three dozen pieces of radical journalism, which he subsequently effaced from his résumé as he prepared to make his debut as the author of *Invisible Man*. Seeking to set the record straight, I exposed my students to excerpts from primary sources like Hosea Hudson's *Black Worker in the Deep South* and Angelo Herndon's *Let Me Live* as well as from secondary sources like Mark Naison's *Communists in Harlem during the Depression* and Dominic Capeci's *The Harlem Riot of 1943*. At this point, historicizing Ellison—in both my teaching and my scholarship—largely entailed setting the novel alongside a historical record that it either ignored or distorted in significant ways.

Even the formal features of *Invisible Man*—which the English professor in me continued to admire—now struck me as rhetorically manipulative. The motif of blinding and not-seeing—from the blindfolding of the youths in the battle royal through Brother Jack's losing his glass eye as he tells Invisible Man that he was hired to talk, not to think—I saw as substituting aesthetic patterning for political argument. The motif of Invisible Man's being continually given slips of paper that define his identity—and that essentially repeat, "Keep This N____-Boy Running" (Ellison, *Invisible Man* 33)—functioned in much the same way. I had come to feel that the novel's metaphorical equation of Jim Crow racists, hypocritical Northern philanthropists, Wall Street imperialists, Garveyite fanatics, and Communist misleaders was the formal accompaniment of the text's repression of the actual historical relationship among African Americans, the class struggle, and the left. I now felt that the universalism invoked by Invisible Man in his closing appeal was founded in a false premise, for readers could be included in Invisible Man's broadcasting audience only if they agreed with Invisible Man's proposition that "Brother Jack and the boys," portrayed as "waiting with their knives" to "ball the jack" of the American eagle, constitute not just one among several antagonists but in fact the principal threat to the health of the body politic—in their way still more dangerous than the goose-stepping police who have murdered Tod Clifton precisely because of the Brotherhood's pretensions to anti-racist solidarity (576).

At this point in my engagement with Ellison, I felt that to teach the patterning of the novel without interrogation of its implied politics was, however inadvertently, to participate in the reinforcement of those politics. To recognize the text's formal parallels was to re-cognize a dominant liberal discourse about totalitarianism that was so taken for granted—so invisible, if you will—as to warrant no scrutiny. In the many essays and interviews gathered in *Shadow and Act* and *Going to the Territory*, moreover, Ellison's chosen vocabulary for designating literary and ethical values—"fluidity," "diversity," and above all "complexity"—struck me as a formalist evasion. While I never denied that *Invisible Man* was, according to widely accepted criteria of literary value, a masterpiece, I concluded that it was no accident that the novel had received the National Book Award in 1952. It was a Cold War classic—and needed to be read as such.[1]

We now fast-forward again, if more gradually. After Ellison's death, there started to appear indications that his involvement with the left—as reflected in his fiction and not just the radical journalism he had disavowed—had been a good deal deeper than he had been willing to admit. *Flying Home and Other Stories* contained several short stories, unpublished in Ellison's lifetime, that showed him to have been quite a skilled practitioner in the field of proletarian literature, of which he would subsequently speak with scorn. Finding that students responded with considerable interest to some of these tales, I re-scrutinized his early literary and political journalism as well as his correspondence with Wright. Ellison, I now concluded, had been not just a leftist but a serious—indeed passionate—Marxist dialectician. In a perspicacious 1941 *New Masses* review of William Attaway's *Blood on the Forge*, Ellison faulted the novelist for having "grasped the destruction of the folk, but missed its rebirth on a higher level" ("Great Migration" 24). In a 1942 letter to Sanora Babb about the draft manuscript of *Whose Names Are Unknown*, her novel about dust-bowl migrants, he pursued this line of reasoning, noting that John Steinbeck, in *The Grapes of Wrath*, was "pleading subtly for the big shots to stop their wrongdoing" (*Selected Letters* 153). Babb, by contrast, was "for the worker, showing his rebirth into a new consciousness." Ellison congratulated Wright in the same year for having produced, in *Twelve Million Black Voices*, "a weapon more subtle than a machine gun, more effective than a fighter plane" and thanked his friend for making him "a better Marxist" (*Selected Letters* 146). Even as I continued to view *Invisible Man* as an urn wrought from static anti-communist political assumptions, I became fascinated by the issue of metamorphosis: how did the man who had expressed such radically anti-capitalist beliefs end up writing a novel that could be so warmly embraced by the Cold War literary establishment?

It was the gradual opening up of access to the Ellison archive at the Library of Congress that led me to rethink not just what I thought of Ellison but how to teach his oeuvre. The early drafts of various stories republished in *Flying Home and Other Stories* indicated that Ellison undertook extensive excisions of leftist political references. Still more provocative were the manuscripts of several unpublished stories and novellas indicating that Ellison was, for a time, dedicated to portraying African American Communists—some professors at Black colleges, others union organizers—in the Deep South. The cartoonish figure of the Black Communist bureaucrat embodied in *Invisible Man*'s Brother Wrestrum is nowhere in evidence in the pages of the 1952 novel; these were mature—indeed, "complex"—political radicals facing profound external dilemmas and internal contradictions.[2]

The real treasure trove in the Ellison archive, however, was constituted by the thousands of pages of notes and drafts of *Invisible Man*, which Ellison worked

92    HISTORICIZING ELLISON

on for nearly seven years between 1945 and 1952. Upon perusing these materials, what I discovered was, to me, utterly astonishing: the novel that I had come to view as a seamless expression of Cold War ideology had begun as a kind of modernist proletarian novel—somewhat satirical of foibles of the left but by no means programmatically anti-communist. Its ordering symbols had not been conceived in advance as a structural scaffolding on which to hang preformed ideas and themes. The novel was instead a process, one from which residues of leftism were only gradually expunged in successive drafts, revealing that Ellison's imagination had been trained in a Marxism that he could not readily relinquish. I chose the title *Wrestling with the Left* for the 2010 book emerging from this research because Ellison evidently had to wrestle down his revolutionary consciousness—indeed, conscience—to produce the novel's prize-winning final draft. But historicizing the novel now meant that I viewed it not as a product but as an embodiment of history—not just to be played off against a factual record that it distorted or masked but as itself containing the historical contradictions by which it had been generated. It perhaps goes without saying that this discovery would lead me to revise my pedagogical approach to the novel—and the rest of Ellison's oeuvre—in significant ways.

I mention here only a few of the findings discussed at length in *Wrestling with the Left*. Suffice it to say that, from beginning to end, Ellison had in mind quite a different conception of his narrative when, sitting in a Vermont barn doorway in the summer of 1945, he first wrote, "I am an invisible man." He originally framed a number of characters and motivations quite differently. When the protagonist accidentally brings Norton to Trueblood's cabin, for instance, he has been distracted by passing the tree where a lynching recently transpired. At the Golden Day, the veteran doctor who addresses Invisible Man was driven insane, we learn, because he attempted to treat Black and white sharecroppers wounded in a shoot-out with sheriff's deputies. Woodridge—mentioned only in passing in the published text—is a barely closeted gay literature professor who has encouraged students to engage in armed resistance by raiding the campus arsenal, with tragic results. The full force of Jim Crow violence, largely passed over in the published novel, is prominently featured in the drafts.

Early drafts and outlines of the Harlem sections of *Invisible Man* challenge the folkish culturalism and anti-communism pervading the 1952 text. On top of Peter Wheatstraw's wagon full of disposable blueprints is a tabloid representation of an American flag. Mary Rambo runs a working-class boarding house whose inhabitants discuss the need for urban rebellion and express interest in the Brotherhood's interracial rallies and dances. Invisible Man sleeps in the room formerly occupied by Leroy, an organizer for a multiracial mariners' union who was murdered by company thugs; it is through reading Leroy's journal that Invisible Man is exposed to proletarian internationalism. Rinehart is primarily an exploitative hustler and pimp, not an embodiment of protean shape-shifting. The Brotherhood escapes demonization. Brother Hambro—originally Stein—bears a tattoo from a concentration camp. Brother Jack's glass eye does not fall out when he scolds Invisible Man. The Brotherhood does not plan—but is naively shocked by—the Harlem rebellion of 1943. Invisible Man enters into a love affair—and in some versions marries—a young, white Communist Party member named Louise. And the novel could have ended quite differently: having fled to the sewer, in one version Invisible Man does not discover in his briefcase handwritten slips of paper revealing Brother Jack to have been his antagonist all along; he simply burns everything except for Leroy's journal. In another outline, he goes on to become the cynical pastor of a storefront church. And in an early draft of the epilogue, Ellison scrawled in the margin, "Bring in grandpa" (Foley, *Wrestling* 37). Apparently, "affirm[ing] the principle" did not motivate Invisible Man—or Ellison—from the outset. Class-conscious anti-capitalism held significantly greater appeal.

Even if teachers have only piecemeal access to the materials in the Ellison archive, I urge them to juxtapose some of the drafts with published portions of the novel. This pedagogical procedure not only reveals Ellison's stage-by-stage transformation during the early years of the Cold War but also comments suggestively about the politics of canon formation. Indeed, it lays bare the process of literary creation itself. If the symbols so carefully paralleled in the published text did not at first constitute a unifying architectural principle, this means that even the best-wrought urn emerges from a process of trial and error. Although my undergraduate students were not about to travel to the Library of Congress to see the Ellison papers, some graduate students were alerted to the importance of archival research in literary analysis; a few of them have gone on to become serious textual scholars. As teachers, we never know what is going to be passed over and what is going to stick.

My interest in how *Invisible Man* came into being made me curious about Ellison's development as a fiction writer after 1952, especially in connection with his never-published—if much-rumored—second novel. After *Juneteenth* appeared in 1999, I assigned the novel twice in semester-long seminars devoted entirely to Ellison. Perhaps I bear more traces of neo-Aristotelianism than I care to admit: despite the novel's extraordinary moments—such as Reverend Hickman's monologue by the bedside of the mortally wounded Senator Adam Sunraider—I viewed the text as a fragment of a larger project whose arc had been lost. No doubt my own lack of enthusiasm shaped my limited ability to arouse my students' interest.

By the time I got around to reading *Three Days before the Shooting . . .* , I was no longer teaching the semester-long Ellison seminar where such a 1,100-page compendium could justifiably have been assigned. Moreover, as was willingly admitted by its editors, John F. Callahan and Adam Bradley, this monster book was itself just the tip of a textual iceberg. Remembering what *Invisible Man* had taught me about Ellison's compositional process, I guessed that a visit to the Library of Congress would be required if one were even to attempt to penetrate the mysteries of what Ellison referred to as the "Hickman Novel." The ten days that I spent perusing the immense archive of Ellison's never-completed second novel validated this intuition. Although I wrote up my findings, I found myself not up to the task of teaching *Three Days*. I imagine, however, that, if one has the energy and persistence, sharing this formidable text with students—most likely graduate students—might prove rewarding, especially if the drafts of *Invisible Man* could be juxtaposed with unpublished portions of the "Hickman Novel." For I found buried in the multiple versions of the assassination plot surrounding Sunraider and his estranged son, Severen, a series of bizarre temporal anomalies that testify to Ellison's continuing preoccupation with internationalist leftism in the merchant marine during World War II. *Three Days* is haunted by the ghost of Leroy. Furthermore, the segments narrated by Welborn McIntyre, a formerly radical white journalist once romantically involved with an African American woman named Laura, indicate Ellison's abiding interest in Popular Front–era interracial love affairs. Louise lingers in the background as well. Finally, the highly probable historical grounding of the race-baiting Senator Sunraider in the fascist theoretician Lawrence Dennis—a light-skinned Black man who passed for white and hobnobbed with Wall Street barons and the Nazi high command—shows Ellison still exploring the shape-shifter as seductive political reactionary. That Sunraider in various fragmentary notes is said to be the son of Bliss Proteus Rinehart establishes a further linkage between *Three Days* and *Invisible Man*. I can imagine that a course thoughtfully conjoining the two texts, with full attention to the changing political outlooks, might be well worth the challenge, to teacher and students alike.[3]

For those who don't have space in a course for the bulky *Three Days* but are interested in teaching political topics in Ellison's other work, I strongly recommend "A Party Down at the Square" (Ellison, *Flying Home* 3–11), a text that I have found useful in both undergraduate survey courses and graduate seminars in literary theory. This proletarian short story, unpublished in Ellison's lifetime, features the first-person viewpoint of a white boy from the North who, visiting his uncle in an Alabama town, is taken to witness a lynching. The then-Marxist young Ellison skillfully frames the story's central events and symbols to convey a class-based analysis of the causes and consequences of racial violence. The lynching bonfire has been lit in the town square, near the courthouse and a Confederate monument, and the sheriff polices the scene. A plane seeking to land in nearby Birmingham, where a cyclone has put out the beacon, mistakes the bonfire for the airport; before swooping upward, the plane strikes a power line that electrocutes a white woman, who is charred black. The man being lynched asks to be put out of his misery but refuses to exhibit weakness. The young narrator vomits at the scene and tells himself that this is "my first party and my last." The tale's coda shows two lean and hungry white sharecroppers ("You'd be surprised how hungry white folks can look") being denied credit at the local store. One remarks that "it didn't do no good to kill the n____ because things don't get no better"; he is told to "shut his damn mouth," but "from the look on his face he won't stay shut long." The story ends with the boy's declaration of backhanded admiration for the man he saw burned alive: "God but that n____ was tough. That Bacote n____ was some n____!" (*Flying Home* 11).

Ellison's use of the n-word is relentless in this tale, yet it serves a purpose at once rhetorical and political. A quintessential product of 1930s literary proletarianism, "A Party Down at the Square" portrays state-sponsored violence and everyday linguistic violence as conjoined forms of racist social control, intended both to intimidate the Black population and to win over those white citizens who, like the electrocuted woman, imagine themselves to be beneficiaries of racial hierarchy and division. Indeed, her turning black in death speaks volumes about not just binary definitions of whiteness and blackness but also illusions that ordinary white people are exempt from destruction by the racism they embrace. The fact that Birmingham is in darkness, moreover, and that even one of the fanciest houses in town has been taken out by the cyclone, suggests the regressive nature of American fascism: power lines, rather than serving the social good, destroy lives indiscriminately. Yet the refusal of one of the white sharecroppers to be satisfied by displays of racial cruelty suggests that the days of ruling-class control, economic and ideological, may be numbered. Had readers encountered this story in *New Masses*—or read it alongside *Uncle Tom's Children*—they could have viewed the hungry white sharecropper as a potential participant in a Red-led multiracial sharecroppers union.

Although it embodies a radical politics that Ellison would abandon, "A Party Down at the Square" gestures toward a moral issue that preoccupied Ellison throughout his career. In "Twentieth-Century Fiction and the Black Mask of Humanity," Ellison castigated the great majority of modern white writers for their near-total obliteration of the figure of the African American from their representations of social reality in the United States. (Faulkner alone escaped Ellison's wrath.) By contrast, key writers of the nineteenth century, from Emerson to James to Twain, had treated the condition of the African American as an index to the moral health of American society—a diagnosis epitomized, for Ellison, in *Adventures of Huckleberry Finn*. Even if Jim did not fully escape from stereotype, his friendship with Huck, symbolized by their raft, signaled a possibility for multiracial democracy. While Ellison evinced little confidence that contemporaneous Black writers would keep the raft afloat—and we may ask whether his own novels, published or unpublished, accomplished this task—"A Party Down at the Square" shows Ellison responding to the Twain challenge early in his career. The boy who narrates, after all, bears a marked resemblance to Huck. Both admire a Black man who manifests more dignity and humanity than any adult white male; both are unable to break from using the n-word in describing this man. But whereas Huck, it seems, will remain confined within the prison house of language, the nameless boy in the 1930s story may have the chance to escape—not least because the class struggle is creating conditions that may enable him to break his linguistic chains.

While useful in historicizing for undergraduates some key features of a Depression-era class analysis of racism, "A Party Down at the Square" can also be taught in a graduate course on literary theory, for it ably illustrates some concepts central to Marxist criticism—namely, Louis Althusser's formulation of interpellation and Antonio Gramsci's notion of hegemony. According to Althusser, to be interpellated—whether by a friend, a police officer, or a text—is to be hailed with the assumption "I know who you are!" (232–72). The "who" here, of course, is a social identity so taken for granted—whether as a Catholic, a pedestrian, or a white person—as to be a form of re-cognition: "Of course!" one replies. According to Gramsci, hegemony consists in a combination of consent and coercion, the carrot and the stick of ruling-class control, of which uninterrogated common sense—a consciousness "inherited from the past and uncritically absorbed"—is the core (333). In Ellison's story, the boy, in witnessing the lynching, is being invited to recognize—that is, re-cognize—himself as white; indeed, his uncle is proposing a ritual initiation in whiteness. While the boy's continuing adherence to the n-word suggests that the ritual may work its magic, the fact that he has vomited and sworn to attend no more such "parties" suggests that he may in the future refuse to be interpellated in this way. The words of the hungry sharecropper indicate, moreover, that, among the poorer sectors of the white working class, there are limits to the efficacy of coercion and consent in maintaining ruling-class hegemony—a lesson that sticks in the mind of the boy as well. Although situated in the historical matrix of the 1930s, Ellison's story ably illustrates theoretical concepts vital to an understanding of the workings of class, race, and ideology in our time.

If my students' overwhelmingly positive response to the story—despite its harsh language—is any indication, historicizing "A Party Down at the Square" in the context of the radical 1930s is not an exercise in nostalgia. Much on our students' minds these days is the continuing practice of state-sanctioned ritual violence directed at Black people. Frequently accompanying this concern, however, is the too-widely-held perception that the great majority of white people objectively benefit from racial inequality, and the corollary that they have no vested interest—material, moral, or psychological—in proclaiming that Black lives matter. Ellison's early works, including the drafts of *Invisible Man*, surely foreground the violence differentially inflicted upon people of African descent. But these texts propose a path to interracial solidarity, not by "affirm[ing] the principle" of US democracy—Grandpa has not yet spoken—but by speaking from the lower frequencies of a class-based understanding of the causes and consequences of racial—and social—inequality.

NOTES

1. In the 1989 edition *Approaches to Teaching Ralph Ellison's* Invisible Man, one critic noted that students "easily recognize the various manipulations of the Brotherhood and can connect them to those of the men at the battle royal and to Bledsoe, Brockway, Kimbro, Emerson, and Norton. This part of *Invisible Man* can be taught very quickly" (Savery 72).

2. As the archive became available piecemeal, I was greatly assisted by Arnold Rampersad, who shared with me the text of his Ellison biography several months before it was published.

3. See Foley, "Becoming"; Horne.

# The Democratic Ideal of Ellison's Jazz-Shaped America

## Sterling Lecater Bland, Jr.

It is widely recognized that Ralph Ellison, the aspiring-musician-turned-writer, regularly used music as a metaphor for the theory of literature and culture that he developed. It was a metaphor that served his thoughts about the relationship between the individual and the collective, between Black culture and white culture, and between the possibilities of democratic liberalism and chaos. In his essay "Homage to William L. Dawson," Ellison claims no particular religious affinity beyond music: "I am not particularly religious, but I am claimed by music" (*Collected Essays* 442).

Regardless of the ways Ralph Ellison's conception of jazz has implications extending broadly across music, literature, and culture, jazz is notoriously difficult to define with any certainty. Its ambiguity may be the very characteristic that makes it such a useful metaphor for the kind of racialized modernity that Ellison embraces. Broadly speaking, jazz is a language disruptive of conventional assumptions of form, structure, ideology, and even meaning. When readers engage that metaphor, it is important to acknowledge the ways the jazz aesthetic permeating Ellison's work is the result of countless interactions between the music itself, geography, migration, and the cultural environment in which the music existed.

One impediment to teaching the relationship of jazz to Ellison's work to all levels of student learners is that students may well be as unfamiliar with jazz (as a musical and cultural form) as they are with Ellison's work. This essay provides instructors with guidance for helping students encounter and broadly consider examples of both. The goal is to help instructors instill an understanding of the ways jazz provides an interdisciplinary set of lenses through which students can understand the themes to which Ellison's work so regularly returns.

## Ellison, Literature, and Cultural Context

Near the conclusion of the introduction to *Invisible Man* written on the occasion of the thirtieth anniversary of the novel's publication, Ellison noted that he improvised on the materials that served as the novel's source "in the manner of a jazz musician putting a musical theme through a wild star-burst of metamorphosis" (*Collected Essays* 488–89). For Ellison, jazz in literature represents democratic possibility. Ellison's ideas were influenced as much by the music he heard growing up in Oklahoma City as they were by T. S. Eliot's "Tradition and the Individual Talent" and literary modernism. For Ellison, beyond its improvisation, the fundamental component of jazz that he found so important was the interaction between the individual and the ensemble. In the truly democratic process that exists between the individual and the collective, jazz becomes crucial for Ellison as a stand-in for Americanism.

The tension between the individual and the collective is as fundamental to jazz as it is to the nation. Individuals in jazz exist in the collective context of their ensemble even as their playing individualizes them. This is strikingly similar to the ways Ellison envisions the very existence of Black people living in America. In his essay "The World and the Jug," Ellison writes that the Black American "is a product of the interaction between his racial predicament, his individual will, and the broader American cultural freedom in which he finds his ambiguous existence. That he, too, in a limited way, is his own creation" (*Collected Essays* 160). Jazz was, for Ellison, more than simply a technique for reading the interplay of components that characterized his work. Jazz was his way of giving meaning to the pluralism that defined American culture. It was a model of the freedom that democracy brought to a nation composed as one from many. Jazz, like the democratic ideal and the literary artist, provides form and order over what appears to be chaos. Ellison saw self-expression as the most potent indication of culture. As Ellison understood it, America is more than a collection of individuals. Cultural pluralism rests at the very heart of the democratic ideal.

## *Bringing Jazz to the Classroom*

The goal of the units described below is to introduce students to different ways of thinking about music (in general) and jazz (in particular). The instruction and discussion should provide students with a basic language with which to discuss music and relate it to literature. Students should be broadly able to distinguish different kinds of music, understand how those distinctions are employed by Black writers, and discern connections of text to music in Ellison's work in particular.

### Introducing Jazz

The learning objective for the unit described in this section is simply to introduce students to jazz. Expect many traditional college students to be relatively unfamiliar with jazz. Most may have a very cursory knowledge about jazz and may have little interest in developing a more extensive knowledge of it. Some students in the classroom may, at best, feel that the music has little, if any, relevance to their lives. It may represent to them a world depicted in movies about a distant, bygone era of American life and culture. Some may consider it overly abstract or may even not particularly enjoy listening to music. There is no reason to expect that Black students will have a greater knowledge about the music than others in the class simply because of their race and because their race reflects the race of some of the music's most influential figures. All of this is to say that in teaching about the relationship of jazz to Black literature, students may well need extensive support in how to listen to it. All students will benefit from a clear explanation of what they are listening to and how to understand and appreciate what they are hearing.

Instructors should begin with a discussion that allows students to express their ideas about music. Broad questions are particularly useful here as a way of facilitating discussion: Do they like music? What qualities make music appealing (or unappealing) to them? Does music serve a purpose in their lives and, if so, what are those purposes? Are there emotional distinctions between vocal music and instrumental music? How do their tastes in music relate to their parents' tastes in music? What styles of music can the students name? And what are the distinctions between those styles? If they agree that music changes over time, have them identify some of those changes. How does technology affect the production and consumption of music? How do visual images like movies, music videos, commercials, or video games, for example, contribute to how listeners process music? It may be useful to play some very brief examples as the discussion unfolds and to list key contributions to the discussion on the board for class reference.

One of the impediments that some find is that jazz is an improvised music that often features extended instrumental solos whose relation to the melody may not be immediately recognizable. To facilitate the transition from a general discussion about music to a more specific discussion of jazz, it may be useful to play brief examples of vocal jazz that have a strong melodic component, as a starting point. To demonstrate how jazz musicians take a theme and create new musical ideas from it, instructors may want to play Rodgers and Hammerstein's "My Favorite Things" and compare it to John Coltrane's instrumental version of the same song. Discussion here should focus on identifying the primary elements of each.[1]

It is best to conclude this unit by directly connecting the preceding discussion of music to the issue of Black American literature. After all, music is an important point of inspiration for some writers, while it plays no role in the work of others. In the work of some writers, jazz is evoked in ways that suggest a very technical understanding. In others, jazz is evoked in ways that suggest something more cultural. In the short story "Sonny's Blues," for example, James Baldwin uses jazz as a way of distinguishing between the social conventionalism of one character and the socially unconventional decisions his brother makes.

With those ideas in mind, instructors may want to begin with a general assessment to gauge what their students are bringing to this content area. Instructors will want to include an assessment at the conclusion, as well. A simple quiz (ideally with a listening section) will help determine student understanding.

## Jazz in Context and Variation

The learning objectives of this content area is to lead students to an understanding of the ways jazz has served both cultural and musical roles and to attune students to the variations contained in the music that is broadly considered jazz.

Before beginning the process of teaching Ellison's relationship to jazz, it will be useful for students to become acquainted with the cultural role that jazz has played. Focus as directly as possible on the ideas most relevant to how the class will explore jazz in relation to Ellison. The arrival of jazz on the nation's cultural landscape generally coincides with the conclusion of World War I and the return of Black servicemen from Europe. In the early decades of the twentieth century, the Black middle class associated jazz far more with brothels, dance halls, and nightlife than with art. It was a music whose roots included New Orleans, Chicago, Kansas City, New York, and Oklahoma City; the latter is where Ralph Ellison first encountered it in his youth. But jazz was not only a music with urban roots; it was a music firmly tied to Black migration from the South and to urban centers across the country. As jazz moved around the country, its sound developed along with its audience, the locations in which it was performed, and the recording, movie, and radio technology that increasingly made it widely available to a broad listening audience.

The small groups of five to seven players that originated in New Orleans in the early part of the century through the 1920s slowly gave way to the more commercially driven swing music that developed during the 1930s. Swing-era bands were generally composed of twelve to sixteen musicians playing highly arranged music that was often used for dancing. The music that developed after the World War II years was less suited for dance and often emphasized small groups, rhythmic complexity, and virtuoso solos: bebop, cool jazz, progressive jazz, and atonal avant-garde jazz. Although the New Negro Movement emphasized the development of Black art, writers associated with the movement were often relatively slow to embrace the music. Langston Hughes was an exception and regularly engaged jazz, as was Sterling A. Brown, whose poems frequently evoked jazz, blues cadences, and spirituals.[2]

Jazz was not widely embraced by Black writers again until the Black Arts movement in the 1960s combined Black nationalism with Marxist ideology and saw jazz as reflective of Black protest. The short story "The Screamers" and the poem "am/trak" by Amiri Baraka (LeRoi Jones), which invokes John Coltrane, are examples.[3] Because this area begins to incorporate music with literature, some examples are useful. Musically, students may benefit from hearing and discussing the distinctions between 1920s New Orleans music, swing-era music, bebop, progressive, and avant-garde jazz. As an exercise, it is useful to have students identify what they are hearing in each. The instructor may want to create and post a general form on the course website to help facilitate and focus student attention. The form should ask students to make basic observations: Can they identify (to the best of their ability) instrumentation? Does the song contain an identifiable melody? What is the mood of the song? Is the song danceable?

As an assessment, have students complete an exercise in which they listen to the lyric version of a jazz song. This will help students who are less familiar with the jazz idiom orient themselves in the form and help them formulate their responses to the exercise. There are numerous vocal versions of Duke

Ellington's "Take the 'A' Train," for example (e.g., Fitzgerald). Have students write what they know (it is about Harlem, Duke Ellington was a famous jazz composer, it has an identifiable melody and a lyric that creates for them a specific response, etc.), what they want to know (e.g., Who is the singer?), and how it relates to what they have learned. This work should be done outside of the classroom. The instructor may want to incorporate their responses into a word-cloud generator to provide a visual demonstration of the words and ideas the exercise generated. The class should consider the importance of the words that have been generated and the frequency with which the words appear. Follow up with examples of jazz standards to strengthen critical listening skills.

## Reading Texts through Jazz

Since writing about music can be challenging, the learning objective of this content area is to get students attuned to using close reading to make basic observations and to connect the text to music. At this point, the class is prepared for close reading of several shorter jazz texts like the poetry of Langston Hughes or Amiri Baraka. What elements connect these texts to jazz? How would students define their form? Are these texts able to incorporate the element of improvisation? How does their form contribute to their meaning? As a class, do a close reading of a poem to illustrate the ways it can be considered. What images are used? Are readers conscious of its sound? Does jazz influence word choice or pattern? What metaphors did the poet choose?

If possible, students can then be divided into small groups and assigned one or two poems to discuss using the same techniques. Each person should be assigned a specific task in the group. Each group will present their readings to the class and each member of the group is expected to make a meaningful contribution. As students are working, the instructor will need to circulate and focus their responses. The same will be true when the group gives its presentation to the class. The instructor should ask probing questions as a way of focusing student thinking and encouraging deeper thought about the poem. These skills will be particularly important when the class moves to its discussion of Ellison.

In assessing this activity, the instructor will need to provide clear rubrics for the presentations so students recognize that they will be assessed on their ability to make clear distinctions about key concepts, participation, evidence of creativity, organization, and their ability to engage their audience.

## Musical Life Experiences

The learning objective for this content area is to examine how Ralph Ellison uses jazz as both content and strategy in his fiction and nonfiction and to recognize and understand the role that music plays in Ellison's work. Ellison's essay "Living with Music" is a very good starting place for discussing music and literature (*Collected Essays* 227–36). In it, Ellison shares some of the roles music has served in his life. The essay suggests a broad association of music with experience. Since

## 102 ELLISON'S JAZZ-SHAPED AMERICA

the same is undoubtedly true for students, it is useful to ask them to compile a list of the music that they live with. They should be encouraged to think very broadly about what that means for them. There is the music that they actively seek out. But, as Ellison notes in the essay, living with music often means living with music that one does not seek out, like the music contained in video games, movies, and religious practice. Sound surrounds us all.

Students should be led to recognize the ways Ellison presents his relationship to music. His essay references Black vernacular music like jazz and blues as well as European classical music: "Perhaps in the swift change of American society in which the meanings of one's origin are so quickly lost, one of the chief values of living with music lies in its power to give us an orientation in time. In doing so, it gives significance to all those indefinable aspects of experience which nevertheless help to make us what we are" (236). How does this shape our understanding as readers of what Ellison says about living with music?

As an assessment, students can be asked to write a brief essay in which they gather some of the music to which they listen and write a reflective essay in which they delineate what the music says about them and the orientation in time it provides them, which is as much cultural as it is musical.

### Jazz in Ellison's Fiction

The learning objective for this content area is to identify how Ellison has brought his own conception of jazz into his fiction. Students should be able to recognize how Ellison uses jazz to contribute to form and meaning. In turning to a discussion of *Invisible Man*, begin with a discussion of Louis Armstrong, his place in jazz, and what his musical and cultural influence means for Ellison.

It is well known that Louis Armstrong's presence frames *Invisible Man* in its prologue and epilogue. Because Louis Armstrong resonates through so much of Ellison's writing as the paragon of jazz possibility and accomplishment, begin with a discussion of Armstrong and his place in the music and in American culture. One useful place to begin this discussion is to have the students watch (outside of class) the section on Louis Armstrong that appears in the Ken Burns documentary *Jazz*. The instructor should play brief excerpts from the film in class that will be relevant to the discussion. Emphasize the context. Useful excerpts to play in class are most often drawn from episode 2, "The Gift."

It is helpful for students to recognize that Ellison features Armstrong's version of a song taken from the revue "Hot Chocolates," which ran from June to December in 1929. Armstrong made his Broadway debut as a musician in the pit orchestra for the show. "(What Did I Do to Be So) Black and Blue," written by Fats Waller and Andy Razaf, is the song to which the narrator listens in the prologue of *Invisible Man*. The song that the invisible narrator takes with him underground is little more than a pop record. In the show, the song is sung by a Black woman with dark skin who laments that men prefer Black women with light skin: "Brown and yallers all have fellers / Gentleman prefer them light" (Reger 17). But Armstrong transforms this from a pitying pop song to a verifiable protest song when he eliminates that verse entirely and instead implies the cultural consequences of being Black and blue in a nation that converts Blackness to invisibility when he sings:

> I'm white inside, but that don't help my case
> 'Cause I can't hide what is in my face
> How would it end? Ain't got a friend
> My only sin is in my skin
> What did I do to be so black and blue?

The main point for students to absorb is that what Ellison does in the novel is to claim Louis Armstrong as a consummate American trickster figure who is as reflective of power and racial attitudes as he is subversive of them. Ellison helps readers recognize this when he writes in his essay "Change the Joke and Slip the Yoke" that "Armstrong's clownish license and intoxicating powers are almost Elizabethan" (*Collected Essays* 107). In this regard, Armstrong serves a role to the invisible narrator that is similar to that of the narrator's grandfather, who offers a deathbed confession of having "been a traitor all my born days, a spy in the enemy's country ever since I give up my gun back in Reconstruction." The grandfather's advice to the narrator is "to overcome 'em with yeses, undermine 'em with grins, agree 'em to death and destruction, let 'em swoller you till they vomit or bust wide open" (Ellison, *Invisible Man* 16). Armstrong reflects to Ellison's audience the uncomfortable elements of minstrelsy the grandfather claims to have displayed, even as he, in Ellison's mind, transcends those limitations.[4]

Part of understanding the theme and variation that Ellison seems to be improvising on here involves understanding the trickster figure and how the trickster uses the forms and materials given and transforms them into something new and meaningful, just as Louis Armstrong has done with "Black and Blue" and, apparently, just as the invisible narrator's grandfather has done throughout his life. Students will benefit from a detailed examination of the ways jazz and Ellison's use of it rely on its power to both reflect and subvert racial attitudes.

What concerns Louis Armstrong in his performance of "Black and Blue" is identity, how to establish it, and how to maintain it in the face of fierce external pressure to change it. This is the point that Ellison's jazz seems to bring to the areas of the novel in which it appears. Since Louis Armstrong specifically appears in the opening and closing areas of the novel, the implication seems to be that the jazz-shaped characteristics of the novel provide a meaningful lens for understanding both the novel and the nation's democratic aspirations.

To fully appreciate Ellison's valuation of the metaphor, it is helpful to recognize that Ellison's consideration of jazz is not limited to *Invisible Man* or his essays on the subject. It extends through his nonfiction writing and through the unfinished second novel, which Ellison worked on for the last forty years of his life. The novel returns to the theme that Ellison had raised in *Invisible Man* emphasizing the centrality of the Black narrative to the American story. It was posthumously published in its unfinished form as *Three Days before the*

104 ELLISON'S JAZZ-SHAPED AMERICA

*Shooting* . . . . While the project lacks a clear narrative structure, a central story involves the relationship between the racist senator Adam Sunraider (who may or may may not have a Black father) and the Black jazz-musician-turned-minister, Reverend Alonzo Hickman, who raised him. The senator and the former jazz musician reminisce after the senator is shot on the floor of the United States Senate while giving a racially charged speech. Much of their conversation is a jazz-inspired call-and-response.

As an assessment, students can be given a brief passage and asked to explicate it in the context of the ways jazz contributes to its meaning. In *Invisible Man*, that passage may be drawn from the "Blackness of Blackness" sermon from the prologue, an excerpt from the Jim Trueblood section, an excerpt from the Harlem eviction scene, or an excerpt from the narrator's eulogy for Tod Clifton. From *Three Days before the Shooting* . . . , instructors may consider excerpting the passage in book 2 in which Reverend Hickman and the senator reminisce about the Juneteenth revival in ways that are equally jazz performance, religious observance, and cultural history (313–29). The emphasis in this passage is on the centrality of collective experience to Black American identity: "They couldn't divide us now. Because anywhere they dragged us we throbbed in time together. If we got a chance to sing, we sang the same song. If we got a chance to dance, we beat back hard times and tribulations with a clap of our hands and the beat of our feet, and it was the same dance" (313). How can the nation deny the influence of Black culture when Black culture *is* American culture? During a section of the novel entitled "Hickman in Washington, D.C.," Ellison creates a scene worth excerpting for students in which Reverend Hickman thinks about the meaning of art as he looks at a tapestry displayed in a hotel: "For being artists, the goal of both jazz musician and weaver was one of using their skills to arouse pleasure and wonder. And both did so by drawing upon that which was left carefully understated or concealed as a means for achieving a transcendent goal" (*Three Days* 595). There is perhaps no better example of how Ellison thinks his reader should hear and see the connections between jazz and literature in relation to what Ellison himself had carefully left concealed in his own prose.

## *Final Chorus*

Ellison invokes a conception of jazz that employs it as both content and strategy throughout his fiction and nonfiction writing. These pedagogical strategies, activities, and assessments are intended to provide an interdisciplinary way of understanding the primary themes and ideas around which Ellison focuses so much of his work. Students are intended to develop a vocabulary of the ways jazz, the music by Black and Creole people that had its origins in New Orleans in the decades following the Civil War and Reconstruction, established a new culture and a new sound reflecting their lived experiences. That music continued to grow and develop and moved from the margins of American culture toward mainstream acceptance.[5]

It is cultural and musical production that its players and their listeners brought to it. Writers like Ellison have embraced it as literary inspiration precisely because of the ways it has crept into so many aspects of America life and culture. For Ellison, it reflects segregation as well as integration and is the nation's best way of organizing its unresolved thoughts about race, class, and national aspiration, dating back to its founding documents, to find unity in its diversity. Jazz characterizes for Ellison the "delicate balance struck between strong individual personality and the group" that is reflected in the highest aspirations of American democracy (Ellison, *Collected Essays* 229). Ellison's use of jazz as democratic metaphor emphasizes the ways Americans exist in a collective environment even as they are defined by their own individuality.

The overall student learning outcome in teaching Ellison and jazz is to encourage students to recognize what jazz, as an art form and as cultural production, has contributed to Ralph Ellison's writing and the ways it can be understood. Rather than relegating this knowledge to a series of academic exercises, students are encouraged to develop the vocabulary necessary to make these connections and to personalize this area of the course content so they can see the ideas presented and discussed in class with actual lived experiences.

NOTES

1. Instructors will find a broad selection of musical examples appropriate for classroom use available on *YouTube* or, sometimes for a fee, on a variety of streaming services.

2. Instructors may want to share a set of poems such as "Jazzonia" (Hughes 34), "Saturday Night" (88), "The Cat and the Saxophone" (89), "Harlem Night Club" (90), "Midnight Dancer" (91), "Lenox Avenue" (92), "Red Silk Stockings" (122), "Trumpet Player" (338), "Juke Box Love Song" (393), "Dream Boogie" (425), and "Jam Session" (691) as examples of Hughes's poetic association with jazz to serve as a precursor to exploring jazz in Ellison's work. Sterling Brown's poems evoking the blues that instructors may want to consider include "When de Saints Go Ma'ching Home" (Jarrett 321), "Memphis Blues" (325), "Ma Rainey" (327), "Tin Roof Blues" (328), and "Cabaret" (329).

3. Baraka's performance of "am/trak" with jazz musicians is also available on *YouTube* ("Amiri Baraka").

4. Minstrel shows regularly featured songs, dances, and formulaic comic routines based on stereotyped depictions of Black Americans and typically performed by white actors who blackened their faces. Though based on centuries of racism, minstrelsy as a form of entertainment originated in the decades preceding the Civil War and reached the height of its popularity in the decades following the Civil War, when demands for civil rights by the recently emancipated triggered racial hostility.

5. The classroom activities included here are drawn and adapted from several sources that address teaching jazz and Black literature. As a way of contextualizing learning about jazz, Burns's film *Jazz* is a very useful place to begin. Though students are not responsible for watching the entire film, this ten-part series is useful for tracing the cultural and musical development of jazz. The curriculum suggestions contained online in Early and "Visualizing" are useful for conceiving and assembling curricular activities, as are "Teaching" and Proulx.

# Listening for the Invisible

## *Jake Johnson*

Writing about sound is as difficult a task as they come. Teaching others to write about the sounds they hear, what sounds might mean, or why they mean what they mean can be a herculean effort.

The tricky part is finding the right approach: metaphor? narrative description? graphic notation? jazz charts? Inclusivity haunts every corner; any one choice risks subtracting an audience from the mix. Music scholars and musicians have struggled with the gives and the takes of talking and writing about music. The literati have heaved against the Goliath, too. "A square stands upon an oblong" is how Virginia Woolf puzzlingly resorted to describing the sounds of a string quartet carving the air like some unsteady scythe (121). The music journalist Tim Rutherford-Johnson lyrically but also flatly likened the rugged music of composer Harrison Birtwistle to "granite in November rain." At some point there just isn't any other way around the problem of sound. Believe me, it's just hard.

But there is also an invitation within sound writing. Incorporating sound into a writing classroom or otherwise-literary space can welcome new, fresh ways of knowing the world. *Acoustemology* is the term the anthropologist Steven Feld gave to this posture: what we can know about the world whenever we listen to it. Listening to our listening is how the musicologist Nina Sun Eidsheim more pointedly describes it. Giving students the opportunity to know how their ears work can be a lifeline for critical, engaged thinking about where our listening factors into issues such as race, sexism, and climate change, for instance. Musicologists and other scholars have tilted their ears in recent years to the listening frameworks we apply to the human voice, judging the race, class, sex, and even physical beauty of a person just through our ears (Eidsheim, "Race"; Stoever). It's not necessarily that the sounds we hear are fundamental to that person, however. It may be more accurate to flip the script on sound and subjectivity; it is the listener who determines someone's identity, not the source who *authors* the sound. Our ears work wonders on determining who, how, and what a sound says.

Which is a funny way to begin asking questions about an actual author, to say nothing of one as esteemed as Ralph Ellison. And yet novel discoveries might still await those who listen to the novelist. In this chapter, I write out loud about Ellison's work. Mine is a noble but humble effort. My task here is not to say with any definitiveness what Ellison's musical background made possible in his writing. I cannot provide all the space required to investigate the full extent of sound in his work, either. My expertise is one of listener. This chapter offers a path of discovery for thinking about and teaching Ellison within a context of musicological inquiry. My goal is in sync with Ellison's: learning to listen for what remains invisible.

It might be useful to begin with the material evidence of sound in Ellison's world. Ellison was most definitely an audiophile. And in the 1950s, audiophilia looked a lot like hoarding. He collected recording and audio equipment, outfitting his living spaces with wires and speaker cabinets and needles and paper sleeves and vinyl discs and storage spaces and AM-FM tuners and turntables and compensators and magnetic cartridges, and I could go on. Ellison sure did. The real estate required for his listening habits was of such magnitude that navigating his and Fanny's already-tiny living spaces meant "it was worth your life to move about without first taking careful bearings" (Ellison, *Collected Essays* 234). His wife, Fanny, was less cavalier about the mess. "Sometimes it's a joke," she wrote to her mother of the clutter, "and sometimes it's sad as hell" (F. M. Ellison, Letter).

What we might call *the materiality of listening*, then, can't help but have invaded the Ellisons in the period when Ralph Ellison's literary light was first dawning. Music clearly meant a great deal to the young writer. In his essays on music, he invokes his early years learning trumpet and listening to traveling musicians in Oklahoma City's bustling Deep Deuce jazz clubs, now long silent. The brass machine touching his lips was but one conductor of his imagination; other machines would follow. Throughout his life, Ellison found ways to use whatever machinery was on hand to channel sound into his understanding of place and character. Like Nietzsche, that first philosopher to discover his thoughts through the interface of a typewriter, Ellison seemed aware that mediation mattered and that any idea worth pursuing must first pass through some motor of sound, whether of brass or metal or plastic-coated copper wires, before passing into the world of silent letters.

The thing about sound is you just can't control where it spills. This is especially true in urban areas where, as the saying goes, there is no noisier party than the one you aren't invited to. In his essay "Living with Music," which first appeared in 1955 in *High Fidelity* magazine, Ellison illustrates this matter in typical lyrical fashion. The thin-walled apartment he and Fanny shared was thick with sound. Noisy neighbors in the walls and traffic sounds below were terribly intrusive. Ellison's description of urban soundscapes offers a sonic corollary to the protagonist Jeff Jefferies's voyeurism in Alfred Hitchcock's film *Rear Window*, which premiered in 1954, one year ahead of Ellison's essay. Jefferies, played by Jimmy Stewart, is homebound due to an injury and throughout the film becomes convinced that a murder has taken place under his lazy gaze into his neighborhood through the apartment's back window. Ellison is also homebound and also unwillingly attentive to his neighbors, but in this case it is he who is driven to homicidal thoughts. The real antagonist of Ellison's story was the upstairs occupant, an operatic singer who took due diligence in daily practice schedules that flatly knocked that delicately balanced square right off the oblong.

At first, Ellison the musician was sympathetic. The singer had to practice *somewhere*, after all. But he had to write somewhere, too. Her routines interrupted his work and soon became a source of frustration. These sounds coming from the ceiling were, for Ellison, in fact, a shot across the bow. "I was forced to listen," he writes, "and in listening I soon became involved to the point of identification" (*Collected Essays* 232).

108    LISTENING FOR THE INVISIBLE

Through a series of comic episodes, Ellison realizes he, too, can weaponize sound in this acoustic tête-à-tête by blasting the singer's repertoire with recordings beneath her feet. This is where the audiophilia begins to develop. The writer assembles more and more audio equipment, converting the apartment into a veritable barricade (an "audio booby trap," as he put it) in his private war with the invisible voice in the ceiling.

I have more to say about this scene later; suffice for now that the picture Ellison the writer paints of his creative process is one where the fact of sound plays on his imagination and, when least desired, holds that imaginative power hostage. Like Hitchcock's nosy protagonist, Ellison cracks the fantastical facade of modernity's tamed chaos and becomes embroiled in the devilish intrusions of the modern world. Only Ellison demonstrates that the listener holds fewer cards than the watcher—absent something like an ear-lid, we are rendered vulnerable in an increasingly noisy world that cannot so easily be shut out. Ellison lived this terrific vulnerability day after day in one of the noisiest cities in the world. No wonder Invisible Man's haunting final message to the world measures its analogy in sound. The shadows of silence may convince us otherwise, but the lower frequencies are where our nameless cruelties are left to vibrate our bones nonetheless. They speak for us. How frightening.

And this is the fulcrum on which I want to pivot. I am a musicologist. Sound is my trade. But in my classrooms I also train musicians to write. In my seminar Writing about Music, I follow established practices in writing studies that privilege process over product, that treat writing as a means of discovery. And, like I mentioned at the outset, writing about sound is one of the hardest and most uncanny things to do—like dancing about architecture, as Frank Zappa put it. But when we attune the ear to the written word—when we pay attention to the alignment of performance and idea—then we have the opportunity to pull into classrooms a resonant theory of community, of belongingness, and of empathy.

What I mean by this is that vibrations connect us to one another. Musicologist Nina Eidsheim has written beautifully of how the *process* of sound is one of bone and flesh vibrating, first in the body of the sound maker and then in the body of the listener (*Sensing Sound*). Pinning down sound as merely a fact of air molecules or sine waves treats sound as some kind of strange specimen of the air instead of the material process where it in fact is most recognizable and familiar to us. Whenever a classroom listens together, it is nothing short of a miracle. In that moment, all bodies collide with one another in vibrational unity. Sound enters our bodies. Our bodies become not unlike Ellison's audio equipment, amplifying signal and conducting one another's energies throughout the room. We are in those moments attuned to one another's frequencies. The intimacy of listening is unmatched.

One way I like to manage this in my classrooms is by listening together to a familiar-enough piece of music (my go-to choice in recent years has been the visually rich and musically stunning opening scene from the 1986 film version of *Little Shop of Horrors*) and then asking pointed questions about students' physical and emotional reactions to that listening experience. Before pushing play, I frame the listening experience by asking everyone to take note of moments where a particular emotional reaction happened for them—maybe this is a specific lyric or a chord change, or even something happening on screen that elicits one response or another. This, I explain, is a mapping technique. We are mapping our reactions to the piece. I give them a moment after the piece is over to collect their thoughts before instructing that, on a second listen, they are then to use their listening maps as a guide to track where, precisely, they felt those moments happen in their bodies. It can at times be uncomfortable to talk about the body's reactions to sounds, but since the body is so often functioning as an unwilling resonating chamber it can be illuminating to pay attention to where, exactly, sound is exerting its forces on us. Upon reflection, we discover that there are often shared moments of excitement from the piece but that often people feel these experiences in different parts of their bodies. And, more to the point, no matter their varied entrances into our bodies, shared reactions often manifest in similar musical moments. We learn something in this moment about how our ears work, and we learn how so very entangled we are in one another's listening experiences.

And so I find it important to help students understand how a particular musician's ears worked before I begin to grasp them or their work. I like to use primary source material when teaching musicians how to write. We read diaries and newspaper reviews and liner notes as well as letters of employment and wills and marginalia scribbled in the staves of a score. These are sometimes stirringly poignant. I ask what you really know of W. A. Mozart's music until you've read his cloying letters begging for work. Musicians are not always the best writers, nor do they always succeed in capturing what sound is doing, but that isn't so much the point. Instead, the way people write about sound tells us something important about how they listen to the world.

It pays, then, to consider Ralph Ellison's many attempts to channel vibrations and frequencies into his work. We know that listening and speaking were important mechanisms through which he wrote. Adam Bradley notes that Ellison and his editor spoke aloud several drafts of *Invisible Man* before publication—sometimes changing prose significantly in the process—and that Ellison spoke into a tape recorder to compose portions of his second and unfinished novel (26). Like the trumpet in his youth and the typewriter in Nietzsche's, audio equipment allows Ellison to listen to his discovery process; its mechanisms reveal through sound what was before hidden in plain sight.[1] Established writers understand that their task, then, is often that of sound-writing. Certainly Ellison's Invisible Man speaks with a musical tone at times, and his descriptions of Charlie Christian's guitar handling in "The Charlie Christian Story" merge into the pluck and strum of its subject—all evidence of an author who can't help but write aloud. Once budding writers grasp something of this phenomenon for themselves, the consequences of mediating the world through their ears give license for something new to develop out of the pen.

110    LISTENING FOR THE INVISIBLE

Ellison, therefore, is not unique in this regard. What makes his a helpful case for writers is how much he understands the necessity of media in a modern world. It's the materiality of his listening that reminds us of the materiality of sound itself, that bone-and-flesh quality, if you will. His audiophilia arises out of disgust with the permeability of sound and his inability to easily control his ears unaided by technological devices.

As this was the case in midcentury America, it almost assuredly has been ever more a concern in the decades since. The search for ways of mediating our world through listening has at times been desperate, and all the more amid the turbulence of the modern age. In Franz Kafka's 1931 telling of the story from *The Odyssey*, for instance, the Sirens are unable to sway Ulysses as he passed by their rocky shore. He trusted vainly in his "handful of wax and fathom of chain" to protect him. If he couldn't hear the world, Ulysses reasoned, then he would be safe from it. For their part, the Sirens grew silent when they realized he could not hear them. They watched his passing ship in awe, never before seeing the complete bliss of someone unaffected by their sound. And for his part, Ulysses was none the wiser, seeing their craned necks toward him as indication that deathly song was reaching from their throats and that his clever waxy implement was saving his life. It *was* working, but it protected him from the Sirens' stunned silence and not from their terrific sound that, unknown to him, existed only in his mind—a tactic that reminds me of a young child's rush to protect themselves from a scary scene on television not by closing their eyes but by clapping their hands over their ears.

Kafka's story moralizes the modern age's growing concern with its encroaching sounds. Our technology has advanced since wax and chains. Machines of all sorts now aid us in curating our personal sound worlds, what with smartphones and earbuds and playlists and the like. Mediation hardly seems the right word anymore. Noise *cancellation* feels more on the nose. Ever vulnerable to the sounds around us, we have ample means of replacing the world imposed on us with one of our own choosing. Ulysses's blissfully triumphant face is now our own. Nature forgot to give us ear-lids, so we have found a way to fashion them for ourselves.

There is, of course, something lost in this calculation. Listening is an important conduit of exchange. We forfeit that opportunity of intimacy, of belonging together, when we stop our ears and sail past one another in silence. Even in my communities of musicians and sound makers, I can no longer assume my students have disciplined their ears to one another. Listening is too obvious, and the effects of our clumsy listening habits simply too invisible. It may be necessary—and this is my point—to rediscover the power of listening through other means. Converting a literature classroom into a sound chamber might be the ticket: giving students the chance to practice listening to the world around them by first attuning to the sonic environments of our richest literary worlds. Drawing attention to what is invisible begins with first learning how to listen for it.

Recall Ellison's villain, that singer on his ceiling whose vibrations drove him nearly to audiophilic madness. There is an important parting lesson here that comes into focus where I left the story. After battling a proxy war of ceiling and floor for a time, Ellison finally meets this nameless, faceless enemy in the hallway. Far from an eruption, their meeting leads to a surprisingly mutual appreciation of Ellison's sound equipment. The singer even compliments him on the artists he has chosen to sling her direction. Ellison notes that, after that chance encounter, the battle continued but their listening changed. On some occasions now, when Ellison's speakers roared in retaliation to her persistent larynx, the singer would pause her vocalizations and, as the recording ended, he could hear her applause bleeding down through the ceiling. They had arrived at a kind of agreement among artists. Ellison came to admire her courage, "for she was neither intimidated into silence nor goaded into undisciplined screaming; she persevered, she marked the phrasing of the great singers I sent her way, she improved her style" (*Collected Essays* 235). In turn, Ellison had rediscovered through the thin membrane of his ceiling a love of sound and the rarefied experience that personal sound equipment affords the modern ears.

The Ellisons eventually moved from that apartment. The audio clutter moved with them, but its function shifted from weaponry to pleasure. This whole story reminds me, in fact, of the media theorist Friedrich Kittler's observation that all entertainment emerges as a misuse of military equipment (96–97). Maybe this is in some part due to the realization that protecting yourself from the sounds of modernity seems a defensive move for most of us. And yet the way we listen in such an environment can also be a way of asking new questions of the world, questions that disarm our instincts to cover our ears and shout louder than the enemy or, perhaps even worse, to ignore one another altogether.

What Ralph Ellison teaches me is that common discomforts of this sort may be an uncommon gift. As Ellison admitted, "we are indebted to the singer and the old environment for forcing us to discover one of the most deeply satisfying aspects of our living" (*Collected Essays* 235)—that is, that listening is a collective enterprise, that vibrating together is one of life's greatest pleasures, and that tuning the ear to those imperceptible resonances can transduce even the lowest frequencies into something we can recognize and feel once more.

NOTE

1. Students can watch and listen to Ellison do one of these recordings in the 1966 short documentary "USA: The Novel," available online.

# SHORT WORKS

# The Voices of History:
# Narrating the Past in Ellison's Short Fiction

## *Keith Byerman*

The publication of an expanded collection of stories in the Vintage paperback *Flying Home and Other Stories* has provided a larger sense of Ralph Ellison as a writer of short fiction. A key theme that emerges from this edition is the significance of the past for him. History has consistently been an element in his work, but several of these short pieces show him employing a range of time periods, geographic settings, and circumstances. Of the stories selected for this analysis, three are set at the time of the Second World War, one occurs during the early twentieth century, and one tells of a hero of the Haitian Revolution. Running through them are three concerns: the problematics of realistic representation, the use of folk material, and the role of women. What emerges from these narratives is the power of the past in shaping Black male identity and the experience of racism. Central to this discussion is the issue of how these often-fraught subjects can be effectively presented in the classroom.

A prime example of the pedagogical difficulties is in "A Party Down at the Square," the first story in the collection. The use of the n-word and variants of it make this story difficult for teaching. While Ellison is very clear here and throughout the collection that the word is only used by white characters, its presence makes the narrative awkward for instructors. Some may choose to avoid it altogether. But to do so is to lose the opportunity to engage Ellison's most explicit presentation of racialized violence. One way to begin the conversation is to discuss the ways in which language itself is a form of violence. Offensive speech acts are used not only against African Americans but also against women, members of other racial minority groups and the LGBTQ community, and even impoverished people of any race or gender. Such language often correlates with physical violence; both serve to insult, objectify, and render powerless those defined as Other. Creating a context for the term can redirect the discussion from simple denunciation of the word to analysis of how the word is used and even why it is used. The point of this exercise is not to render the word in any way acceptable; rather, it is to clarify its dangerous power, as the story demonstrates.

The fact that it is used unselfconsciously by the narrator, who is from the North, suggests the universality of the racism that pervades the story. "A Party Down at the Square" is a lynching narrative that initially follows in the realistic tradition of Theodore Dreiser ("N\_\_\_\_ Jeff") and Richard Wright ("Big Boy Leaves Home"). It is told by a young white man from Cincinnati who is visiting with relatives in eastern Alabama, apparently not far from where Ellison attended school at the Tuskegee Institute. He describes the white crowd gathering from as far away as Phenix City, the excitement that they display, and the insults to the Black man who is their victim. All of this detail serves to create the expectation of a story of America's holocaust, in which the laws against homicide are flagrantly ignored in the name of white supremacy.

But the narrative then takes a series of turns into the surreal that subvert notions of normality at the heart of realism. The event takes place late at night, during a cold rain. The fire designed to kill the Black man has to be fed repeatedly with gasoline: "You could see the flames light up the whole square. It was late and the streetlights had been off for a long time. It was so bright that the bronze statue of the general standing there in the Square was like something alive. The shadows playing on his moldy green face made him seem to be smiling down at the n\_\_\_\_" (Ellison, *Flying Home* 4). This passage offers a number of oddities. The green Confederate officer comes alive as the Black man is being put to death. Curiously, the narrator associates the green with mold rather than verdigris, which would be the natural source of the color, thereby creating a Poe-esque effect of the living dead. The smile is ambiguous: is it approval of the violence against the victim or is it an act of sympathy? The general's place on the pedestal is, after all, the result of the past and present sacrifices of Black lives.

The flames are also the cause of the chaos that comes to dominate the story. The platform on which the man is being burned falls through, and the man, still on fire, rolls into the crowd. He comes to a stop at the feet of the narrator: "I jumped back so he wouldn't get on me. I'll never forget it. Every time I eat barbeque I'll remember that n\_\_\_\_. His back was just like a barbequed hog. I could see the prints of his ribs where they start around from his backbone and curve down and around" (9). The Black body here becomes an object to be consumed, suggesting symbolically that violence against Black people is a means of feeding and nurturing white supremacy.

114    VOICES OF HISTORY

The most extreme incident in the story is that the flames create a sense of deceptive space. The brightness of the fire causes the pilot of a plane to believe that it has reached an airport and therefore begins its descent:

> Her motors stopped altogether and I could hear the sound of branches cracking and snapping off below her landing gear. I could see her plain now, all silver and shining in the light of the fire with T.W.A. in black letters under her wings. She was sailing smoothly out of the Square when she hit the high power lines that follow the Birmingham highway through the town. It made a loud crash. It sounded like the wind blowing the door of a tin barn shut. She only hit with her landing gear, but I could see the sparks flying, and the wires knocked loose from the poles were spitting blue sparks and whipping around like a bunch of snakes and leaving circles of blue sparks in the darkness.                                    (6–7)

What is anomalous here is the presence of the plane at all. Trans World Airlines was a transcontinental carrier that made refueling stops in large cities, such as St. Louis. It would not be expected to be preparing to land anywhere near a small Alabama town.

The downed wires create panic among the townspeople, and that disorder itself causes more destruction. They run toward the downed wires, and in the confusion a woman is pushed against one of the wires: "It must have killed her right off. She was lying in a puddle stiff as a board. [. . .] Her white dress was torn, and I saw one of her tits hanging out in the water and her thighs. [. . .] The shock had turned the woman almost as black as the n____" (7). The shared color and the death by fire create an identification between the Black man and the white woman. The exposure of her body hints at but subverts the assault on white women that was the usual justification for lynching. The exposure of the woman's body also suggests the ways that racist violence manipulated white women's bodies as justification for lynching.

More than in most lynching narratives, which tend to rely on realistic depictions to reinforce an ideological stance, Ellison disrupts that pattern, creating an apocalyptic narrative that points to the failure of racism to construct a social order and in fact its creation of chaos.[1] The very effort to construct a racialized history in which whiteness dominates produces an even greater sense of the centrality of Blackness. As the narrator concludes, "I was right there watching it all. It was my first party and my last. God, but that n____ was tough. That Bacote n____ was some n____!" (11). The very language of insult becomes the language of admiration. It should not be surprising that this is his only lynching party.

The choice of this narrative voice is an important question in a discussion of the story. The narrator is young, white, supposedly innocent (even naive), a Northerner, sociable, and attentive to details. While he uses racist language, it is clear that he has not yet been hardened by the white supremacist ideology that shapes his relatives and their community. He is something of an outsider to this community and thus can be both shocked and intrigued by the events. For some white student readers, he has qualities similar to theirs, even if they have no comparable experience. For students of color, he is far more problematic, since he both adopts the racist language of his environment and takes a passive stance in regard to the violence. The role of the instructor involves negotiating these very different perspectives by pointing to the narrator's admiration of the Black man and failure to do anything about his suffering. The ability to identify is important in connection with two aspects of the conclusion. The first is his acknowledgment of the victim's toughness, a desirable quality associated with manhood. The second is his socialization into the discourse of racism, so that it is natural for him even as he questions some of the values of it.

"A Party Down at the Square" is followed by a grouping known as the Buster and Riley tales, which includes "Afternoon," "That I Had the Wings," and, most famously, "A Coupla Scalped Indians." These reverse the first story by making the focal characters two young Black boys from the South. One effect is to shift the emphasis to the Black community, making white characters marginal in the narratives. In doing so, Ellison presents everyday life, as opposed to the violence and chaos of the first story. The contrast enables the author to point to the ordinary humanity of African Americans, something that the white narrator of "Party" barely glimpses.

"Mister Toussan" is distinct in this group for incorporating a legendary version of Toussaint L'Ouverture, the most famous leader of the Haitian Revolution. In the story, he serves as the counter to mundane white racism. The story opens with Buster and Riley experiencing frustration at the meanness of their white neighbor. Old Rogan, as they call him, has several cherry trees in his yard but will not allow the boys to get the cherries that have fallen to the ground, let alone to pick better ones off the trees. At the same time, he tolerates birds flying in and out, consuming as much of the fruit as they want. Interestingly, Buster identifies the birds as mockingbirds, which carry the symbolic significance of innocence or endurance of the spirit. They also mimic the sounds of other animals and thus carry the connotation of multiple forms of expression.

This reference is immediately linked to Riley's mother, who is singing the spiritual "All God's Chillun Got Wings" as she does some sewing for the white family she works for. Her singing leads the boys into a call-and-response performance that shifts them away from their frustration with Rogan. In it they imagine their escape from their town to major cities, "'Or anywhere else colored is free'" (*Flying Home* 25). They imagine flying back to Africa, but this leads them to the falsehoods that pass as history in their schoolbook. They first joke about cannibals but then enter the realm of other stereotypes: "'Shucks, man, they couldn't catch me, them suckers is too lazy. The geography book says they 'bout the most lazy folks in the whole world,' said Buster with disgust, 'just black and lazy!'" (25). Riley angrily rejects this view, regardless of what the book says.

116    VOICES OF HISTORY

His contradiction is based on the word of his father: "'Cause my old man says that over there they got kings and diamonds and gold and ivory, and if they got all them things, all of 'em caint be lazy" (25).

Implicit in this dialogue is Ellison's repudiation of a history based on racist ideology; in doing so, the author is taking up in fictional form the contentions made by W. E. B. Du Bois in the same time period (the 1940s) within the profession of history. Even if the source (the father) is not authoritative, nonetheless, "[i]t was good to think that all the Africans were not lazy" (25).

The text returns to the school to offer a more concrete narrative that solidifies racial pride. Buster remembers that his teacher told his class about Toussaint L'Ouverture, an "African guy" who defeated Napoleon. At first Riley does not believe him, asserting that he is lying. But then he changes: "Riley looked hard at Buster and, seeing the seriousness of the face, felt the excitement of a story rise up within him" (26). They revert immediately into another call-and-response as a means of communicating the history. It becomes a secular version of sermonic performance, casting Buster as preacher and Riley as the engaged congregation. They blend the discourses of historical information and biblical reference. In their mutual telling, Toussaint becomes Joshua fighting at Jericho. But instead of dependence on Yahweh, their Black hero trusts his fighting skill and his voice. They impersonate him and the defeated French soldiers.

But Riley cannot quite believe in the story they have constructed: "Riley's voice was unbelieving, and there was a wistful expression in his eyes that Buster could not understand" (28–29). What he doubts is the ability of adults to get the story right, so the two of them must take responsibility for completing it. They embody Toussaint as a man who, along with his enslaved comrades, just wants to be left alone to live his life. He is unafraid to challenge the French, including Napoleon himself, who fail to accept Black humanity. The boys then express respect for the teacher who started them on this narrative journey, in part because Black heroic history is not in the books that constitute the education they receive. They must generate that past out of the scraps that become available to them. Significantly, the story is halted by Riley's mother, who is concerned with how white people view her family: "'I says I want you all to go round the backyard and play. You keeping up too much fuss out there. White folks says we tear up a neighborhood when we move in it and you all out there jus provin' them out true. Now git on round in the back'" (31). Her worries are the opposite of Toussaint's bravado and remind them of the effect of the white gaze on their everyday lives. At the end, Buster imagines that they can "'slip around and get some cherries'" (32). This desire is his small way of claiming for himself the heritage of Black manhood.

It is worth noting that folk narratives almost universally incorporate challenges to existing authority.[2] Those considered weak or unimportant or dirty, among other negative qualities, can be imagined to be more quick-witted or skillful than those who oppress them. Classroom discussion of this point could enable students to critically examine racist thinking about the Other; in that thinking, it is essential to not only denigrate and dehumanize the powerless but to make them unworthy of empathy. Related to this process is the insistence on victimhood, making the oppressed incapable of significant response to their situation. Making the Other intelligent and skillful, perhaps more so than their oppressors, instills a sense of humanity, equality, and perhaps superiority. The use of young boys as the protagonists offers students an opportunity to rethink the nature of power. Ellison begins and ends this story with ritualized language that announces it as a folktale. By doing so, he places Buster and Riley in the tradition of vernacular storytelling; their narrative is improvised by combining bits of history with self-empowering speech acts that enable them to transcend the diminishment of young Black lives lived in a world of white oppression.

In contrast to these stories of childhood, "In a Strange Country" and "A Storm of Blizzard Proportions" focus on Black manhood and race in the context of war and international environments. They address the question of how Black identity works in situations where race is not a primary factor. Ellison raises the question of whether it is possible to free oneself of the American curse. Significantly, the stories offer very different responses. The stories are set at the time of World War II in Wales, where a Black sailor awaits transport home after completing his tour of duty. On his way to a pub in the first story, he is accosted by a group of white American soldiers who insult and assault him. He is saved by some Welsh civilians on their way to the pub. There he meets and converses with Mr. Catti, the owner and bartender, who expresses sympathy for his experience. He then invites the sailor to a performance by a men's chorus. Throughout this period, Parker, the sailor, goes through conflicting emotions of hatred of white people and appreciation for the help and kindness of his hosts. He initially refuses the invitation to the concert, but then Mr. Catti assures him that it is a private club open only to members and their guests. The implication is that he will not have to deal with any Americans.

Parker finds himself enthralled by the quality and emotion of the music. But he also is troubled by his own racial history: "And as the men sang in hushed tones he felt a growing poverty of spirit. He should have known more of the Welsh, their history and art. If only we had some of what they have, he thought. They are a much smaller nation than ours would be, yet I can remember no song of ours that's of love of the soil or of country. Nor any song of battle other than those of biblical times" (Ellison, *Flying Home* 142). His reaction can be read in two ways. One would be the racist perspective that stereotypes Black people as having little depth of feeling, a view that goes back at least as far as Thomas Jefferson. The other, more likely reading is that African Americans, having been forced to work the land under threat of the whip or even death, had no reason to have a spiritual connection to the soil; it was never theirs to love and care for. Similarly, they have little reason to love the nation that put them in bondage. Why would they create battle songs in praise of such a country?

The chorus then sings "God Save the King," the "Internationale," and then, in his honor, "The Star-Spangled Banner." Initially, he misreads the moment, believing that "they were enticing him into some unwilled and degrading act, from which only his failure to remember the words would save him. It was all unreal, yet it seemed to have happened before. Only now the melody seemed charged with some vast new meaning which that part of him could not fit with the old familiar words" (145–46). Somehow, in this "strange country," he becomes fully an American: "For the first time in your whole life, he thought with dreamlike wonder, the words are not ironic" (146). What is ironic is that his countrymen make him feel alien, while the foreigners grant him a sense of national identity. It is an epiphany: a simple act of recognition of shared humanity provides him with a more complete sense of who he is.

If "In a Strange Country" enhances the meaning of being Black and American, "A Storm of Blizzard Proportions" subverts that meaning. In both stories, there is an enticement to become an expatriate, in order to save the focal character from the damage that a return home would inflict. "Storm" is a romance that is inflected with racial history. The focal character appears to be a version of Parker, with very similar experiences, circumstances, and attitudes, who has developed a relationship with a Welsh woman who works with the Red Cross.

The story opens with a discussion of the protagonist's obsession with the boxer Jack Johnson, a skilled and notorious fighter of the early part of the twentieth century. He became the world heavyweight champion by breaking the color line that restricted that title to white men. In addition to the fame and wealth that came through those achievements, he was also defiant in his preference for marrying white women. He gained notoriety when he was charged and found guilty of violating the Mann Act, which prohibited taking women across state lines for illicit purposes. It is this refusal to accept the rules of white supremacy that make him important in the story: "They didn't praise him as they do Joe [Louis], but what I like is that he went where he wanted to go and did what he wanted to do. No matter what they said. That's what a man has to do" (Ellison, *Flying Home* 149).

The irony of the story is that the protagonist lacks the courage to tell the woman, Joan, that he is going to leave her. She begs him to stay or to take her back to Ohio with him. But he pretends that she is the weak one; he even calls her a child because she so openly expresses her love and hopes. He cannot be Jack Johnson when it comes to matters of race. In place of a home with her, he can only think of returning alone to where his mother is buried and where the snow is falling. He obviously fears the repercussions of a cross-racial relationship. He lacks the intensity of either Jack Johnson or Joan. They both embrace life, whatever the risks, while he can think only of the snow, the emblem of death and surrender in the story.

The teaching of these stories would be enhanced by inclusion of the experiences of Black men in the American military during World War II, especially the irony of their being asked to defend a nation that refuses to grant them full citizenship and to do so in a military that was segregated and insistently racist in its treatment of Black soldiers and sailors. This could then be linked to the very different treatment they received from British and European allies.

Specifically, Wales as a setting serves to show how a country can be dominated by a more powerful one (in this case England); thus a parallel is created with the Black American experience.

The final protagonist, both in this discussion and in the collection of stories, is Todd of "Flying Home." It is a narrative of the Tuskegee Airmen, who trained under white officers during World War II. One of the purposes of locating them in Alabama, even though a significant number were from the North, was to constantly remind them of their restricted status in American society regardless of their achievements, skills, or contributions to the war effort. This strategy is crucial to the story, since Todd takes his sense of worth from the white gaze.[3] To understand the consciousness of this main character, Ellison makes use of all of the elements—realism/distortion, folklore, and women—found in some combination in the stories already discussed.

Todd has had to crash-land his training plane when it is hit by a bird; in the process, he breaks his ankle and goes in and out of consciousness. The narrator is very clear about the level of his pain and his frustration at not being able to return to the airfield. What emerges almost immediately is his embarrassment at having crashed, even though he is not at fault. This turns almost immediately to a form of racial self-hatred, at the old man who has been helping him, at the possibility of having to ride to the doctor's office on an ox, and at the memory of a letter from his girlfriend in which she questions the attitudes of white society:

> I don't need the papers to tell me you had the intelligence to fly. And I have always known you to be as brave as anyone else. The papers annoy me. Don't you be contented to prove over and over again that you're brave or skillful just because you're black, Todd. I think they keep beating that dead horse because they don't want to say why you boys are not yet fighting. I'm really disappointed, Todd. Anyone with brains can learn to fly, but then what. What about using it, and who will you use it for? [. . .] I sometimes think they're playing a trick on us. It's very humiliating . . .
>
> (Ellison, *Flying Home* 159)

He immediately turns her insights against her, thinking that she cannot understand because she has never been to the South, and then, significantly against Jefferson, "this old black ignorant man" (159).[4] Because Todd measures himself by white recognition, he cannot accept any other ways of looking at himself or his experience.

Todd's sensibility is contextualized by two narratives, one personal and one folkloric. The first is a memory from his childhood, in which his mother tries to keep him in the realm of reality. When she takes him to the fair, he becomes obsessed with a model plane that is flying around the top of the exhibit hall. From that point, he is constantly bothering her about getting him one like it; she regularly refuses because it would be too expensive. He then attempts to build models out of the scraps of wood around their house. One day, he hears and then

120   VOICES OF HISTORY

sees a small plane overhead. He believes that it is another model and climbs up the screen door to try to grab it. He falls to the ground and injures himself. When the doctor comes, the mother asks him if her son has a mental problem, based on this obsession. She then has to explain to her son that what he saw was a real plane that was "a hundred miles" up in the air (175). Her exaggeration only serves to give us a sense of why he becomes a pilot, even at the cost of being condescended to by the white officers. It links his personal history to the larger engagement of Black men with the Tuskegee training.

The second narrative appears to be the opposite of the first, in that it is a fantastical folktale told by Jefferson.[5] In it, the old man claims to have died and gone to heaven, where he is outfitted with wings. He is reassured when he sees that there are other Black angels but notes that they are wearing harnesses. He rejects the harness and soon discovers that he is highly skilled at flying; he can in fact fly better with just one wing than others can with two. He soon disrupts heaven by flying fast and doing all kinds of tricks. Soon the white angels complain about him, and Saint Peter gives him a warning: he is to slow down and always fly with two wings. But, as he tells it, he soon forgets and is back to his old tricks. For this second violation, his wings are taken away, and he is returned to Alabama. Before he leaves, he has the final word: "Well, you done took my wings. And you puttin' me out. You got charge of things so's I can't do nothin' about it. But you got to admit just this: While I was up here I was the flyin'est son-of-a-bitch what ever hit heaven" (169).

Todd misreads the tale as an attack on him, not understanding that it is an act of praise for his skills and courage. It acknowledges all the restrictions placed on the Black trainees but demands respect for their ability and effort. By the end of the story, he has begun to understand. He begins to feel connected to "the world of men." As Jefferson and his grandson carry him to the ambulance, Todd sees a buzzard fly over. But instead of reminding him of his humiliation, he "saw the dark bird glide into the sun and glow like a bird of flaming gold" (182). Out of this troubling history, he has a moment of epiphany, in which the world is transformed into something mysterious and beautiful.

In these stories, Ellison uses women—mothers, girlfriends, teachers—to ground men in reality, to push them to grasp the actuality of the world, society, and the past. But these young men, conditioned by that very history, are often uncertain or confused or self-doubting. Then the author disrupts this pattern with the eruption of the surreal or the folkloric, as in children's call-and-response, in folk music, or in folktales. These stories, several of which were written around the time Ellison was working on *Invisible Man*, might be seen as ways of trying out these elements for their usefulness in the larger work. "Flying Home" can be taught as preparation for the novel, both for the protagonist's uncertainty about his identity and for the use of folk figures who challenge that uncertainty. "A Storm of Blizzard Proportions" could be used as a way of exploring relationships between Black men and white women in a different context from *Invisible Man*. "A Party Down at the Square" explores surreal elements that recur in the novel.

It is also the case that these texts can stand alone as Ellison's efforts in the short story form. Some of them could be included in a unit on war stories and others on narratives of childhood, both of which have little place in the novel. Thus, this set of texts offers a variety of possibilities for the literature classroom.

NOTES

1. Ellison consistently makes use of a dialectic of chaos and order. One example from *Invisible Man* involves the Brotherhood's deliberate provocation of the riot in order to discredit Ras, their main opponent in the Harlem community.

2. On Ellison's use of folklore generally, see Blake; O'Meally, *Craft*.

3. A phrase from the story, "his need to measure himself against the mirror of other men's appreciation" (Ellison, *Flying Home* 161), is a close paraphrase of the famous words of Du Bois's *The Souls of Black Folk*: "this sense of always looking at one's self through the eyes of others" (8). Thus, Todd experiences what Du Bois referred to as double consciousness.

4. For other comments on Ellison's use of folk material in "Flying Home," see Lucy; Ostendorf.

5. The old man's name is indicative of Ellison's play with naming practices. As a student of folklore, he would have known that newly freed slaves repudiated their experience as property by taking the names of Americans associated with freedom: Washington, Franklin, and Lincoln are primary examples. The choice of the name Jefferson is typical of this pattern. But it conjures also the relationship between Thomas Jefferson and Sally Hemings, which carries with it the reality of white control over Black lives. Jefferson's name and his tale, as well as other comments, are ways of representing the dichotomy of freedom and white control.

# Teaching Intergenerational Conflict and Technology in "Flying Home" and "Cadillac Flambé"

*Paul Devlin*

Stanley Crouch, when he was twenty-four or twenty-five, credited Ralph Ellison with cultivating in him an awareness and appreciation of an elder generation, writing in a preface to a poem about Howling Wolf that Ellison had "opened my eyes to the strength and substance of old Black men."[1] In that moment life imitated art, and Crouch became like a young protagonist of one of Ellison's short stories while placing Ellison in the role of one of his own elder characters. Ellison was interested in intergenerational conflict as a phenomenon in human affairs and as subject matter with literary potential; *Invisible Man* and *Three Days before the Shooting . . .* can both be read as extended meditations on this topic. In the short stories "Flying Home" and "Cadillac Flambé," intergenerational conflict is intertwined with technology—the relation of young men to technology that befuddles older people—in a way that makes the stories a valuable pair of texts for teaching. Many students can relate to an elder's skepticism of technology or lack of facility with it. In the plot of each story, a seemingly out-of-touch elder offers transformative lessons for a younger generation. As such, these stories can range from a window into what literature can offer, for introductory students, to an example of evidence for understanding intergenerational tension as a productive theme within African American literary traditions, for students in a course focused on African American literature. The juxtaposition discussed in this chapter provides a model for how an instructor might use these stories—among Ellison's most accomplished—to explore some concerns present in much of his work. Neatly spanning World War II and postwar affluence and consumerism, together they create productive possibilities for class discussion.

"Flying Home" and "Cadillac Flambé"[2] both feature elite African American protagonists in their twenties or thirties. Todd, the protagonist of "Flying Home," is a trainee pilot during World War II. LeeWillie Minifees, in "Cadillac Flambé," is a successful jazz musician. Both are (overly) proud operators of state-of-the-art vehicles (a plane and a new Cadillac), both of which get destroyed—Todd's by accident, LeeWillie's in an act of public arson to make a multifaceted statement. They both have their worldviews and presumptions questioned and adjusted by older African American men, reminders of folk experience offering alternatives to pride taken in technology. Although the stories take place approximately ten years apart, LeeWillie and Todd are of approximately the same generation—the first to grow up with mass media and a rapidly homogenizing national culture. In each story, an elder tempers the hubris of the hotshot protagonist. Todd and LeeWillie both imagine that recently produced vehicles can (and do) elevate their social standing, while each older man deflates each protagonist's arrogance.

These stories can be paired effectively in an introduction to literature course, a survey of African American literature (perhaps framed around Ellison—e.g., his influences and those he influenced), a course on Ellison alone (perhaps focused on the topsy-turvy American social dynamics explored in "The Little Man at Chehaw Station"), or a course centered on *Invisible Man*. They could also provide American flavor to a world literature course on the theme of tensions between traditional and contemporary societies.

"Flying Home" and "Cadillac Flambé" should be understood and taught within specifically African American cultural and historical contexts, but a crucial theme of the stories—the hubris of talented young people whose egos are inflated through their mastery of technology—is urgently relevant to first-generation college students of all backgrounds. While both stories should be contextualized for students in terms of the African American experience, first-generation students from Asian, Latin American, African, Caribbean, and European backgrounds, for example, can recognize the intergenerational tensions Ellison explores. Many of them can identify with the protagonist at the outset of each story. Like Todd and LeeWillie, some are looking to technology to change their own social positions, even if they have not yet necessarily articulated this idea to themselves.

"Flying Home" begins with Todd awakening in his plane, which he had just crashed after colliding with a buzzard. (The story alludes to the Tuskegee Airmen and suggests that Todd is training to become one. There is no other way to understand the setting in terms of history, although neither Tuskegee Army Airfield nor its training program are specified in the story.)[3] Jefferson, an elderly African American man, and Teddy, a young boy accompanying him, discover Todd in the plane in a remote area. Todd is suffering from a horrendous ankle injury. Yet he is too arrogant to appreciate that the honest and capable old man, sincerely eager to help, is his only chance of being rescued.

Students find it startling to see the blunt, rude language with which Todd thinks of the old man, who is merely trying to figure out how to move him from wreckage (and possibly save his leg in the process): "That buzzard knocked me back a hundred years, he thought. . . . With all I've learned, I'm dependent upon this 'peasant's' sense of time and space" (Ellison, *Flying Home* 160). Students may ask why "peasant," which registers as pejorative, is in quotation marks. Suggestive of Todd's familiarity with Marxist theory, this moment provides several opportunities: to speculate (lightly) about Todd's educational background, to give an overview of how the American South was theorized (e.g., in terms of feudalism) in American Communist circles in the 1930s and early 1940s, to give an overview of Ellison's own background in Marxism,[4] to explore the way he thought about the rural-urban divide in African American culture at that time,[5] and to explain concepts in literary criticism such as free indirect discourse and structures of feeling. Todd's point about "time and space" can also lead to productive

124    "FLYING HOME" AND "CADILLAC FLAMBÉ"

class discussion about the global upheavals occasioned by modernity, specifically by the combustion engine and its collapsing of distances through trains, planes, automobiles, and ships.

The plane has become part of Todd's identity. He thinks, "I'm naked without it. Not a machine, a suit of clothes you wear" (160). A bit later, Jefferson asks Todd why he wants to be a pilot. The narrator conveys Todd's thoughts: "because it makes me less like you" (162). Jefferson proceeds to tell Todd a rambling tall tale about flying to and around heaven, which amplifies Todd's irritation. Eventually, the racist owner of the land, Mr. Graves, wants Todd removed from it immediately. Todd eventually comes around to an appreciative perspective on Jefferson, recognizing him as his "sole salvation in an insane world of outrage and humiliation" (181). As Jefferson and Teddy carry Todd off on a stretcher, the narrator notes, "A new current of communication flowed between the man and the boy and himself" (181). Jennifer L. Lieberman observes that "Ellison does not simply celebrate the sensibility of old-timers like Jefferson. Instead, the author writes these two characters in a productive dialectical tension" ("Ralph Ellison's Technological Humanism" 20).[6] Todd learns a finely shaded and subtle lesson.

Todd and LeeWillie are anxious at the outset of each story. Despite their ease with advanced technology, they are ill at ease with themselves as upwardly mobile young men, still defensive about their social positions despite significant preliminary achievements. Ellison has Todd and LeeWillie learn through their elders about the instability of the sign(s) around which they have constructed their identities. Students may ponder parallels here with social-media-platform and smartphone addiction. The stories teach a lesson about breaking away from objects and learning how to once again see and hear people, particularly people previously marginalized within each protagonist's respective worldview.

The juxtaposition of the two stories can form a case study for examining major midcentury shifts in literary sensibility (and how Ellison's career arc tracks a wider trend)—a shift away from realism toward exercises of the imagination narrating outlandish scenarios, metaphors, and behavior patterns. "Cadillac Flambé" is generally thought to take place in the 1950s,[7] but it feels more like a work from the mid-to-late 1960s (if not exactly postmodern by many definitions), mirroring the conditions and atmosphere of the time and fitting well into a literary landscape then dominated by figures such as Kurt Vonnegut and John Barth rather than, say, Richard Wright or Sinclair Lewis.

"Cadillac Flambé" is a more surreal and flamboyant story than the tightly controlled and somber "Flying Home," a stylistic development perhaps reflective of Ellison's having proven himself artistically with *Invisible Man* in the years between the stories. In most of the short stories in *Flying Home and Other Stories*, Ellison's writing is basically realist with naturalistic elements or forays ("King of the Bingo Game" is the notable exception). He was still some years away from the modernist surrealism that ebbs and flows across *Invisible Man*, and students might notice how that surrealism reemerges in his work thereafter, with "Cadillac Flambé" as a sample.

The first things students might observe about "Cadillac Flambé" vis-à-vis "Flying Home" is the different tone and absence of free indirect discourse. Welborn McIntyre, the first-person peripheral narrator of "Cadillac Flambé," is a professional journalist. (This may lend credence to his ability to capture so many details of the chaotic scene that LeeWillie creates.) A first-person peripheral narrator is often a staid figure on the case of a mysterious, unpredictable character (see *Lord Jim, The Great Gatsby, All the King's Men*), and while the conundrum troubling McIntyre lies elsewhere (the mysterious relationship between Reverend Hickman and Senator Sunraider), LeeWillie fits the pattern and is McIntyre's misguided focus for a while. (Here, if one is giving the class a précis of the plot of *Three Days*, one might take the opportunity to explain what a red herring is.)

In the story, LeeWillie Minifees is a jazz musician traveling through Washington, DC, on his way home to New York after playing in Chattanooga. He hears Senator Sunraider, a racist demagogue, ranting on the radio about the Cadillac brand of automobile, which he refers to in the singular as a "coon cage" (Ellison, *Three Days* 1091). This racist description generates significant cognitive dissonance in LeeWillie: "That Senator up there wasn't simply degrading my Caddy. That wasn't the *point*. It's that he would low-rate a thing so truly fine as a *Cadillac* just in order to degrade *me* and my *people*. He was accusing *me* of lowering the value of the auto, when all I ever wanted was the very best!" (1092) The Cadillac had represented the apex of the automobile, in addition to signaling his own hard work, thrift, and good sense (see his description of the story that appears a few lines above the quoted passage). It is jarring for him to hear it referred to in such a disrespectful manner. Desiring "the very best" was, after all, in the bull's-eye of the ethos of the postwar "affluent society." (On this point, students may relate to the experience of having a consumer good they initially coveted and were proud of acquiring later mocked for being passé.) LeeWillie ponders this and concludes that he has been duped into buying a Cadillac by slick advertising. He then proceeds with flair, ceremony, and speechifying to incinerate his Cadillac on Sunraider's lawn.

In addition to feeling like a work of literature of its time, "Cadillac Flambé" is also suggestive of the related cultural upheavals of the 1960s that helped to create an audience for a more freewheeling sort of writing. Upon reading how LeeWillie Minifees sets his Cadillac ablaze in protest on the lawn of Senator Sunraider in Washington, DC, students sometimes make analogies with the flag burning or draft-card burning of the Vietnam era, and occasionally one will know about Thích Quảng Đức, the Buddhist monk who lit himself on fire in 1963 and was photographed in the act.

Intergenerational friction is the unmistakable central theme of "Flying Home," but in "Cadillac Flambé" it plays a subtler role, behind questions of race, advertising, and media. Readers might not associate "Cadillac Flambé" with

126     "FLYING HOME" AND "CADILLAC FLAMBÉ"

intergenerational friction, but Ellison weaves it in when LeeWillie recollects seeing a man with a mule along the highway:[8]

> "I found myself rolling toward an old man who reminded me of my granddaddy by the way he was walking beside the highway behind a plow hitched to an old, white-muzzled Missouri mule. And when that old man looked up and saw me he waved. And I looked back through the mirror as I shot past him and I could see him open his mouth and say something like, 'Go on, fool!' Then him and that mule was gone even from the mirror and I was rolling on.
> "And then, ladies and gentlemen, in a twinkling of an eye it struck me. A voice said to me, 'LeeWillie, that old man is right: you are a fool.'"
>
> (1091)

The entire long section, a small portion of which is quoted here, should be explored in detail in class. The man and his mule become a rhetorical fulcrum through which LeeWillie can catapult himself out of the trap of consumerism, the cult of having the latest thing. A significant difference between the stories is that Jefferson, the old man in "Flying Home," is an actual personality that Todd interacts with, whereas LeeWillie constructs the personality of the man with the mule from seeing his lips form one brief sentence. He may or may not have said, "Go on, fool!"—that could have been in LeeWillie's imagination or merely a plausible fiction to form the basis of his anecdote. Nevertheless, he knows the type and is able to build a scenario around him, allowing the mule to speak, too, in a humorous touch.[9]

A beast of burden also appears in "Flying Home." Teddy suggests that Todd could be transported into town on an ox named Old Ned (Ellison, *Flying Home* 158), creating anxiety for the image-conscious (or image-mad?) Todd about the potential embarrassment of such a situation. "Uncle Ned," incidentally, was one of several metonymic nicknames for older African American men, listed by Albert Murray along with Uncles Bud, Doc, and Remus as the "legendary uncles" of African American culture (*Albert Murray* 728). The narrator notes, "Thoughts of himself riding an ox through the town, past streets full of white faces, down the concrete runways of the airfield, made swift images of humiliation in his mind" (Ellison, *Flying Home* 159).[10] A decade before the present of "Cadillac Flambé" and within a specifically African American context, a beast of burden would have been viewed as symbolic of a rural past by the type of ambitious young man Ellison is trying to relay on the page.

The man with the mule seen by LeeWillie may be keenly aware that technology has passed him by. Perhaps he represents a person financially unable to give up his mule, or perhaps he is unwilling; maybe he likes his mule or the mule makes his work flow in the way he finds most comfortable. In any case, committed to old-fashioned farming as he is, he sees (so LeeWillie thinks, reading lips) the young man in the fancy car as a "fool," perhaps not just for riding in a car but in an expensive one, the short-term resale value of which is depreciating by the moment. LeeWillie, an urban sophisticate, is startled by the coeval residual culture of rural African Americans. Arguably, the man with the mule is essential to the plot of the story, as LeeWillie's thought process about the Cadillac and what should be done with it could not have developed as it does without his recollection of the old man.

Students respond enthusiastically to both stories in which lived experience cracks the ideological shells of the protagonists and often find both illustrative of issues they themselves have been pondering amorphously or unsystematically. They are often aware that generational friction today is often amplified by social media and can be at odds with lived experience. But Todd and LeeWillie have their worldviews skewed by information coming from other social vectors; generational tension can be amplified by social media but is not solely a product of it. The intergenerational discussion can be a way to break the ice about more difficult subjects, such as race, class, and economic development.

When teaching the stories in a course on Ellison or another course with *Invisible Man* on the syllabus, "Flying Home" can be used to prefigure the protagonist's encounters with elders such as Lucius Brockway, Peter Wheatstraw, Mary Rambo, and Brother Tarp, while "Cadillac Flambé" can show how these issues both lingered and evolved in society and in Ellison's consciousness. But there are significant differences between the way these issues are approached in the stories and in *Invisible Man*. In the stories, technology makes generational differences more pronounced, as generational differences become compounded through technology. While intergenerational friction and the protagonist's interest in technology both exist in *Invisible Man*, they do not interlock as they do in these stories, making the stories both relate to and stand apart from *Invisible Man*. (One might point out the metaphorical use of "current," suggestive of electric current, in "Flying Home" and the narrator's interest in and experiences with electricity in *Invisible Man*.)

The stories can also be a window into Ellison's position in a tradition of African American writing in which educated or otherwise-talented African Americans encounter and often struggle with feelings of alienation from elders without formal educations, pronounced dramatically in the chapter "Of the Coming of John" in *The Souls of Black Folk* by W. E. B. Du Bois, which is itself critiqued (I believe) by James Weldon Johnson in *Along This Way* (discussed below). Frank discussion of these issues in all their complexity can be beneficial for first-generation college students dealing with similar concerns. This is often especially interesting for science majors from traditional backgrounds who have been thinking about these topics and perhaps did not previously know that literature was a place in which they have received sophisticated consideration. Students from all over the world, from Africa to Asia to Latin America to Appalachia (and not always necessarily first-generation students), all have stories about the persistence of folk beliefs. Their feelings may continually oscillate as to the relative merits behind the cold, homogenizing rationalism of academia and ways of

128    "FLYING HOME" AND "CADILLAC FLAMBÉ"

knowing from their traditional heritage, perhaps navigating, like the narrator of *Invisible Man* (after encountering the boisterous folk figure Peter Wheatstraw and suddenly being intrigued by a world he had suppressed in his consciousness), the thin, ambiguous line between "pride or disgust" (177), which moves toward the acceptance and reveling in the yams in chapter 13.

With this in mind, a possible text to teach alongside "Flying Home" and "Cadillac Flambé" is Saul Bellow's novel *Henderson the Rain King*, written while he was housemates with Ellison during their time teaching at Bard College and featuring a major character, King Dahfu, straddling the worlds of science and folk belief.[11] Other texts with comparative potential include August Wilson's *Gem of the Ocean* and *Radio Golf*. Mahashweta Devi's short story "Arjun," about the persistence of folk beliefs and values (vis-à-vis shortsighted economic interests) in a village in India fits well with these texts, as does Alice Rohrwacher's movie *Happy as Lazzaro*.

There are also students whose grandparents may be from "the old country" but whose parents have sought to suppress folk traditions in an attempt to assimilate or leave behind a society they associated with various forms of repression, a lack of resources, or general backwardness. Some parents do not want their children hearing about folk beliefs from grandparents or other relatives. There are many subtle and complicated concerns potentially in play here in the classroom. Folk beliefs must be respected and taken seriously but not necessarily lionized. At the same time, modern science developed out of folk science.[12] The point would be to help students form an understanding of the content being presented in the texts and thereby to use such content to attain new perspectives on their own experiences.

One possible short writing assignment could be a brief reflection paper on students' own intergenerational experiences vis-à-vis technology. Students often have examples of teaching an older relative how to use the new or trendy device or platform. Beyond the specificity of a particular tool or process, students may wish to reflect broadly on intergenerational experiences of modernity. Students may come from backgrounds in which folk beliefs, superstitions, and sympathetic magic hold sway and offer compelling modes for making sense of reality. Or, if they don't, it can be a valuable experience to learn about those who do. In order for this to work in the classroom, there must be a straightforward, unironic, non-rationalized discussion of traditions. If brought into the classroom, they must be taken seriously and treated without laughter or irony, unless a student chooses to introduce either in their description of their own background.

If teaching Ellison in terms of his influences and his influence on others, or if trying to find a through line within African American literature, one might look to James Weldon Johnson's autobiography *Along This Way*.[13] Sharing the following excerpt from *Along This Way*, in which Johnson, from Jacksonville, Florida, then a mid-sized resort town, finds himself teaching at a school in rural Georgia, could be a way to alert students to the manner in which Ellison is working within or perhaps commenting on an aspect of the African American literary tradition. One might have students look to the past and then to the future by assigning "Of the Coming of John," "Flying Home," "Cadillac Flambé," the following excerpt from *Along This Way*, and "The Little Man at Chehaw Station"—in that order. This is also a useful order if the ultimate goal is the exploration of the ambiguities of identity through the Ellisonian ethics of "The Little Man at Chehaw Station." That is to say, if a goal is to introduce students to that essay's major theme—that democratic societies contain variable, unpredictable, and often unnamed social strata—the sequence of texts mentioned above can be a good way to go about it. Here is a section from Johnson's *Along This Way* that sounds rather Ellisonian:

> Mr. Woodward interested me and I liked to talk with him. He was an uneducated man, but one with a good share of native intelligence—a cotton-field philosopher. He frequently delighted me with his original phraseology. I remember asking one morning for his forecast of the weather. He looked up, and pointing to a mass of cirrocumulus clouds, said, "Fessar, see them rain eggs up there; hatch out 'fore noon." And they hatched out. . . . In talking with him I learned that he was an elder brother of Sidney Woodward, the celebrated Boston Negro tenor, and that Sidney had been reared in the locality. (262–63)

This is the very sort of fellow that Todd and LeeWillie encounter in their respective stories—farmers with folk wisdom—but the way they learn from their elders is slower and more dramatic than the way Johnson learns from Mr. Woodward.

But Johnson is writing about himself—a person far savvier than the average person, a person able to use his intelligence and imagination to grasp how someone from his own ethnic background yet with a different educational background attained practical knowledge and contributed to society. And Mr. Woodward was real. (Indeed, where would the human race be without self-taught meteorologists and "cottonfield philosophers"? Someone had to make guesses and predictions based upon previously observed phenomena in order for agriculture to have developed.)

Ellison is writing about characters. These characters are not meant to be representative, but perhaps it is fair to say that they are unremarkable, a type of person who existed in a given time—a type Ellison knew (see his letter to his wife, Fanny, on 2 July 1953, in which he discusses his cousin Maybelle's husband, a man who might relate to Mr. Woodward or to Jefferson or the man with the mule; *Selected Letters* 329). Todd and LeeWillie, despite being men of some achievement, are not especially remarkable either, prior to the unusual incidents that expose their respective blind spots.

The difference between Mr. Woodward and his brother, Sidney, is the sort of family dynamic that would have surprised the somewhat pretentious young Ellison, as depicted by the older Ellison in "The Little Man at Chehaw Station" when he describes his younger self as "purged by the revelation" that a group of

130   "FLYING HOME" AND "CADILLAC FLAMBÉ"

blue-collar African Americans he meets in Manhattan are opera buffs who learned about opera by moonlighting as extras (*Collected Essays* 523). He adds that "my appreciation of the arcane ways of American cultural possibility was vastly extended" (523). Sidney Woodward was not just a celebrated tenor but a "Boston" tenor, a singer who had succeeded in and was associated with a capital of culture, a place that was practically a by-word for progress, technology, and modernity. (Mr. Norton in *Invisible Man* is described as a "Bostonian" first and foremost.)

If one wishes to frame literature as an ongoing colloquy or discourse community across time, this would be one way to go about it in the context of the African American tradition. Ellison seems to be searching for a middle ground between the morose, prickly young student described by Du Bois in "Of the Coming of John," who becomes alienated from his community through attending school, and Johnson's sunny description of himself—a shrewd up-and-comer with an open mind, happy to recognize intelligence and practical knowledge where he finds it. On this topic of the relation between young, educated African Americans and other African Americans without formal educations, Ellison seems more interested in an exploratory process engendered by a dramatic situation. For Du Bois and Johnson, both situations feel fairly automatic. In other words, Ellison avoids the mechanistic lament of Du Bois, who paints education as a tragic, unavoidable tradeoff, and Johnson's matter-of-fact egalitarian eclecticism. Here one might point students to Ellison's character Revern' Murray in *Three Days before the Shooting . . .* (as described by Hickman): "that little Negro Murray, who had been to a seminary up North and could preach the pure Greek and the original Hebrew and could still make all our uneducated folks swing along with him. . . . Revern' Murray's education didn't get him separated from the folks" (328). Not letting education get you separated from the folks: this a consistent theme throughout Ellison's work and thought, along with reconnecting with the folks on the terms of one's education. And it is an unnamed, almost always untheorized, yet viscerally urgent question for many students from backgrounds where folk beliefs and practices hold sway.

These stories taught consecutively can function as an introduction to Ellison, as brackets for *Invisible Man*, as representative works in literary history, and as approaches to a consistent theme in African American literature. They elicit spirited discussion and evoke personal experiences from across the generational technology gap, perhaps giving literature a new dimension, and as such can be an especially rewarding pair in an introduction to literature survey. In a best-case scenario, they may even create "a new current of communication" between generations (*Flying Home* 181).

NOTES

1. "Black" is capitalized in the original.

2. "Cadillac Flambé" was published as a short story in *American Review* in 1973 and also appears as chapter 4 of book 1 in *Three Days before the Shooting . . .* (35–48). The

*Paul Devlin* 131

1973 version cited in this essay is in the appendix to *Three Days* (1085–97). This version was also reprinted in *Callaloo* and is available on *JSTOR*. Some students are intrigued to find LeeWillie reappearing later in *Three Days* (216–30) when he is interviewed by Welborn McIntyre about the incident.

3. Murray writes in his preface to *Trading Twelves* about a contemporaneous exchange he had with Ellison about the story around 1944 (xxii–xxiii). Murray was a training officer at Tuskegee Army Airfield in 1944–45. From Murray's comments in his preface, it can be inferred that Ellison had done his homework on the story's setting. Todd flies an "Advanced Trainer" (Ellison, *Flying Home* 162). Murray notes that as a single-engine plane, an AT-6 Advanced Trainer could crash if hit by a buzzard, but a "twin-engine medium bomber" flying out of Tuskegee had in fact hit a buzzard in real life and had not crashed (xxii). The implication (not at all the point of Murray's anecdote) is that Ellison had been reading up on the Tuskegee Airmen.

4. An important text to assign here in an advanced course could be Maxwell, "'Creative.'" For an example of Ellison theorizing about "feudal-folk forms of the South" (343), see "Working Notes for *Invisible Man*" in his *Collected Essays* (341–49). Another essay of interest here could be O'Meally, "On Burke and the Vernacular," which reads "Flying Home" in terms of Todd's re-encounter with the vernacular.

5. Optional reading on rural African Americans encountering life in the urban North could include Ellison's essay "Harlem Is Nowhere," about the difficulties rural migrants face when trying to adjust to Harlem life, and Murray's celebratory essay "Image and Unlikeness in Harlem" (*Albert Murray* 65–70).

6. Lieberman's article is one of the best and most accessible studies of Ellison and technology and could be assigned with the stories or recommended. Lieberman recognizes Ellison's ambivalence toward technology, casting his approach as "polyvalent" ("Ralph Ellison's Technological Humanism" 9). Ellison's personal curiosity about and occasional admiration for emerging technologies does not translate into his fiction as propaganda or boosterism. Lieberman correctly adduces that Ellison's "fictional representations of technology were too multifarious to be uniformly favorable" and argues that "Ellison's capacious technological and humanist imagery undermines the popular model of equating technological development with freedom—particularly freedom from fear" (11, 21). This dissents from impressions that could be gleaned from works such as John S. Wright's *Shadowing Ralph Ellison* and Adam Bradley's *Ralph Ellison in Progress*.

7. LeeWillie's mention of "SPACE SHOES" complicates this widely accepted chronological setting (Ellison, *Three Days* 1094).

8. "Flying Home" and "Cadillac Flambé" are like inversions of the themes of "Harlem Is Nowhere"—instead of emphasizing the shock of the city, the stories delineate an encounter with down-home wisdom. LeeWillie has prior experience with rural life, noting the man with the mule "reminded me of my granddaddy" (1091), who also plowed with a mule. LeeWillie is a Harlem resident, suggesting (in terms of probability) that either he or his parents participated in the Great Migration. This could be a starting point for discussion of the Great Migration in class. Or, if students already know about it through previous texts, then it is possible to discuss LeeWillie—trapped by his lifestyle choices in a way that the man with the mule is not—as part of a later countermovement in African American culture against the desire to move to northern cities, as also reflected (for example) in the 1971 song "Country Living" by the Stylistics, about leaving the city for the country.

9. The mid-to-late 1950s were when wheeled tractors began to outnumber mules. See the table "Farm Mechanization: 1900–1997" (United States, Department of Agriculture).

10. It could be worth pointing out to students how this is possibly a riff on the story of Sir Lancelot and the cart, which is featured in Arthurian romances, also perhaps implying a narcissistic sense of heroism in Todd.

11. Greif suggests that Ellison may have been Bellow's inspiration for King Dahfu (202–03). While this is certainly possible, some of Bellow's essays show that he was also personally invested in questions of folk beliefs versus modernity.

12. If one wanted to take the discussion somewhat further afield, students could be pointed to Holmes on the folk origins of Romantic-era science, described in his book *The Age of Wonder*—specifically, the way the grand impresario of science Joseph Banks (1743–1820) paid "the wise women of country lanes and hedgerows, the gypsy herbalists" for their knowledge (8).

13. Incidentally, Fanny Ellison helped Johnson to prepare the text for the printer when she was his student assistant at Fisk. See Johnson's inscription in the copy in the Ellisons' library, Rare Book and Special Collections Division, Library of Congress.

# Is Resistance Futile?
## Exploring "King of the Bingo Game" in a Secondary ELA Classroom

*Aimée Myers*

In 1990, *Star Trek* first introduced the phrase "Resistance is futile." The Borg, a colony of cyborgs, used this phrase to warn victims of impending assimilation and forced service. The phrase "resistance is futile" has become an embedded part of our culture. It has been adopted by countless films, books, and television shows. Despite the phrase being ingrained within American culture, art and media often present resistance as a worthy and admirable fight. This can be seen in the plethora of films glamorizing the civil rights movement and using the historical moment as consumable entertainment. The glamorizing of resistance is also prevalent within school curricula. Throughout most of the literature read in K–12 classrooms, there is no question of whether resistance is worth the battle. The worthiness of resistance is encapsulated in classic pieces like Henry David Thoreau's *Civil Disobedience*, Kate Chopin's *The Awakening*, and Christopher Paul Curtis's *The Watsons Go to Birmingham*. The virtue of resistance is even seen in popular young adult literature like *The Hate U Give* by Angie Thomas and *The Book Thief* by Markus Zusak.

While much of mainstream film and literature romanticizes the concept of resistance, Ralph Ellison's work often depicts the struggle against the status quo as insurmountable. His work thrusts readers into the gray areas of life. Through Ellison's stories, the weariness and desperation of resistance are revealed through characters who have unsuccessfully attempted to oppose the system, thus pushing readers to question whether resistance is worth the personal costs.

The theme of resistance, along with identity and agency, is prevalent in most of Ellison's works. Resistance is incredibly salient in his short story "King of the Bingo Game." This story, found in Ellison's *Flying Home* collection and in many literary-anthology textbooks, uses an unnamed protagonist to reflect on the darker side of resistance. Through the main character, Ellison illustrates how the status quo alienates and marginalizes the Black community in the United States. Additionally, the rest of the characters in the story, who are also unnamed, act as cogs within the symbolic machine.

This essay explores the contextual elements of resistance in Ellison's "King of the Bingo Game" while also sharing pedagogical strategies for a high school English language arts (ELA) classroom. Using culturally and historically responsive literacy (CHRL) as a theoretical guide, this essay discusses approaches to Ralph Ellison's short story that make the work even more relevant to twenty-first-century students. This essay presents the theoretical foundations of CHRL, along with a detailed exploration of its five branches, and shares examples of concrete classroom applications of the CHRL framework to Ralph Ellison's work.

## 134 "KING OF THE BINGO GAME"

## *Approaching the Story*

While "King of the Bingo Game" reflects elements of naturalism through the use of fate or luck, it also demonstrates that ultimately the system has unyielding control (see Hoeveler; Urquhart). The unnamed protagonist is a man who is down on his luck, struggling with poverty and a sick wife. He visits a movie hall in an attempt to escape reality. Even though he has seen the movie three times, he is still enthralled by the scene where the hero saves the woman tied to the bed.

The theme of resistance and its futility is present immediately. The setting alone plays deeply into the idea of resistance being a fantasy because movies are fictional and create a false sense of reality. While the protagonist dreams of saving his wife from her illness, this is interrupted as he falls asleep and encounters a terrible nightmare. The nightmare is one of the many symbolic moments that remind readers that resistance is futile. He is woken up by a fellow movie watcher who yells at him, "Wake up there, buddy! What the hell do you mean hollering like that?" (Ellison, *Flying Home* 125). The fellow next to him reminds him that making any noise is merely disruptive to the status quo. The system tells us to sit quietly and passively engage. Another moment early in the story indicating that resistance is futile comes as the protagonist watches the light of the movie projector. He quietly reflects, "But they had it all fixed. Everything was fixed" (124). The protagonist cannot help but notice how the beam always lands exactly where "they" want it and how this reflects an individual's position in society.

As the movie ends, the story shifts toward the bingo game, which is the entertainment to end the evening. The protagonist's first act of resistance is bringing in five cards, which is against the rules. Despite his subversion, he is still aware that "[e]ven with five cards he didn't have much of a chance" 126). Despite his skepticism, the protagonist wins a full bingo and gets called down to the stage to spin the prize wheel. Here again, Ellison offers readers a quick reminder that resistance is futile against the system by having the bingo host and audience make the protagonist the butt of the joke even within his joyful moment of hopefulness (Hoeveler 41; Doyle 172). As the protagonist moves toward the stage, trembling with excitement, the bingo host declares, "[L]adies and gentlemen, he's one of the chosen people!" (Ellison, *Flying Home* 128). The audience erupts into laughter at the host's sarcastic comment.

The protagonist is now in the hands of fate, which is symbolically represented through the prize wheel. All he has to do is press the button that spins the wheel and let go to see where it lands. His hope is that the wheel will land on the jackpot and his winnings will save him and his wife from their hopeless situation. However, he is soon overtaken with the power he feels by holding the button down. He knows the moment he lets go of the button, the system takes back over and his fate is out of his hands. He refuses to let go of the button, and the audience grows irritated, hurling insults. He declares that this power is the closest thing to God. He finally feels like he is "running the show" (132). The audience and host shift from irritation to rage. Their rage only further fuels the protagonist into holding the button down as he thinks to himself, "He was running the show, by god! They had to react to him, for he was their luck" (132). The protagonist realizes that the only way to gain power is to reject the rules. The moment of resistance ends when two uniformed men attempt to forcibly remove the protagonist from the stage. This turns into a physical altercation and ends with the protagonist taking a blow to the head.

The theme of resistance cannot be explored without including the concept of identity. Identity plays a huge role in the protagonist's ability, or lack of ability, to resist (Doyle; Urquhart). In "King of the Bingo Game," the protagonist's identity is that of a Black man living in poverty. Not only is he oppressed, he is completely displaced within society. First, the man has no name. He is merely another face. His displacement is obvious from the beginning when he feels isolated and a lack of connection to the people sitting around him in the movie house. The displacement only deepens with his attempts to resist the system. As he refuses to let go of the button that spins the wheel, even other Black individuals in the audience turn on him and begin yelling insults with the rest of the audience: "All the Negroes down there were just ashamed because he was black like them" (Ellison, *Flying Home* 132). The system controls individuals' identities so much that it leads people to disconnect from their kinfolk and disconnect from themselves (Doyle 165). In the end, the protagonist screams out "Who am I?" and reminds readers that the Black audience members who have turned on him "didn't even know their own names, they were all poor nameless bastards" (133). Despite the temporary power and sense of self he began to feel while holding the button down, he knows that his identity does not matter.

An additional concept related to resistance is that of agency. Resistance is typically a reaction meant to disrupt. On the other hand, agency consists of transformative moments where an individual gains enlightenment mentally and then makes choices to act based on new understandings of power (see Archer; Hollander and Einwohner; K. Wilson). The narrator alludes to the dubious situation that the protagonist is approaching early in the story. Several times, the narrator uses the word "slippery" to describe the environment that the protagonist is entering. Once the protagonist realizes that he is standing on "the slippery brink of some terrible embarrassment," it is too late (Ellison, *Flying Home* 128). The system is already moving its gears into motion. While his hope and sense of power feel very real to him, the setting of the movie theater reminds the reader that this is all fantasy. Rather than taking agency over his situation, he leaves his hands in the fate of the system that was already set up against him.

## *Approaching the CHRL Framework*

Gholdy Muhammad's CHRL framework can be utilized as both a theory and a model that supports educators in moving students beyond academic skill development and toward relevant and authentic learning. In her book *Cultivating Genius*, Muhammad defines culturally and historically responsive literacy as "the

136 "KING OF THE BINGO GAME"

ideologies, language used, instructional materials, and instructional practices that honor and are authentically responsive to students' histories, identities, and literacies" (50). While rooted in the literacy histories of Black people, the framework serves as a guide that can shape instruction through the intersectionalities of all students' identities.

The development of CHRL is deeply rooted in culturally relevant pedagogy, which was born out of a resistance against Eurocentric content that was at the center of curriculum and pedagogy in the United States (Banks; Ladson-Billings, "Toward a Theory"). Educators who are responsive to their students' cultural needs and backgrounds continuously think about how they teach, not just what they teach. The CHRL framework consists of five branches that guide teachers in developing authentic learning experiences for students (Muhammad and Mosely). Below is a brief definition of each branch:

1. Identity: Students are supported in their learning in regard to their sense of self.
2. Skill: Students develop key academic skills necessary to approach rigorous texts.
3. Intellect: Students utilize higher-order thinking that is connected to prior knowledge and lived experience.
4. Criticality: Students are engaging in critical reflection, interrogating issues of power, and problematizing the status quo.
5. Joy: Students focus on solutions to issues found in the literature and extend that knowledge to the world around them.

## *Merging CHRL with Literature*

While it is important for students to engage in literary analysis of Ellison's work, it is also just as important that secondary students are encouraged to explore the text in a way that is relevant to their lives. Teachers can assist students in identifying Ellison's use of symbolism and themes of resistance, agency, and identity by utilizing the CHRL framework. Ellison's short story "King of the Bingo Game" demands that we reflect on our own identities, where we are positioned within the system, and whether resistance is worth the risk. The CHRL framework can serve as a vehicle for students to evaluate historical and contemporary ideas of resistance while also engaging in literary analysis of Ellison's work.

While this piece is set during the Depression, resistance is still deeply ingrained in our society today. Systemic racial violence took center stage for young people when the original Black Lives Matter protests started in Ferguson, Missouri, with the 2014 police shooting of Michael Brown and continued more recently in Minneapolis with the killing of George Floyd. During the past few years, students have faced continuous social injustice. Furthermore, constant access to social media and digital resources emboldens young people to reconsider what resistance can look like. This last section will guide educators through an application of the CHRL framework alongside Ellison's short story and offer extension learning ideas to deepen student knowledge. It is important to remember that this framework is not a lockstep curriculum or a linear manual. Rather, the CHRL framework provides educators with a guide for exploring literature that can lead students through a meaningful experience with Ellison's work.

## 1. Identity: Students explore their own identities and how these identities relate to resistance.

The "identity" branch of the CHRL framework is focused on individual student identity and the identities of others. Engaging students in their own identities and how their identities shape their worldviews is an imperative starting point for engaging with literature (Morrell). Muhammad also reminds us that an additional focus of this branch of CHRL is "identifying truth and excellence in marginalized communities" (194). Rather than only dwelling on the suffering of oppressed people, the identity component also encourages connecting with moments of victory and brilliance. Before exploring the identities of Ellison's fictional characters and their relationship to resistance, it is important for students to be given the space to explore their own identities and how they relate to the world around them. It is also important for educators to remember that identity is fluid, dynamic, and intersectional.

One way for students to engage in this process is graphing their identities and the salience of those identities within their current place and space. To assist with this understanding, educators can use a visual similar to the "model of multiple dimensions of identity" (Abes et al.; Jones and McEwen). This graphical template allows students to visually comprehend how identities intersect. Additionally, they can plot their multiple identities on the template and move the identities closer to the core or further away based on their environment. For example, a student's identity as a Latina might be more salient when she is in a room of predominately white students and less dominant when she is home with her family. After students explore the salience of their identities based on their environment, teachers can adapt the template to reflect the idea of resistance. Students can then create a new graphical representation plotting their identities with the core being the need to resist. These shifts in identity movement would be based upon their lived experiences. The identity exploration could be extended to the development of multimodal assignments like digital storytelling.

## 2. Skill: Students identify Ellison's use of symbolism and apply symbols toward thematic understanding.

Culturally responsive approaches do not disregard academic skills and academic excellence. Rather, they engage students in a holistic approach to learning while still holding students to high standards. Educators must support academic skills while also engaging in equitable practices and being willing to meet students where they are (Alim and Paris). CHRL recognizes that high academic standards are essential in the classroom, no matter the background of the student population. However, educators must acknowledge that additional support and practice often need to take place through instructional scaffolding in order to lift students toward high expectations.

Through the "skill" branch, teachers facilitate an exploration of key academic skills necessary for approaching Ellison's text and tie them in with the students' lived experiences. The skill development here focuses on understanding an author's use of symbolism to support theme interpretation. Teachers can scaffold student understanding of symbolism and theme by giving a passage of the text to annotate. Students can work in small groups to identify and label different types of symbolism that reflect the themes of resistance and identity.

Additionally, teachers can facilitate a class discussion of how resistance is different from agency through vocabulary exercises. Once students have gained a foundational understanding of these two terms, they can begin to search the text for symbolic examples that represent resistance versus agency. A Venn diagram or an H-chart can be used as a visual guide.

Once students have had an opportunity to practice the skills of analysis of symbolism and theme, they can be led through an activity called the Bento Box (Wilson et al.). A bento box is a compartmentalized container of Japanese origin that holds a meal. The bento box is a strong visual image to help students understand how smaller components develop a larger concept. For example, within a bento box, a person might pack edamame, fruit, and sushi rolls. These three smaller edible components make up an individual's lunch. Similarly, piecing together multiple symbolic elements from the story assists with supporting an overall thematic interpretation. As an extension assignment, students could convert their bento box ideas into a CER essay (McNeill and Krajcik). *CER* stands for claim, evidence, and reasoning. Students will make a claim about the theme within "King of the Bingo Game," support that claim with symbolic examples for their evidence, and offer commentary for their reasoning as to why they chose those symbolic examples.

### 3. Intellect: Students investigate ways Black communities experienced marginalization during the Great Depression.

Through the "intellect" branch of the CHRL framework, teachers guide students toward higher-order thinking. In addition, classroom curriculum and instruction should "respond to or build upon students' knowledge and mental powers" (Muhammad 194). This branch revolves heavily around sociocultural approaches to teaching (see Vygotsky). In taking a sociocultural approach, educators recognize that knowledge is constructed within interconnected cultural and social spheres.

When teaching "King of the Bingo Game," teachers can allow time for an independent exploration of historical and sociopolitical context for the story. No story is written within a vacuum. Similarly, our identities are not developed in a vacuum. Through a sociocultural constructivist approach to the text, students can research how Black communities were marginalized during the Great Depression. Students can work as a class to develop a "data dump" that will guide their investigation of American history and how it may have influenced Ellison's short story. Kelly Gallagher explains that in a data dump, students do a quick research dive and pull as many examples as they can. These examples are then accumulated into a larger classroom list, which would include aspects like food shortages, racist hiring practices, Jim Crow laws, housing discrimination, hate groups, and suppressive voting practices. Once the data dump has been completed, students identify one key area they would like to pursue in more depth with a small group. Small groups work together to research their chosen topic and develop a presentation to assist the rest of the class with developing new knowledge. The "intellect" branch can be further extended to include individual synthesis essays wherein students formulate a thesis by merging their knowledge of the short story and their historical research.

## 4. Criticality: Students interrogate different oppressive systems that sought to control individuals who were leading resistance movements.

Criticality heavily involves the concept of liberation pedagogy and the use of critical consciousness to support students' investigation of their sociopolitical realm in order to emancipate themselves from oppressive systems (Freire). Through criticality, teachers use literature to encourage students' interrogation of injustices in the world and then explore how they can become disruptors.

In this fourth branch of the CHRL framework, students interrogate power structures, identify how those structures produce oppression, and evaluate the actions of individuals who attempted to push back. Studying oppression without investigating the oppressor does not lead to social change. By interrogating power structures and oppressive practices, students can be more aware of how their own actions may play into the system.

Students begin practicing criticality by using what I have termed the ICE method. By "icing" a text, students use three investigative skills: identify, connect, evaluate. First, students work through Ellison's text to *identify* which key power structures were in place throughout the story. Second, students can *connect* oppressive actions that were a result of the power structures. Third, students *evaluate* the main character's attempts at resistance and offer alternatives.

Once students have practiced the ICE activity with the text, they can extend their knowledge to real-world application. Students begin by identifying key power structures in society today. Next, they make connections to oppressive actions associated with those power structures. Last, students evaluate how various historical individuals have led resistance movements against oppressive power structures. To extend the assignment for criticality, students can create visual representations that consider what those individuals could have done in different circumstances. Using the "if this, then that" concept, students can

140 "KING OF THE BINGO GAME"

develop infographics showing different paths of resistance and agency the individual could have developed.

### 5. Joy: Students share different forms of media that support their identity through resistance and agency.

Within the last branch of the CHRL framework, students look toward possible solutions to oppressive practices but also toward current forms of media that make them feel supported and empowered. They can also focus on finding resources for self-empowerment and communal support. By allowing students to find moments of inspiration, educators increase their love of learning and establish a positive engagement with academic content (Ladson-Billings, "Toward a Theory"). This branch encourages students to connect positively with the text and the humanity represented within it.

Teachers can begin this process by having students revisit Ellison's short story and examine the main character's interaction with the film being shown in the movie house. Examples of guiding questions are as follows:

> Why would the main character seek out a movie house?
> What emotions developed for him while watching the film in the movie house?
> In what ways was the film beneficial to the character?

After reviewing Ellison's use of the movie house in the short story, students engage in conversations about how different forms of media are an outlet for individuals or a guide for them to take action.

After discussing the use of media in the story, students explore their own relationships with specific media that support their identities, make them feel empowered, and encourage agency. Examples of media that students can explore are music videos, documentaries, television shows, *YouTube* channels, social media platforms, news outlets, and magazines. Students should be reminded that media are often used as a vehicle for the people. Academic sources of information are incredibly important; however, popular media allows the average citizen to share their experiences and connect with others. After students identify a specific source of media that brings them a sense of empowerment, they should discuss how this media source moves them beyond resistance and toward agency. Teachers can extend the instruction by having students work through the seven stages of problem-based learning ("Gold Standard PBL").

The short story "King of the Bingo Game" gives students a glimpse into the literary legacy of Ralph Ellison. While many of Ellison's works were published decades ago, his thematic elements around resistance are still relevant for today's youth. Due to recent injustices involving police brutality and the COVID-19 pandemic, the current sociopolitical environment is rife with feelings of detachment, alienation, and disenfranchisement. Many young people are feeling as if resistance is futile. However, Muhammad's CHRL framework provides a guide for teachers to use to engage students in social justice work. Through a close reading of Ellison's work framed by CHRL, students can begin to consider ways they can find empowerment through their intersectional identities and establish themselves as agents of change.

# Navigating Freedom with "Uncertainty and Daring": Reading Ellison and Writing Memoir in a Prison Classroom

*Agnieszka Tuszynska*

Thirty-five years after Ralph Ellison's essay "An Extravagance of Laughter" was published and over eight decades since the events it describes took place, the text evokes an unsettling jolt of familiarity. Centering his own migration to New York City from the South in 1936 as the nucleus of the essay, Ellison turns it into an occasion to explore the vast terrain of the nation's racial relations. The essay anchors its panoramic analysis in a specific incident during Ellison's early days in New York: a moment of his own "embarrassing" laughter, which he fails to control in the midst of a comedic performance at an integrated Broadway theater he attends at Langston Hughes's invitation (*Going* 190). Ellison poses the concept of "offensive" Black laughter as a test of restrictions imposed on Black freedom in the North during the Jim Crow era (145), ultimately scrutinizing the character of American democracy and testing its principles against the realities of Black lives. Given our own historical moment's reckoning with the unevenness of American freedom, we would do well to bring Ellison's essay about America's confused relationship with its own ideals into college classrooms, and while any college-level literature student would benefit from Ellison's probing of America's warped democracy, here I explore the pedagogical possibilities of using the essay as a departure point for a deep reflection on the subject of freedom with students whose relationship to freedom—and to *un*freedom—shapes their daily realities in very particular ways: students impacted by the criminal legal system.

The idea of bringing "An Extravagance of Laughter" to this specific educational context was born when I introduced a small group of incarcerated students to the essay as part of a college-level reading workshop at a New York City prison. What became clear almost immediately was the students' sense of their special stakes in Ellison's indictment of American freedom. The essay's detailing of the cruelties of the Jim Crow South and its recounting of the limits on Black freedom Ellison found in New York led the students to draw parallels between Ellison's migration and the experience of transition from incarceration to life on parole and beyond. "An Extravagance of Laughter" offers a platform for exploring the sociopolitical and psychological dimensions of the transition from unfreedom to its supposed opposite with students who are in prison or formerly incarcerated and who have an interest in writing autobiographically. I therefore envision a course or a workshop series in reading and writing memoir taught at a prison, jail, or in an educational space serving formerly incarcerated individuals, in which Ellison's essay would serve as the central text around which to build a conversation about freedom in the context of race and incarceration. While a text *about prison* may seem like a more obvious choice, as educators working with students who have experienced carceral spaces, we should strive to extend to them the same access to the exploration of the human condition within its many contexts as we do for students in our traditional classrooms. This essay describes a course design that centers the text and low-stakes written reflections about the reading in the first portion of the course, then gradually prioritizes students' own memoir writing.

One fruitful starting point for the discussion of Ellison's essay in the context of this specific course design is to consider how Ellison outlines the parameters of freedom by spatializing it. Students gain a sense of Ellison's broader ideas by focusing first on the essay's language related to mobility and both material and psychological restrictions that may prevent one's movement and ability to occupy space. A useful frame for this task of identifying the discourse of movement, spatiality, and spatial restrictions could be provided to students with information about the prominence of the problems of mobility and mapping in African American historiography (Dobbs 913). Such highlighting of spatial questions also sheds light on the parallels with the discourse of incarceration, where the regulation of movement—through imprisonment itself, remote locations of prisons, relocation across prisons, post-release deportations, spatial restrictions of parole, and more—marks the experience of both incarcerated and formerly incarcerated people.

Ellison frames his recollections within the larger narrative of the Great Migration to challenge the idea of the movement from the South to the North demarcating the transition from unfreedom to freedom. Early in the essay, Ellison portrays his younger self as an excited college-aged man, "[f]resh out of Alabama," whose exploration of the Northern city—just "[a] few weeks after my arrival in New York"—is already in full swing. Ellison points to the socially liberating implications of his migration, describing himself "enjoying the many forms of social freedom that were unavailable to me in Alabama" (*Going* 146–47), a contrast that becomes even more clear later in the essay where he describes the racial terror accompanying Black people's physical movement in the South. However, almost immediately, Ellison also notes that the absence of any "agreed-upon rules of conduct" with regard to race makes navigating New York an unpredictable experience (151), and therefore dangerous in its own right. He comes to understand that New York is ruled by its own, more obscure set of racist codes and that he therefore needs to "improvise a makeshift map of the city's racially determined do's-and-don'ts" (148). Unlike the collective effort behind the creation of *The Negro Motorist Green Book*, a guide for Black travelers published the same year Ellison arrived in New York, Ellison is alone in his endeavor to configure New York's racial topography. Consequently, during this "journey without a map" around New York (163), Ellison begins to deconstruct the assumption about the dichotomy between the racial relations in the South and those governing the North.

Ellison's previous "dreamlike" notion of New York "as the freest of American cities" undergoes a revision as he realizes that "Northern freedom could be

144    NAVIGATING FREEDOM

grasped only by my running the risk of the unknown and by acting in the face of uncertainty" (147, 156), which implies a presumption of ubiquitous danger. Disappointed with "Northern freedom," which, to use Dobbs's fitting metaphor, "is in fact shot through with the ghosts of the South" (Dobbs 911), Ellison casts New York as a flawed paradise. He radically revises the thesis about New York as the beacon of freedom by portraying it as seemingly a land of plenty and liberty that is nevertheless full of prohibitions and constraints. I would guide students to focus on two different paradise analogies that allow Ellison to delineate the complex dimensions of the restrictions that Black Americans are subjected to in the North. The first has Ellison confessing to feeling "as though I had come to the Eden of American culture and found myself indecisive as to which of its fruits were free for the picking" (*Going* 148). Here, Ellison gives voice to the psychological trauma of previously experienced discrimination acting as Foucault's panopticon—an important link between Southern Jim Crow and prison.[1] He precedes this vision of New York as an Eden by confessing, "I had discovered, much to my chagrin, that while I was physically out of the South, I was restrained—sometimes consciously, sometimes not—by certain internalized thou-shalt-nots that had structured my public conduct in Alabama" (148).

A second paradise metaphor reveals that, even in the North, Black freedom, to borrow the historian Stephanie Smallwood's apt wording, is "an impossible category" (see "Slavery, Race"). Ellison writes:

> [T]here were moments when I reminded myself of the hero of the old Negro folktale who, after arriving mistakenly in heaven and being issued a pair of wings, was surprised to learn that there were certain earth-like restrictions which required people of his complexion to fly with one wing strapped to their sides. But, while surprised, the new arrival came to the philosophical conclusion that even in heaven, that place of unearthly perfection, there had to be rules and regulations.        (*Going* 149)

By relating the African American folktale about heaven welcoming Black arrivals with what is essentially a form of shackles, Ellison recognizes that even if New York is indeed "the freest of American cities" (147), that freedom—or American freedom in general—has specific ramifications that categorically rule out his inclusion.

These references to movement and mapping, as well as ones identified by students, provide a fruitful start for memoir writing. I begin by modeling some idea-generating questions: What are some similarities and differences between Ellison's experience of moving from the South to the North and the students' own transition from a more restricted to a more "free" environment, as they either remember or imagine it? Considering what Dobbs writes about Ellison's view of the Great Migration, that it was "a series of physical, social, and psychological movements" (914), to what extent is coming back home from prison a series of such movements? How can the experience of unfreedom condition one to internalize its restrictions? Reflecting on Ellison's portrayal of the long reach of the Jim Crow South, what is the reach of the carceral state? To what extent does it permeate structures of American society, and what are the material, social, political, and emotional limitations on access to freedom for formerly incarcerated people and people of color? What are some intersecting conditions of unfreedom associated with race and incarceration? Can transition from prison to the "free world" be considered a sort of migration? Finally, given the disorientation described by Ellison upon migrating to the uncharted territory of New York, if the students' memoirs were to be considered their own maps of the journey through freedom and unfreedom, what would these maps look like? What would they include? What place would the city occupy in them? And, finally, what if these map memoirs went beyond reflection of what has taken place in the students' lives and became also charts of the students' visions of freedom?

## *Grasping American Freedom and Unfreedom*

It may seem ironic that an essay that at first presents a "delighted" Ellison excitedly readying himself for his "introduction to Broadway theater" and closes with a scene, at the play's conclusion, of Ellison "grateful" for a chance to have laughed at the comedy's white Southern characters, in an integrated theater, "without the threat of physical violence" (*Going* 146, 197), is primarily devoted—fifty pages of it, no less—to recounting the indignities and fear caused by racial discrimination, not only in the South but also, importantly, in what is supposedly "the freest of American cities" (147, 159). Clearly, Ellison refuses to subdue the story of racial oppression in the interest of celebrating the relative gains of liberty in the North. His refusal to do so points to a larger conversation about the very nature of freedom in the United States and the contradictions it encompasses. "An Extravagance of Laughter" also rejects the theory of freedom as linearly progressing, inevitably unfolding and expanding, inviting a discussion of freedom's exclusionary character and vicissitudes.

In addition to Ellison's exposure of the conditional and limited Northern freedom, students also benefit from recent scholarship by historians who, like Ellison a few decades earlier, have concluded that the "from slavery to freedom" narrative needs an amendment. Smallwood, for example, stresses the need to "[reckon] with the tenuousness of black freedom and the 'afterlife' of slavery that resonates to the present day" ("Slavery and the Framing").[2] Walter Johnson's work—critical of the notion of American freedom's linear progression—"aim[s] to expose the metanarrative of 'freedom,' the story that organizes so many of our histories of slavery, reassuring us that the succession of the latter by the former was somehow inevitable rather than contingent, complete rather than unfinished, a matter of the past rather than the present" (44). Johnson also points out a dangerous ideological slippage inherent in the conceptualization of slavery as predestined to lead to freedom: it makes the oppressed appear as the

146 NAVIGATING FREEDOM

means to purposes larger than their own (42–44). These writers and activists help cast the unfreedom of system-impacted people as not only a fitting parallel to the story of sanctioned racial persecution but an actual continuation of that persecution.

The misleading metanarrative of freedom as self-propelling, or progressively unfolding, as described by both Ellison and race theorists, conceals another suspect trait of American freedom: it is exclusionary—by design. The "from slavery to freedom" narrative obscures the fact that it was "slavery [that] produced freedom in America" ("Slavery, Race") and that the American theory of freedom "used racial exclusion" to define what freedom would be (Smallwood, "Freedom" 112). As thusly defined, freedom was never meant to be for everyone. That fact is eclipsed by the abstract terms in which freedom is defined in most dictionaries, which focus on freedom as an idea, or a personal feeling of being unconstrained, rather than on "the materiality of the specific contexts through which freedom has attained its central place" in the West (111).

Smallwood explains that the understanding of freedom in the West emerges as an individualist and *possessive* value around the seventeenth to eighteenth centuries. It is individualist in the sense that it emerges as a concept of autonomous, rights-bearing individuals against the absolute rule of a sovereign. It is possessive as it is "conceptualized as something that resulted from an individual's ability to possess things" (Smallwood, "Freedom" 111), which also includes John Locke's idea that "every man has a property in his own person" (qtd. in Smallwood, "Freedom" 111). However, this concept of freedom involved a paradox from its inception: "The individual celebrated by the modern Western theory was male, and his purportedly self-produced economic independence derived at least in part from the labor" of others "whose political subjectivity was subsumed" (Smallwood, "Freedom" 111).

Freedom emerged as a value that was never meant to apply to everyone. Smallwood explains the categorical impossibility of Black freedom by showing that even when many of the revolutionary-era figures, including Thomas Jefferson, eventually arrived at an antislavery position, the only way they could conceive of Black people's freedom was if, after emancipation, it existed outside of the borders of the United States, an emigration idea that would also capture Abraham Lincoln's imagination several decades later ("Freedom" 112). The gains in Black freedom appear always to have been accompanied by new measures to restrict it, including the use of mass incarceration in the past forty years. Mass incarceration, then, can be thought of as the next "logical" step in the story of exclusionary American freedom.[3]

In "An Extravagance of Laughter," Ellison describes his realization that he would need to accept the uncertainty and risk of navigating New York's racial scene "if I were to grasp American freedom" (*Going* 157). The wording here is startling. Unlike his use of the phrase "Northern freedom" elsewhere in the text (156), Ellison's choice here suggests that his movement is not just one from the restrictions of the Jim Crow South to the liberating conditions of the North but rather movement around the fence of a seemingly impenetrable space of "American freedom." The phrase reveals his visceral sense of being on the *outside* of freedom's boundaries, like a visitor to a foreign land who may try to "grasp" useful linguistic expressions and elements of customs but who will nevertheless remain an onlooker rather than a participant.

## Visibility, Invisibility, and Power

Ellison studies the notion of exclusionary freedom by employing the trope that preoccupied him throughout his life and that he had previously used to lay the foundation of his only published novel: invisibility. He illustrates what it means to move around a social scene as someone who is in some ways hypervisible and often perceived as out of place—or not in his proper place—and yet, in the process, to be simultaneously rendered invisible as an individual. It is this engagement with the concepts of visibility and invisibility with respect to the production of unfreedom that provides the most direct link between the subject of Ellison's essay and the problem of the carceral state.

In his biography of Ellison, Arnold Rampersad notes that Ellison reflected on the white people of his youth in Oklahoma City and concluded that they had "God-like power to make blacks feel, well, invisible" (34). For anyone unsure of the intended meaning behind the metaphor his name has become synonymous with, Ellison offers this straightforward explanation: "they treated you or could treat you as though you had no personal identity" (qtd. in Rampersad 34). In "Extravagance" he recalls a similar impression of white people in Alabama during his Tuskegee days: "whiteness struck at signs, at coloration, hair texture, and speech idiom, and thus denied you individuality" (Ellison, *Going* 172). Yet here, as I would encourage students to note, the recounting of the racialized group characteristics—such as skin tone and speech patterns—points to what may appear as a counterintuitive basis for Black Americans' invisibility in the white mind: the fact of their being *seen*. Understanding this seemingly paradoxical relationship, both as Ellison illustrates it and as it has been theorized by Michel Foucault in the context of prison, would form the basis for the next portion of our course.

Ellison's sense of being hypervisible and subject to scrutiny does not leave him upon his migration to New York. Hungry for the cultural wealth of New York's museums and art venues, he visits them with an acute awareness that they are "areas of the culture where few of my people were to be seen" (*Going* 158). The apex of his examination of white people's perception of his appearance in those spaces coincides with the incident that gives the essay its title and anchors Ellison's dissection of American freedom: the Broadway play he attends in his first few weeks in New York. With our discussion of American freedom's history and Ellison's insistence on stressing the limits it imposes on Black liberty, students examine how those restrictions play out in the essay's central event and how visibility and invisibility figuratively stand for American freedom and unfreedom.

148    NAVIGATING FREEDOM

Ellison writes that, when visiting New York's cultural institutions, "in my dark singularity I often appeared to be perceived more as a symbol than as an individual, more as a threatening sign . . . than as a disinterested seeker after culture" (*Going* 158). While he is invisible as an individual, Ellison's essay shows him as simultaneously hypervisible and out of place—not in "his place"—in the cultural spaces marked as white, and that is, in and of itself, an encroachment on those white spaces, and therefore a violation of white freedom. Ellison tells us this to prepare us for the Broadway theater episode around which his essay revolves. A comedic scene depicting morally depraved Southern white characters performing a grotesque sexual act leads Ellison to react with "helpless laughter," which "distracted the entire balcony" (186). He describes his mortification by calling it "a terrible moment" and noting that "more attention was being directed toward me than at the action unfolding on the stage" (186). This not only causes him "soul-wracking agony of embarrassment" but also transports him mentally back to the racial terror of the South: "Then it was as if I had been stripped naked, kicked out of a low-flying plane onto an Alabama road, and ordered to laugh for my life" (187, 186). Ellison describes the horrors of Southern roads haunted by both "lynch-fever stirred up" by the Scottsboro trial and the casual daily persecution from cops resembling slavery-era patrols (167).

Furthermore, Ellison relates the story of "laughing barrels," literal and symbolic containers of Black laughter used by white Southerners during slavery to restrict and bar themselves from the invasion of Black expression. By describing white viewers reacting indignantly to his laughter at the theater—Black laughter that "demonstrate[s] his social unacceptability" (187)—Ellison draws a parallel between the inventors and enforcers of the laughing barrel and the white people surrounding him at the theater. Despite his laughter being the expected audience reaction to comedy, it is made abnormal by the fact of his Blackness. Ellison's laughter at the theater forces the white viewers to acknowledge his "dark singularity" as personhood, and they resist, seeing his laughter as a violation of their space, their freedom.

I encourage students to focus on one specific passage in the essay, where Ellison stresses the real material consequences of figurative invisibility:

> Most Negroes are characterized—in the jargon of sociology—by a "high visibility" of pigmentation which made the group easily distinguishable from other citizens and therefore easy to keep in line and politically powerless. That powerlessness was justified and reinforced by the stereotypes, which denied blacks individuality and allowed any Negro to be interchangeable with any other. (*Going* 174)

Here, Ellison underscores the sociopolitical dimensions of invisibility. Just as freedom is more than a feeling or an abstract idea, so is the erasure of subjecthood that Ellison speaks about. In this passage, he helpfully brings full circle his point about the symbiotic relationship between hypervisibility as vulnerability and invisibility as oppressive power and employs the discourse of discipline to do so, showing how categorization is a tool of control and agential loss. Ellison's language provides an organic connection to one of the most definitive theorizations of the Western penal systems: Michel Foucault's *Discipline and Punish*.[4]

Foucault actually mentions life writing, setting it up against the contrast of documentation involved in the mechanisms of objectification. He explains that the prison system "reversed" the relation between individuals and writing and "made of the description a means of control and a method of domination" (191). He compares subjecthood-affirming life writing—"[t]he chronicle of a man, the account of his life, his historiography" (191)—to the documentary function of disciplinary description and concludes that the latter's "turning of real lives into writing . . . functions as a procedure of objectification and subjection" (192).

Autobiographical writing by those who have been subjected to mechanisms of objectification represents a reclaiming of the agential function of writing. Ellison devotes a lot of thought to the strategies one may employ to reclaim one's identity from subjecthood-erasing systems of oppressions. In "Extravagance," he quotes W. B. Yeats's explanation of "masking" as crucial. But Ellison suggests revisions to the text to make it fit the context of Black life in America. My altered quotation below illustrates the changes Ellison suggests to Yeats's words: "if [an Afro-American] cannot imagine ourselves as different from what [many white people assume an American Negro to be] and assume the second self, we cannot impose a discipline upon ourselves, though we may accept one from others," and "active virtue, as distinct from the passive acceptance of [prevailing racial attitudes], is the wearing of a mask" (Yeats qtd. in Ellison, *Going* 163; bracketed phrases are Ellison's replacements, 163–64). Ellison, then, adopts "masking"—a common trope in African American literature—as a defense against not just physical harm but the psychic damage of being robbed of the right to self-define.

## Carceral Citizenship and Freedom Dreaming

The last unit of the course focuses on the direct implications of Ellison's insights and American freedom in the lives of the students. It combines textual analysis, optional guided or assisted research, and writing, with increasing emphasis on the latter. While students' work on their memoir essays is the ultimate goal, the scaffolding of that larger task continues to involve reflection-style responses to readings combined with personal narrative.

In the process of carefully studying and pairing Ellison's indictment of America's commitment to Black unfreedom with Foucault's discussion of disciplinary power, another parallel regarding the carceral state and the racist order is likely to organically emerge: the long reach of both. Ellison uses his essay's meandering narrative—with its expansive timeline and spatial breadth—to show that the combination of hypervisibility and invisibility he first experienced in the South is hardly a Southern phenomenon. Similarly, anyone familiar with the socio-legal intricacies of the so-called reentry process, and especially individuals who have

150 NAVIGATING FREEDOM

themselves experienced it, understands that the tentacles of incarceration have a firm grip on people's lives beyond the spatial limits of prison or the temporal boundaries demarcated by "time," keeping system-impacted people in what could be seen as a perpetual state of unfreedom.

Part of the lasting effect of racism and incarceration is in the psychic trauma both cause. Ellison refers to his "jimcrowed psychology" leading him to occupy balcony seats in integrated New York theaters, following the dictates of internalized Southern racial order ("Adventures" 29). Such "invisible aspects of racism" (Cheng 122), which do not always translate into physical or material damage, unsurprisingly find their corresponding psychological injuries among people who have experienced incarceration and who have internalized certain limitations of their agency. Foucault writes, "[T]he major effect of the Panopticon [is] to induce in the inmate a state of conscious and permanent visibility that assures the automatic functioning of power" (201),[5] which is to say that those subjected to such power are never actually outside of its reach. In "Extravagance," Ellison underscores the ubiquity of that power and the necessity to learn how to live with it: "while racial danger was always with me, I lived with it as with threats of natural disasters or acts of God" (*Going* 179). The limitations of Ellison's freedom in New York are very much real, and the same is true of system-impacted people outside of the walled jails and prisons, where criminal checks, public registries and records, and the vast net of socioeconomic implications of the parole system continue to play the role of the "laughing barrel" or panopticon.

Dobbs writes that "[t]o control the movement of a person's body, and the body of people, is to disempower and dehumanize" (913). Criminologists Reuben Miller and Amanda Alexander's term "carceral citizenship" captures a similar process in the lives of formerly incarcerated people. Carceral citizenship is based on a presumption of illegal activity (Miller and Alexander 296). Just as, according to Smallwood, Black freedom is precluded within the racialized conception of American freedom, the freedom of system-impacted people appears as an impossible category within the ramifications of carceral citizenship. Having introduced Miller and Alexander's work, I hand over the authority to direct the conversation to the students, who choose the extent to which they are willing to share autobiographically while discussing the legal scholarship. For students interested in data and systematic analyses of issues related to carceral citizenship, I would offer recent statistical research, analytical reports, and helpful examples of legislation.[6]

In this part of the course, writing dominates students' time. As a way of helping students bring together various threads of our engagement with Ellison's essay and other texts to create their memoirs—or narrative maps of their journeys through freedom and unfreedom—I introduce them to the historian Robin D. G. Kelley's term "freedom dreams," or visions of a different society, a better world, "that [enable] us to see beyond our immediate ordeals" (45). I also invite students to begin by considering the following question: If the oppressive systems' tracking and restricting of the movement of Black and system-impacted

Agnieszka Tuszynska 151

bodies is a tool of control and dehumanization, then—to quote Dobbs—"What happens . . . when the subaltern takes over as cartographer? What alternative maps emerge?" (914).

The final set of ideas and examples I share with the students are models of "freedom dreams" from social movements discussed by scholars and from Ellison himself. When Kelley discusses "freedom dreams," his interest lies in progressive social movements that "compel us to relive the horrors" and "enable us to imagine a new society" (9). That necessity to sit with the harm done in order to "imagine something different" brings to mind the activist and academic movements that prioritize recognizing the flaws of the freedom narrative and challenging the completeness of its stated goals (Kelley 9). Similarly, Ellison's "second self" is no Jay Gatsby vision of donning a more socially desirable persona—not even an available option, given his "dark singularity"—but rather a rejection of the way America has opted to conceive of him. Therefore, Ellison's theory of "masking" is not outward-facing; instead, it is focused on the bold possibility of alternative planes of existence for Black Americans and superimposing them onto the entrenched racist reality.

The last text I submit for students' consideration is another of Ellison's New York essays, "Harlem Is Nowhere" (*Shadow and Act* 294–301). The remarkable concurrence of this title and Kelley's assertion that freedom dreams originate in the space that could be described as "nowhere" uncovers the possibility of reading Ellison's title beyond its apparent bleakness. Ellison paints a vivid and grim image of Harlem's "crimes, its casual violence, its crumbling buildings with littered areaways, ill-smelling halls and vermin-invaded rooms" (295). "Harlem is a ruin," Ellison writes, and its status as such, in the midst of New York's grandeur, makes it also "the scene and symbol of the Negro's perpetual alienation in the land of his birth" (295, 296). But the essay notably opens with a description of a much more optimistic vision of a parallel universe that exists underneath Harlem's desolate landscape: a basement psychiatric clinic, Lafargue, which "is the only center in the city wherein both Negros and whites may receive extended psychiatric care" and which to Ellison "represents an underground extension of democracy" (295).

Having considered how freedom dreams—or alternative maps—have been both theorized by scholars and imagined by Ellison, students are left to create their own in the form of autobiographical writing. As a way of maximizing the range of their expressive choices, I expand the definition of memoir to encompass mixing verbal text with visual or graphical elements. I take the time to ask students how they perceive the very fact of their work on the memoir in relation to notions of visibility and invisibility. If the young Ellison was out of place in New York's museums and theaters during the Jim Crow era, what are analogous situations and spaces where system-impacted people are not supposed to belong? What does it mean for them to claim rights as college students, as readers of Ralph Ellison and Michel Foucault, as authors of their own stories? I hope these stories will lead us to some place—a kind of "nowhere"—where American freedom gets a do-over.

## NOTES

1. The panopticon is a feature of penal architecture and a symbol of disciplinary order theorized by Michel Foucault in *Discipline and Punish: The Birth of the Prison.*

2. Smallwood points to "the crisis in racialized policing, mass incarceration, and other forms of growing racial disparities" to question "whether slavery's chokehold on black life was ever fully extinguished" ("Slavery and the Framing").

3. Orlando Patterson's analysis of a national survey he conducted in 2000 on the subject of freedom revealed that, although obscured and repressed, the meaning of freedom as power persists. In response to a question that "asked respondents to say how much more or less free they felt compared with the past" (Patterson 8), white men were the ones who said that they had less freedom than previously, which Patterson interprets as "a zero sum view of freedom: the fact that women and minorities have more of it may be taken to mean that white men have less" (10).

4. The thematic boundaries of the course described here do not necessitate the reading of *Discipline and Punish* in its entirety (although some students may choose to do so), but Ellison's use of the tropes of visibility and invisibility and the course focus on freedom certainly invite an introduction to the text and a careful study of some excerpts from the section of Foucault's book devoted to discipline.

5. I normally preface a reading from any text that includes racial slurs with a short reflection that I share with students on the destructive power of dehumanizing language. Given the unfortunate wording of some sections of Foucault's text, where the translation uses the word "inmate," I would include a similar preface here.

6. Sources might include Cerda-Jara et al.; sample data from the National Inventory of the Collateral Consequences of Conviction (nij.ojp.gov/topics/articles/national-inventory-collateral-consequences-conviction); Craigie et al.; Couloute; and new legislation advancing in New York State known as the Clean Slate Bill, which proposes automatic sealing of certain convictions.

# Epistolary Ellison:
# Letter Writing as Pedagogy

## *Clark Barwick*

Although Ralph Ellison may not have been as prolific as many of his contemporaries in terms of publishing fiction, he in fact wrote all the time, and a significant portion of his literary energy was devoted to letter writing. Ellison's correspondence, which has become far more accessible in recent years, spans more than six decades—including more than four hundred available letters—and stands as its own significant body of work within his oeuvre. From his "Dear Mama" letters, written during his years at Tuskegee, to his endearing and complicated letters to his beloved wife, Fanny, to his intellectual exchanges with Albert Murray, Richard Wright, Stanley Hyman, Kenneth Burke, Saul Bellow, and others, Ellison reveals so much about his development as a person, writer, and thinker. In ample turns, we find one of America's greatest and most revered novelists as perceptive, wise, knowledgeable, challenging, humorous, vulnerable, charming, exasperated, generous, hopeful, ambitious, angry, caring, gossipy, wistful, and, ultimately, human.

By all indications, Ellison took letter writing extremely seriously. In 1953, Ellison wrote to Wright that he was "more [himself] when writing a letter than at any other time" (*Selected Letters* 309), and the writing we find in his letters is often as carefully conceived and crafted as anything he ever published. (Ellison was known to revise and sometimes draft multiple versions of a given letter [Callahan, General Introduction 14].) While Ellison's letters can be deeply intimate and contain feelings that he would not have wanted broadcast to the world, Ellison did imagine his letter writing as part of his greater literary project. As early as the 1950s, Ellison proposed publishing a collection of letters between Murray and himself (*Selected Letters* 559–60). Ellison kept carbon copies of his typed letters, allowing for at least the possibility of future readers (Callahan, General Introduction 13). Moreover, Ellison scholar and executor John F. Callahan suggests that Ellison may have imagined his letters as his de facto autobiography, as he sensed that he would not live long enough to write a proper story of his life (4).

Yet how many of us who regularly teach Ellison's work ever introduce his letters? In this essay I explore Ellison's epistolary archive and examine the immense value that his correspondence can bring to instructors and students alike. I begin with an overview of Ellison's letter writing and identify how and where his vast correspondence can be found. Later, I examine the contents of Ellison's letters and focus on how their various themes and topics can resonate with contemporary students. I conclude with some pedagogical strategies for employing Ellison's letters to engage students and encourage analysis and reflection.

## Accessing Ellison's Letters

The vast majority of Ralph Ellison's letters reside at the Library of Congress in Washington, DC. Upon Ellison's death in 1994, his papers, including his correspondence, were carefully collected from Ellison's New York City apartment and catalogued by library archivists. According to Callahan, Fanny Ellison deserves a lot of credit for the preservation of Ellison's letters, as she was initially responsible for organizing his correspondence and later ensured its transfer (General Introduction 12–13). For those in the vicinity and interested in introducing students to primary source research, Ellison's letters are open to the public. Others of Ellison's physical letters are housed at archives and libraries across the United States.[1]

Ellison's letters are also available in two published collections. A good starting point is *Trading Twelves: The Selected Letters of Ralph Ellison and Albert Murray*, edited by Murray and Callahan. This volume, which completes the epistolary collaboration that Ellison once imagined, is useful as it focuses on a single relationship over the course of a particularly tumultuous and eventful decade (1950–60). Helpfully, *Trading Twelves* places Ellison's and Murray's letters side by side, giving the reader a full sense of their back-and-forth exchange.

The most expansive and definitive collection of Ellison's letters is *The Selected Letters of Ralph Ellison*, edited by Callahan and Marc C. Conner. *Selected Letters* features much of Ellison's extant correspondence between 1933 and 1993 and includes only letters written by Ellison. With access to so many letters, readers can easily follow Ellison's growth as a person and writer, and the collection offers insight into almost anything—from his friendships to literature to jazz to politics to photography—that mattered to the writer. In fact, by the end of *Selected Letters*, readers feel as if they actually know Ellison—how he talks, what he cares about, how he is likely to respond to a given subject—even if the silences in his letters also leave remaining questions. While this thousand-plus-page compendium is too long to assign to undergraduates, the volume is invaluable for strategically pulling out content pertaining to Ellison's biography, writing process, thoughts on America, and any number of other topics. *Selected Letters* also provides images of some of Ellison's letters, which emphasizes the intimacy of this medium, and Callahan includes beneficial introductions before each decade of letters to help readers contextualize what they will encounter.

## Learning through Ellison's Letters

Ellison's letter writing offers an immense archive for approaching and understanding his background and his work. Yet even before we delve into the richness of his correspondence, Ellison's letters have the potential to open a new genre of writing to our students. Rebecca Solnit, referencing Virginia Woolf's famous quotation, writes that "in or around June 1995 human character changed" with the rise of the Internet (32). While email did not exactly kill letter writing, the function of "postal" communication had been evolving for a long time. For centuries, letter writing served as the primary mode for long-distance human interaction. However, technological developments—the airplane, the telephone, the personal computer (which Ellison started composing on in the 1980s), and, much later, the cell phone—made the world smaller. Speed and efficiency became the goals for communication, rendering the personal letter far less popular for transmitting everyday information. As a result, many of our students, now born in this millennium, have likely never written or received a handwritten letter.

Therefore, Ellison's letters offer an opportunity to explore a bygone yet enduringly powerful mode of connection. During Ellison's life, letter writing was deeply intimate and deliberate. Until his late age, Ellison wrote letters by hand or on a typewriter, on actual paper that was finite in supply. His letters could take hours or days to write. When Ellison penned a letter, he knew exactly who his reader would be (unlike with his fiction or essays), and he tailored his tone and writing—which might include private information—for this very specific audience. Yet, unlike with today's texting, efficiency was not the point. Ellison's letters could be long and sometimes wander from subject to subject. Nonetheless, his correspondence, in the tradition of the letter writing of many of America's greatest authors, could also be as vivid, beautiful, entertaining, and perceptive as anything written for the public.

When it came time for Ellison to send a letter, uncertainty abounded. One of his missives could get lost or be misdelivered. It might be intercepted. (When writing from Italy in the 1950s, Ellison feared his mail was being opened [*Selected Letters* 431].) A letter could be damaged or become illegible. Its contents would almost certainly be dated upon arrival. And there was always waiting involved, as letters were generally delivered only once per day. But this antiquated process also produced a tangible artifact—a physical symbol of a relationship that could be held, kept, and reread. So, for our students, Ellison's correspondence introduces a totally different reading and writing experience from what they now expect in their private communication. Therefore, as Jonathan Ellis explains, "the history and nature of letter writing in the past may help us to understand our habits and methods of communication today" (1).

As students become familiar with letter writing as a genre, Ellison's correspondence offers innumerable entry points for exploring his life and work. The first is as a means for learning Ellison's biography. His letters demystify "the great novelist" and inform us about his lived experience, with all of its ups and downs. We learn about Ellison's formative relationships—with his mother ("tell me everything," he asks her [*Selected Letters* 81]), his brother Herbert, and his Oklahoma City relatives and friends. We find a young man acclimating to life first at Tuskegee (dealing with homesickness and even abuse), then in Harlem, later abroad, and finally back in New York City for good. We watch as Ellison transforms from a trumpeter-turned-writer, with ambition but self-doubt, into a bona

156   EPISTOLARY ELLISON

fide literary celebrity, who enjoys new stature and opportunities (the American Academy of Arts and Letters fellowship in Rome, offers for high-profile publications, appearances on the covers of magazines, requests for lectures, meeting the Queen of England) but also feels accompanying pressures and demands (the anticipation for a great second novel, expectations that he will speak on behalf of his race, attacks from a younger generation of Black artists). We witness Ellison falling in love on a few occasions, most notably in the mid-1940s with Fanny McConnell, his future wife. In his many letters to Fanny, which begin with a stirring letter on 4 October 1944, we find a deep and abiding love that bends but does not break with the eventual "cruel thing" of Ellison's infidelity thirteen years into their relationship (*Selected Letters* 514). We observe Ellison developing trusted friendships with Albert Murray and Saul Bellow, with whom he shares a range of private thoughts, concerns, and needs. (Ellison was known to ask Murray and other friends for money.) We are privy to how Ellison experienced his greatest successes, such as the events surrounding the National Book Award he won for *Invisible Man* in 1953. We also find him dealing with tragedy, as when his home in Plainfield, Massachusetts, burned in November 1967 and destroyed portions of his second novel. But above all we encounter Ellison as a human being. We learn of his daily routines, and we are introduced to his passions ("listening to jazz from two a.m. to 4" [552]) and preoccupations. As with any honest life portrait, we also encounter flaws. Ellison's occasional unvarnished comments concerning women and homosexuals are troubling and indefensible. Yet students will find the wholeness of Ellison to be relatable. Ultimately, Ellison's letters offer a biography of his unmediated thoughts and feelings—one that should be read as a necessary companion to biographies such as Lawrence Jackson's *Ralph Ellison: Emergence of Genius*, Arnold Rampersad's *Ralph Ellison: A Biography*, and any future renderings of Ellison's life and career.

Ellison's letters also provide great insight on writing. Students may be amazed—and potentially relieved—to learn how hard Ellison worked at his craft. His letters reveal the writing process to be a constant struggle that never managed to abate with experience. We learn that Ellison had bouts of writer's block ("Things ain't coming worth a damn" [*Selected Letters* 320]), and he had anxieties about the quality and meaningfulness of his work. However, we also witness how seriously Ellison took his art. Nothing in his fiction—from structure to character names to symbols—seems to have been unconsidered. In his letters, Ellison repeatedly refers to his writing in terms of problem-solving, and we see the extent to which Ellison lived with his work—to the point where he refers to some of his characters as if they were actual people (e.g., Rinehart 320; Hickman 581). In numerous letters, we find Ellison workshopping ideas for future stories or essays. One such passage appears when he launches into a transcendent and haunting description of returning to Oklahoma for his cousin's funeral (342), which seems to spark an urge to write more about the land of his boyhood. And in other moments, he discloses his influences and inspirations. For instructors teaching *Invisible Man*, Ellison writes extensively about his novel—about its conception, its content, its reception—which will prove invaluable to students.

Ellison's letters also tell us about his literary world. We learn about his self-education in the stacks of Tuskegee's library. We find him being mentored in New York by Langston Hughes and Richard Wright. We see him establishing relationships with contemporary writers (Murray, Bellow, Robert Penn Warren, Richard Wilbur, Shirley Jackson, John Hersey, and others), and we observe him in combat with others (notably, Norman Mailer). Ellison was devoted to the concept of American literature, and we constantly encounter him trying to articulate its foundations, its canon (Ellison writes about Stephen Crane, Herman Melville, T. S. Eliot), and its meanings. We are also privy to what Ellison was currently reading at any point in time, and we gain access to Ellison's private reviews and assessments, which were unflinching. Ellison was in frequent conversation with academics and critics, too—notably, Stanley Hyman and Kenneth Burke—and some of his most impassioned commentary appears in these exchanges. In his later letters, we find Ellison giving guidance to younger writers and thinkers, including James Alan McPherson, Michael S. Harper, Robert O'Meally, and Henry Louis Gates, Jr. (Ellison encourages Gates to "reveal to us dummy's [sic] the extent, if any, the old Mose is hiding in Henry James's word-pile" [824]). We also see Ellison teaching literature to college students—an undertaking he found alternatingly energizing and frustrating ("They all expect to be entertained" [552]). Given this context, Ellison's letters help us situate his work within his own twentieth-century milieu.

By reading Ellison's correspondence, we also gain a deeper understanding of how he perceived America and its racial past. Ellison was proud to be an American but believed the country had too often ignored its African American roots and had a long way to go on matters of race. In his letters, Ellison writes about his painful firsthand encounters with segregation. For example, during a stay in New Orleans in the 1950s, he was forbidden from riding in "white" taxis or spending the night in decent hotels (351). Elsewhere, Ellison discusses the civil rights movement ("something is happening . . . Mose is fighting and he's still got his briar patch cunning" [417]) and monumental Supreme Court decisions (Ellison was "wet-eyed" upon learning of the *Brown v. Board of Education* decision [360]). Ellison continually expresses his deep connection to Black culture—its food, its music, its storytelling—and he longs to hear "the idiom" when he is away, such as during his time abroad in Europe.[2] Ellison's letters reveal his thoughts on a range of race-related subjects that students may find valuable—the NAACP; Martin Luther King, Jr.; racial violence; and the rise of Black nationalism. Above all, Ellison insistently cultivated his "own particular American style" (491) that explored the human experience through the lives of African Americans. "If you're lucky," Ellison wrote to Murray, "you have shared your vision; if not, you still haven't wasted your time for the Negro material will have been thrown into its wider frame of reference and the reader can pick it up" (290).

## 158  EPISTOLARY ELLISON

## *Letter Writing as Engagement*

With this array of themes and contexts in mind, how can we now use Ellison's letters to engage students in active learning and writing?

One effective strategy is to provide students with a single Ellison letter and ask them to analyze and respond to what they find. Letters can be strategically chosen to coordinate with Ellison's fiction or essays. Each of Ellison's missives— and especially his longer, more contemplative ones—can feel like its own contained world, piquing curiosity and lending to close reading. Who is the audience? What kind of relationship does Ellison have with them? What leads you to this conclusion? What is the purpose of the letter? What is the tone? How would you describe Ellison's writing? How does this letter inform or differ from our other Ellison readings? How does Ellison use his letter writing to explore grander literary and cultural ideas? What questions do you now have? What are the limitations of our eavesdropping?

This assignment is eminently adaptable. It can be completed by individuals or groups. It can function as a warm-up to a larger discussion of Ellison's writing, or it can serve as the focus for its own sustained discussion. Students can prepare this assignment for homework or complete it during class. If research is important, instructors can ask students to annotate a letter or write a contextual essay that "explains" the letter. This exercise could also be incorporated into a final-paper project, such as a comparative essay that requires multiple sources or contextualization. And it can work in any number of classes, from an expository or creative writing course to a literature or cultural studies seminar.

Any number of Ellison letters would be fruitful for this activity. However, I will suggest a long and multifaceted letter that Ellison sent to Albert Murray on 9 April 1953. Ellison opens, "Dear Murray," and he launches into a description of his recent speaking tour through the South: "Man, I hope you received my postal from Greensboro, as I was so close to a cotton patch as I have been in sixteen years, and I wanted you to know just in case those crackers jumped salty" (*Selected Letters* 317). Ellison, who had recently become one of America's most distinguished and celebrated writers, writes with his guard down, in the casual language of a man who is shooting the breeze with his buddy. His tone is humorous and entertaining as he details what he has encountered in North Carolina. "Boy," he declares, "their local versions of some of the fancier men's fashions knocked me out; the cat who started that fancy vest business should be jailed, because there are one or two studs in Greensboro who have taken it and committed a crime against the western aesthetic!" (318).

Yet when Ellison begins to recall a speaking engagement at Bennett College's Homemaking Institute, his tone shifts. In a passage that echoes *Invisible Man*, Ellison depicts in vivid and poetic detail how Dr. Jones, the leader of the women's college, duped him into giving a sermon before the student body. With an imposing organ bellowing behind him and "the Gothic space and upturned faces" in front of him, Ellison writes that his past hit him "like a ton of bricks":

[I]n spite of everything the emotions started striking past my defenses, not a religious emotion, but that of <u>remembering</u> religious feeling—that perhaps is little different. Anyway, there I was in a black robe, sharing a hymnal with the doctor (LL.D) with my throat throbbing and my speech notes rendered worthless because of the atmosphere. Someone had been so naive as to select "achieving peace through creative experiences" as the theme of the institute, and I knew that I wasn't going to tell them that creative experience brought peace, but only a fighting chance with the chaos of living. I looked down there at those chicks, man and felt that I was a repentant Rinehart. I was full of love for them because they were young and black and hopeful and, like all the young, prepared to be swindled by another four flusher who had no idea of what it meant to be young, idealistic and willing to learn. I could hardly talk, but I tried to level with them; tried to direct them towards reality and away from illusion. Once I heard my voice and, Jack, it was as sad and gloomy a voice as I've ever heard; and I knew then why even the most sincere preacher must depend upon rhetoric, raw communication between the shaman and the group to which he's spiritually committed is just too overpowering. Without the art the emotion would split him apart. (319–20)

Then, as if awakened from this "nightmare" (319), Ellison shifts gears again to discuss his work on the second novel ("it looks like a much more complex book than [*Invisible Man*]" [320]) and an essay he's working on for *Partisan Review* that involves Richard Wright and James Baldwin ("Take a look at their works, I don't think either is successful, but both are interesting examples of what happens when you go elsewhere looking for what you already had at home" [320]). Before the letter concludes, Ellison manages to also describe how Duke Ellington once hit on Fanny at a party (Ellington went after her "like a glad dog making for a meat wagon" [321]) and his recent meeting of William Faulkner. With its numerous historical, cultural, and literary allusions, this letter provides a rich opportunity to ask students to identify Ellison's references and their relevance to his life and work. Over the course of this single letter, we encounter multiple "Ellisons," writing in a variety of styles about a range of subjects, all in a way that feels true to the complexity of real life.

Other possibilities exist for using letter writing to teach Ralph Ellison's work. A second strategy would be to flip the dynamic and ask students to write a letter to Ellison. Ellison loved debating literature and art in his correspondence, and he was known to take fan mail seriously, sometimes responding to letters from strangers. (Some of these are included in *Selected Letters*.) One approach would involve asking students to read one of Ellison's writings—an essay, a short story, or a passage from *Invisible Man*—and to then compose a letter to Ellison in response. This activity, unlike a standard response paper or journal entry, establishes a certain intimacy with the author. It also requires students to really understand a reading (there's an invested reader on the other end!) and to think

160  EPISTOLARY ELLISON

through a host of questions that they might not otherwise consider. How should Ellison be addressed, and what tone should be used? Why? What questions is Ellison uniquely qualified to answer? What topics is he likely to avoid? If a claim or critique is made concerning his work, what evidence would be most persuasive? What, if anything, is necessary to convey to Ellison about yourself?

For more advanced undergraduates and graduate students, another variation on this assignment would be to ask students to respond to a letter that Ellison actually wrote. This version of the assignment requires students to understand both the specifics and the context of a given letter as they respond to Ellison's observations or concerns.

## *Letters as Productively Unfinished*

In reviewing Ellison's *Selected Letters*, the poet Kevin Young declared the volume to be "another Ellison magnum opus, one necessarily unfinished" (68). While Young's comment makes direct reference to Ellison's never-completed second novel—an incompletion widely regarded as a negative, if not unfairly as a shame—the "unfinished" nature of Ellison's letter writing can be productive and exciting. In one sense, Ellison's body of letters have the "living" compositional quality of Walt Whitman's *Leaves of Grass*, with the author adding and revising until death. With no expectation for closure, Ellison's letters allow for personal growth, experimentation, contradiction, and responsiveness to the changing times. As readers, we benefit from all of this. Ellison's letters are also productively unfinished, too, in the sense that a new letter could quite easily appear at any time in an attic, antique bookshop, or online. Therefore, we will never have the sense that we "have" every single one of Ellison's missives, and the scholarly search can always continue, allowing for discovery and surprise. Ellison's letters are also unfinished in that they leave so much unsaid. His correspondence has silences, gaps, missing responses, ellipses, unknown subtexts, and intentional omissions. Again, this incompletion leaves room for scholarly work and innovative interpretation.

But perhaps most importantly, Ellison's letters offer students and scholars a vast territory of material that has yet to be explored. Whereas so many areas of Ellison's work feel as if they have been exhausted—the familiar debates, the well-worn topics, the now-obvious questions—the scholarship on his letters is far from finished. Any given letter offers the potential for novel analysis, which can lead to new directions in the classroom as well as a richer understanding of Ellison's writing and its meaningfulness to our lives.

NOTES

1. Ellison's correspondence can also be found in the special collections of Duke University, Harvard University, the Huntington Library, Penn State University, Princeton

University, Syracuse University, the University of Chicago, the University of Michigan, the University of North Carolina at Charlotte, the University of Rochester, the University of Texas, the University of Virginia, Washington University in St. Louis, and Yale University, among other institutions and e-commerce platforms.

2. This connection to Black culture in Ellison's letters is particularly important to contrast with popular characterizations of Ellison's supposed removal from contemporary African American life. In *Ralph Ellison: A Biography*, Arnold Rampersad writes that Ellison was increasingly at a distance "from his fellow blacks" (513) and from "the black social reality about him" (315). However, as we see here, Ellison's letters complicate (and sometimes altogether disprove) the narratives of race betrayal and social climbing that continue to define and misrepresent his relationship with African American culture.

# VERSIONS OF THE SECOND NOVEL

## Reflecting on the Mysteries of Ellison's "Unfinished" Project

### *Keyana Parks*

More than seventy years after its publication, Ralph Ellison's *Invisible Man* continues to enthrall students and instructors. As a visiting assistant professor at Kenyon College, I learned students had been requesting a course dedicated to Ralph Ellison—to *Invisible Man*, to be exact—for some time. In constructing the course syllabus, I felt confident in my ability to teach Ellison's 1952 magnum opus. I initially encountered it as a middle schooler, at the suggestion of my older brother. My first critical engagement with the novel came as an undergraduate at Spelman College, through the course Introduction to African American Literature, and later, when I was a graduate student, my own research became indebted to Ellison's preoccupation with humor and irony in *Invisible Man*. But what about Ellison beyond *Invisible Man*? What twenty-first-century course could possibly do justice to the political, cultural, and literary complexities of such a luminary without at least gesturing to his posthumously published work? How does one go about teaching an unfinished novel compiled from multiple manuscript drafts, notes, and previously published excerpts spanning forty years? What possible configurations exist? This essay narrates some of the pedagogical and logistical decisions I made in teaching *Juneteenth* and offers some alternative ideas for future undertakings of a similar offering.[1]

At the suggestion of my Kenyon colleague Ted Mason, who had previously taught versions of an Ellison course, I adopted Eric J. Sundquist's *Cultural Contexts for Ralph Ellison's* Invisible Man as a starting point for building students' historical and cultural knowledge.[2] I also heavily relied on *The Collected Essays of Ralph Ellison* and taught several of Ellison's short stories collected in *Flying Home and Other Stories*. I opted to teach *Juneteenth* over *Three Days before the Shooting*... in part because of my own adherence to the novel form as a discrete, knowable entity and my nascent familiarity with the latter. However, even with the support of *Cultural Contexts* and *Collected Essays*, preparing to teach Ellison's *Juneteenth* proved to be a difficult task. I did not possess the same kind of rapport or history with that novel. I wondered how I was not only going to interest my students in an unfinished text but also help them make sense of what *Juneteenth* potentially illuminates about Ellison as an African American male writer and his views on American literature, exceptionalism, individualism, and democracy for a twenty-first-century audience.

Attempting to teach *Juneteenth* is no small feat. This is, in part, because *Invisible Man* looms so large in students' cultural frame of reference. Their investment in Ellison is inherently tied to reading and understanding his canonized novel. Indeed, teaching *Juneteenth* without knowledge of and substantial reference to his other writings may be an unachievable endeavor. You must decide how *Juneteenth* builds on, connects to, or relates to Ellison's first and only published novel, his critical essays, and his short stories. You must consider its editorial process. You have to contend with not only Ellison's characteristically dense, imagery-laden prose but also a Faulknerian fragmentation that can only be understood as potentially exacerbated by the wrought and fragmentary nature of the novel's (re)constitution.

As it turns out, the answer I was looking for was to be found precisely in the mystery and intrigue behind *Juneteenth*'s long, complicated production. As the back cover suggests, mystery is an essential aspect of the narrative.[3] Entering the text through the mystery of Ellison's burned manuscript captivates students' attention and motivates them to work critically through difficult prose and plot.[4] It also concretely connects them to the mystical element pervading the novel, or what John F. Callahan describes as the "mysteries of kinship and race" surrounding the relationship between the novel's two main characters, Bliss/Adam Sunraider and musician-turned-reverend Alonzo Hickman (Introduction [*Juneteenth*] xxvii). How are they related? What kind of kinship do they share? What compels Hickman to take responsibility for Bliss? How might we read the mystery of Hickman's sense of responsibility in concert with Ellison's own views on a writer's obligation to narrative, language, and style? to a people, a nation, an American ideal? However fraught it may be to rely on authorial intent, it proves to be a productive and accessible place to begin.

What accounts for Ellison's "failure" to produce a second novel? Was the 1967 loss of a portion of his manuscript to fire an insurmountable setback? Was it the pressure of completing another great work? What other explanations account for *Juneteenth*'s posthumous publication?[5] Whatever the case, approaching *Juneteenth* through the guise of a mystery in need of solving primes students to want to read it and prepares them to think about Ellison's writing craft after *Invisible Man*. To that end, an instructor might set out to demystify the infallible genius

164    ELLISON'S "UNFINISHED" PROJECT

ascribed to Ellison in order to make the mysteries of his posthumously published novel more legible.

Opening the class with Ellison's unpublished 1948 essay "Harlem Is Nowhere" and viewing images from Ellison's collaboration with the photographer Gordon Parks is an engaging and interactive way of introducing some of the central themes and questions running through much of his work. Written on the occasion of the opening of New York City's Lafargue Psychiatric Clinic in 1946, the collaboration provides students the opportunity to visually contemplate how the semester's texts would reflect Ellison's preeminent interest in aesthetically probing boundaries of African American identity politics and the rejection of "the second-class status assigned to them, [where] they feel alienated and their whole lives have become a search for answers to the questions: Who am I, What am I, and Where?" (Ellison, *Collected Essays* 323).[6] Asking students to reflect on how the photographs speak to the complexity of what seemed to be simple, straightforward questions will prompt discussions about Ellison's preoccupation with the "psychological character" of the individual and the search for identity.

Ellison's essays "Twentieth-Century Fiction and the Black Mask of Humanity" (*Collected Essays* 81–99), "Society, Morality and the Novel" (698–729), "The World and the Jug" (155–88), and "The Novel as a Function of American Democracy" (759–69)—all of which we returned to time and time again throughout the semester—were invaluable resources. Reading each of these essays early in the course quickly acquaints students with Ellison's philosophy of the novel and the complicated, sometimes contradictory and idiosyncratic evolution of his ideas. "Twentieth-Century Fiction and the Black Mask of Humanity" helped resolve some of the aversion students felt when reading about Ellison's distinction between literary ancestors and relatives in "The World and the Jug." Ellison's claim of white male writers like Ernest Hemingway and William Faulkner as ancestors—those who influenced his writing style—and Black writers like Langston Hughes and Richard Wright as relatives—those with whom he shared a racial designation—can sometimes foreclose critical engagement with Ellison's argument.[7] The essay illuminates how Ellison's investment in writers' precision of language and form (like that of Stephen Crane and Mark Twain) by no means excused the writers from using the figure of the Black person to justify the incongruencies between their "democratic beliefs and certain antidemocratic practices" (*Collected Essays* 85).[8] It also foregrounds how Ellison viewed the novel as arbiter around questions of identity, democracy, and race. So, from early in the semester, students question historical representations of Ellison as a static, self-assured, and always already evolved writer. This proves useful later when asking students to think about suspending and upsetting the indomitable consensus that views Ellison's posthumous novel as a blight on his literary career.

The first two units of the course, "Ancestors" and "Relatives," included Herman Melville's *Benito Cereno*, Fyodor Dostoyevsky's *Notes from Underground*, and excerpts from Wright's *Native Son* and Ann Petry's *The Street*. In the course reviews, one student expressed the wish for less preliminary material before finally reading *Invisible Man*, and there is certainly a case to be made for that. Still, my decision to open the class with a detailed interrogation of what Ellison meant by "ancestors" and "relatives" aided students' comprehension of Ellison's stylistic representation of the alienated individual. We also probed Melville's representation of the "Black" by returning to Ellison's admonishment of the "Negro stereotype [. . .] a key figure in a magic rite by which the white American seeks to resolve the dilemma arising between his democratic beliefs and antidemocratic practices, between his acceptance of the sacred democratic belief that all men are created equal and his treatment of every tenth man as though he were not" (*Collected Essays* 85). Useful here might be Bradley Ray King's claim that Ellison's preoccupation with Melville was due in part to his understanding that allusions and references to Melville's work carried with them a form of cultural capital that enabled him to "perform his loyalty to American values" in a way that "figures [Ellison] as a democratic joker who affirms the canon only to repudiate the racially exclusionary hermeneutic practices of post war Americanists" (128). This consideration complicates Ellison's claim to "ancestors" as connected to inserting himself in a traditionally white-male-dominated literary space instead of an outright dismissal of African American writers and their work.

Before beginning *Juneteenth*, students read Cheryl Alison's "Writing Underground: Ralph Ellison and the Novel" as a way to contemplate a stylistic through line from Ellison's first novel and short stories to his unfinished text. The article explores what Alison describes as Ellison's complex relationship with the "novel form's potential for capaciousness" (329). In other words, Ellison's episodic style not only points to the formal constraints on his writing but also troubles our idea of the novel as a unified whole. Through her argument, students returned to moments in *Invisible Man* where transitions between chapters seemed to depart from Ellison's typically complex and elaborate sentence construction.[9] I asked them to seriously consider what possibilities there are for reading and interpreting *Invisible Man*'s epilogue if we, as Alison suggests, give up "wondering whether the narrator makes it out or not" (333). In some sense, students resisted this idea because of the ways an indefinite hibernation can point to a failure of individual social and political responsibility, but this is precisely where I wanted them to go as we moved to consider Ellison's struggle with his second novel. I asked them how moving beyond a binary critique of Invisible Man's return from the underground releases us from constructing his hibernation as success or failure, and what that says about how we read and engage with the development of Ellison's literary craft over the next forty years.

In one sense, I am guiding students to think about Alan Nadel's assertion that "Ellison's unpublished works bring us to an impossible impasse guaranteeing that the limits of Ellison's second novel will be no more clearly defined and finalized than the subject of that novel: America" (400). More importantly, Alison's article prepares them to approach *Juneteenth* as a construction of a coherent text mediated through Ellison's decade-long process of revision as well as John Callahan's suturing of drafts and previously published excerpts. Melanie Masterton

166   ELLISON'S "UNFINISHED" PROJECT

Sherazi's article is also particularly instructive here when teaching *Juneteenth* or *Three Days before the Shooting . . . .* In a similar vein, Sherazi moves to deconstruct scholars', critics', and audiences' reliance on the aesthetic notion of a complete novel with clear authorial intent by reading it as an "unbound" novel, where "the themes of Ellison's unbound novel demonstrate the tension between belonging, or being bound, to the historical time of the nation-state and a resistance to normative citizenship, or being unbound, which is sometimes forced and sometimes self-selected and championed" (7–8). These are themes with which students should be well acquainted after reading *Invisible Man*, left, as they were, with the narrator contemplating a return to a "socially responsible role" and wondering "who knows but that, on the lower frequencies, I speak for you?" (581).

When finally reaching *Juneteenth*, it is necessary to give important historical and contextual background information. Informing students Ellison spent four decades, from 1954 up until his death in 1994, working on his second novel leads them to reflect on all he witnessed over those forty years and what those events might illuminate about his complicated relationship with writing the novel. As either a short mental exercise before reading, a mini assignment, or a final course product, you might consider discussing and having students design their own version of Sundquist's *Cultural Contexts* for *Juneteenth*.[10]

Whether teaching *Juneteenth* or *Three Days*, you will inevitably engage with Ellison's archive. I benefited greatly from Callahan's publication of *The Selected Letters of Ralph Ellison*, particularly "Letters from the Sixties" and "Letters from the Seventies" (567–748). As the introductory note remarks, the letters of the sixties remain preoccupied with *Invisible Man*, and, on the rare occasions they mention Ellison's second manuscript, they communicate his dissatisfaction with the novel's development (567–71). There is much to be learned from Ellison's correspondences on *Invisible Man* as they point to what he may have been grappling with while attempting to rework *Juneteenth*. In one letter, Ellison discusses the figure of Trueblood—whose voice offers the only interruption to the novel's dominating first-person point of view—and how unfortunate it was that *Invisible Man*'s protagonist took too long to recognize and understand Trueblood's message (*Selected Letters* 589–90). How does thinking about Ellison's relationship to Trueblood help students consider Ellison's struggle with the overpowering figure of Alonzo Hickman? Why do folk figures, figures who appear to exist as relatives—connected to a folk history, way of life, and storytelling— loom so large that they almost take over the narrative? What does it mean that Ellison struggles with this in both novels?

It is also in the letters from the sixties that Ellison first mentions the fire on 29 November 1967 that destroyed "a section" of his manuscript at his Plainfield, Massachusetts home (*Selected Letters* 641).[11] What we do not know is how much was lost, how heavily Ellison had to rely on what was still fresh in his mind and "imagination" in order to recover what was burned, or the psychological toll. In the initial mention of the fire, the loss does not appear to be a major source of distress. But, according to Ellison biographer Arnold Rampersad, this story changes over time—from a "minor setback" to "the loss of 365 pages" (715–16). What we do know for certain is Ellison's ability to publish pieces of the larger work. Ellison published eight excerpts—"And Hickman Arrives"; "The Roof, The Steeple and the People"; "It Always Breaks Out"; "Juneteenth"; "Night-Talk"; "A Song of Innocence"; "Cadillac Flambé"; and "Backwacking, a Plea to the Senator"—all of which are collected and published in *Three Days*.

Continuing to interrogate the future novel as a series of episodes supposedly heading toward a cohesive whole will help students remark on what Callahan describes as the "paradox [that] haunts [Ellison's] work on his second novel"— his upbeat confidence on the novel's progress and its actual state and frustrations (*Selected Letters* 576). Indeed, in the introductory remarks to the next decade of Ellison's correspondence, Callahan references the publication of the excerpts as where "one senses narrative drive as well as a luminous, haunting, melancholy power, [but] between the lines of the seventies letters there is an edgy fear that the second novel as a whole may be approaching the status of missing in action" (663). Exploring the contours of Ellison's incomplete novel requires entertaining multiple and varied explanations for the state of the manuscript he left behind. Do the episodes point toward the possibility of a composed text or negate it? *Three Days* is a rich resource for probing this possibility through questions students might ask of Ellison's archive. For example, although "And Hickman Arrives" was published in *The Noble Savage* as a polished excerpt, *Three Days* includes eleven variants students can compare to the public piece.

*Juneteenth* opens with a group of Southern Black church folk seeking an audience with Senator Adam Sunraider. However, given his race-baiting exhortations, those close to Sunraider do not understand what business the group could possibly have with the senator and turn them away. As the opening continues to unfold, we learn Senator Sunraider is the child Bliss, who was raised in the Black church by Alonzo Hickman—revival preacher and former bluesman. Hickman and his congregation traveled to the nation's capital, seeking to warn Sunraider of an assassination plot against his life. Unable to do so, they witness him be gunned down while delivering a speech on the senate floor.[12] In *Juneteenth*, the assassin's motive and relationship to Sunraider/Bliss is not evidently clear, but in *Three Days* readers expressly learn the gunman is Severen, the abandoned son of the movie-man-turned-senator.[13]

The novel's main action transitions to the hospital as Sunraider/Bliss and Hickman move between storytelling and internal reflection on the past through a stream-of-consciousness narrative style. Even as the novel traverses time and space, it is important to draw students' attention to the novel's background setting—the hospital bed. The space itself is barely perceptible, overshadowed by the antiphony that facilitates flashbacks and recollections of times and places gone by. As students struggle to keep track of the movement among Sunraider reminiscing about his childhood, his time as a movie man, Hickman's retelling of the Juneteenth revival, and the story of Bliss's mother, they can always reorient

168   ELLISON'S "UNFINISHED" PROJECT

themselves around knowing the shifts occur within the space of an exchange between two men in a hospital. I have them regard the hospital as the space of the story and storytelling. Similar to the ways Ellison's drafts, some lost forever, reflect a chaotic layering of past, present, and incomplete future, the dueling moments of reflection on and rejection of the past unfold chaotically in the shared recollections of Hickman and Sunraider. In teaching *Three Days* as a stand-alone text or in concert with *Juneteenth*, instructors might consider directing students to map out the changes in narrative voice to provide a generative space for them to consider Ellison's novel as unfinished. What does it mean that only on his deathbed is Bliss/Sunraider compelled to remember, recollect, and reconcile with his past? This may also be an inroad to discussing structural parallels and differing framing techniques between *Juneteenth* and *Invisible Man* or exploring the major thematic, aesthetic, cultural, political, and social preoccupation of Ellison—history.

To that end, it can be generative to approach the novel and the history it tells and engages with by reflecting on Fanny Ellison's musing to Callahan when he begins compiling Ellison's notes for publication: "'Beginning, middle, and end' [. . .]'Does it have a beginning, middle, and end'" (qtd. in Callahan, Introduction [*Juneteenth*] xxiv). Several scholars discuss the Juneteenth revival scene as the novel's center. As such, you may consider supplying your students with this as a narrative anchor. However, the move toward that center is punctuated with flashbacks. Indeed, which history, if any, is the "beginning" composed of? Variations of "And Hickman Arrives" call into question the very notion of a definitive beginning. Directing students to mark shifts in time, place, and point of view makes the sequencing of the text manageable and, as one student noted in their discussion post, attunes them to the elimination of "the middle ground between event and perception." It helps them register the Faulknerian sense of fragmentation that explains the childlike viewpoint of Bliss as blended with the present recollection of the adult Sunraider and how those are two inseparable perspectives. This shift can be more deeply explored in *Three Days*, as it provides a fuller description of Bliss/Sunraider's days as a filmmaker.

The marking of temporal spaces within the narrative structure compels students to reflect on Ellison's continued preoccupation with the boomerang of history from *Invisible Man* through to *Juneteenth* and beyond. In *Juneteenth*, Ellison describes time as a "merry-go-round within a merry-go-round" (99). Although the metaphors differ, they both reflect Ellison's ideas about temporality, the cyclical nature of history, and the ways in which understanding the present requires a layered simultaneity of the past. Bliss/Sunraider, even on his deathbed, must return to his past, must "recall to himself an uneasy dream," however fragmentary, to answer and confront the self (41). Consider how Bliss differs from *Invisible Man*'s protagonist and discuss how both engage with the motif of running to guide observations about the narrative impact of perspective—first-person versus third-person, free indirect speech—and explore what that means in terms of Ellison's evolution as a writer and his view of individual power in the face of history.

Another important extratextual component of *Juneteenth* is Callahan's inclusion of Ellison's draft notes in the novel's back matter. Particularly informative is the note describing an interaction between Bliss and Hickman as the "antiphonal section, or Emancipation myth, if spun out in [the] hospital where Senator confesses to Hickman under pressure of conscience, memory and Hickman's questions and it takes form of Bliss's remembered version versus Hickman's idiomatic accounts" (Ellison, *Juneteenth* 351). Apart from engaging students with important literary vocabulary, such as *antiphony* and *idiom*, you will be able to lead students on an exploration of how Ellison uses Hickman and Bliss to take part in the African American tradition of call-and-response while simultaneously employing Hickman to signal Bliss's proximity and distance from Blackness. You might also lead students to contemplate Ellison's choice of the word "confess." Can this then also be read as a confession narrative? For whom?

One such example of antiphonal exchange opens with Hickman leading Sunraider toward the past:

> "Bliss, I watched them bringing you slowly down the aisle on those young shoulders and putting you there among the pots of flowers, the red and white roses and the bleeding hearts—and I stood above you on the platform and begin describing the beginning and the end, the birth and the agony, and . . ."
>
> Screaming, mute, the Senator thought, Not me but another. Bliss. Resting on his lids, black inside, yet he knew that it was pink, a soft silky pink blackness around his face, covering even his nostrils. Always the blackness. Inside everything became blackness, even the white Bible and Teddy, even his white suit. Not me! (Ellison, *Juneteenth* 143)

Discussing this antiphonal exchange can lead students back to questions about the invisible protagonist's closing "statement in the form of a question" (Spaulding 498). Who is Ellison speaking to, about, and perhaps for in his second novel? What does the antiphonal structure of exchange and the idiomatic expression of Reverend Hickman in sermonic idiom illuminate, and who does it implicate in the assumed Blackness of the American "you"?

When reaching the "middle," the section of the novel detailing the Juneteenth revival, Nadel's reading of Bliss/Sunraider as "not only Christ but also America, both sacrificial spirit and the historical embodiment of democracy" will help the class ponder what kind of work Ellison's inclusion of a delayed celebration of African American emancipation performs in the novel (402). What does it mean that Bliss is simultaneously the resurrected and on his deathbed? What does this positioning say about Ellison's attitude toward American racial politics? Also, you might redirect students to the motif of mystery as they encounter the white, redheaded woman who interrupts the revival and claims Bliss as her child. Her surreal disruption of the revival stirs Bliss's desire to forsake and deny his relationship to Hickman, rejecting a Black religious tradition and history, and

170 ELLISON'S "UNFINISHED" PROJECT

potentially redemption. How does the fragmentary nature of Bliss's memory and his refusal to go "Back to that? No!" encapsulate American cultural memory surrounding its history of enslavement; deep, abiding connection to Blackness; and refusal and perhaps terror at having to address its failed democratic promises (Ellison, *Juneteenth* 143)?

The novel's "end," the chapters following the revival, requires interrogating what mysteries, if any, are resolved. Turning to discuss the power and alluring mystery of the image as represented through Bliss's desire to see a movie can help begin that journey. Before Hickman takes Bliss to see a film, Bliss confesses wanting "to leave the place unentered, even if it has a steeple higher than any church in the world, leave it, pass it ever by, rather than see it once, then never enter it again—with all the countless unseen episodes to remain a mystery and like my mother flown forever. But I could not say it, nor could I refuse it; for no language existed between child and man" (235). From these episodes, what do we learn about his identity as Mr. Movie Man? What is this interim identity? His introduction to whiteness and white power? How does it bridge Bliss with Sunraider? How does the image stand up against the word as wielded by Hickman?[14]

Hickman's internal revelation of how Bliss came into his care returns the class to the question of kinship, of relatives versus ancestors. What is significant about the fact that Hickman, through a storied internal dialogue where he refers to himself in second person, relays what he knows of Bliss/Sunraider's familial history to readers and yet refuses to divulge this information directly to the child and the man? What does it mean that even as Sunraider is turning toward death, neither character can make sense of their connection and history? Musing upon the moment Bliss's mother demands he raise the boy, Hickman exclaims:

> Ha! Hickman, you had wanted a life for a life and the relief of drowning your humiliation and grief in blood, and now this flawed-hearted woman was offering you two lives—your own, and his young life to train. Here was a chance to prove that there was something in this world stronger than all their ignorant superstition about blood and ghosts. [. . .] Maybe the baby *could* redeem her and me my failure of revenge and my softness of heart, and help us all (was it here, Hickman, that you began to dream?).   (311)

This passage can lead students to reflect metaphorically on Ellison's relationship to writing, his staunch individualism, and his selection of ancestors as an attempt to "redeem" the American canon. Does the fact that Ellison was unable to finish his second novel suggest he was met with the same betrayal as Hickman? Does his ability to form episodes instead of a cohesive whole reflect the reality of Ellison's relationship to writing instead of his dream?

The dreamlike and delirious state of Sunraider in chapter 16 interestingly calls to mind Invisible Man's movement through a fragmentated series of events in the prologue while under the influence of marijuana. At one point in his dream, after riding atop a speeding train and jumping off to escape some unknown Black figures that charge toward him with a gun, Sunraider encounters two foxes in an idyllic wooded area and thinks, "All this I've known, [. . .] but had forgotten. . . . Then in the sudden hush, accented by a pheasant's cry, he felt as though no trains nor town nor sermons existed. He was at peace. Here was no need to escape nor search for Eden, nor need to solve his mystery. But again he moved, somehow compelled to go ahead" (330). This Edenic state, however, is followed by Sunraider noticing a plane writing in the sky:

> N___s
> Stay
> Away
> From
> The Polls   (330)

Here, when attempting to interpret this jarring break in formal structure, we discussed how even in this dreamlike state the reader is faced with the racist politics of 1955 and, considering ongoing efforts to undermine voting rights, the present. Both Hickman and Sunraider grapple with compelling pressure of history and redemption, both individual and collective.

Again, although I did not teach from *Three Days* in this particular iteration, I believe mentioning the Cadillac-burning scene that was excised from *Juneteenth* would be extremely useful in helping students understand the surreal and symbolic ending. Published as an excerpt in 1973, "Cadillac Flambé" is written in the first-person perspective of white male journalist Welborn McIntyre and offers further opportunity to discuss the novel as episode, contemplate Ellison's use of point of view, and perhaps "identify the revolutionary political conviction that both animates Ellison's insistence on a 'division of labor' between art and activism and defines his commitment to civil rights and American democracy" (Mills 150). How does the inclusion or exclusion of the scene impact the novel's development? or our understanding of Ellison's individual politics?

To close the novel, a return to Fanny Ellison's question—"Does it have a beginning, middle, and end?"—and Sherazi's argument about the novel's construction as "unbound" instead of unfinished leads to a revision of the question: Does it *need* a beginning, middle, and end? What do we do with an "unbound" novel?

There is an infinite, dare I say boundless, number of ways to teach *Juneteenth*. It is possible to teach it without including *Invisible Man* by focusing on method and archive and having students engage with *Three Days before the Shooting . . .*, independent chapters published in journals and periodicals, and his published letters. Although I did not cover this here, my students and I also spent a good deal of the class discussing issues of gender and sexuality across Ellison's work— from *Invisible Man* to his short stories, essays, and *Juneteenth*. If my own foray into teaching it is any indication, you can expect a much richer, more nuanced understanding of *Juneteenth* when placing it in conversation with his larger body of work. May our future examinations carry the spirit of its mystery and process

172   ELLISON'S "UNFINISHED" PROJECT

and hopefully continually compel us to reflect critically on Ellison's vision of literature, American democracy, and individualism.


NOTES

I gratefully acknowledge and thank the students who greatly contributed to this essay through their active and eager engagement with Ellison's work, even after the COVID-19 pandemic derailed our in-person sessions. Thank you to Ted Mason; Jene Schoenfeld; Kenyon's English department, for encouraging me to undertake this fruitful endeavor; my numerous writing groups that carried me over; Thea Autry, who shared this opportunity with me; and Tracy Floreani, for generous editing.

1. This essay cites the 1999 edition.

2. It can be useful to pair the short entries from Sundquist's text with longer contextual and critical readings. For example, when we arrived at the moment of Invisible Man's journey from the South to the North, we read the short entries on the Great Migration as well as several on vernacular culture alongside excerpts from Farah Jasmine Griffin's *"Who Set You Flowin'?"*

3. "And behind it all lies a mystery: how did this chosen child become the man who would deny everything to achieve his goals?"

4. Students may also be interested in the technological loss Ellison suffered when transferring work to an IBM computer. See the October 1988 note in "Chronology of Composition" (Ellison, *Three Days* xiv).

5. See Bradley; Harriss, "One Blues"; Rampersad.

6. The longer quotation proposes that the condition of Black life in Harlem requires "new definitions for terms like *primitive* and *modern, ethical* and *unethical, moral* and *immoral, patriotism* and *treason, tragedy* and *comedy, sanity* and *insanity*" (Ellison, *Collected Essays* 323). It is helpful to ask students why the condition of Black life requires this and what those new definitions might be.

7. See Ellison, *Collected Essays* 185–86.

8. See Nadel.

9. See Alison 336–37.

10. Some contexts to consider include the culture wars, integration, the Cold War, the legacy of *Brown v. Board of Education*, multiculturalism, affirmative action, the Black Power and Black Arts movements, Ronald Reagan, the rise of film, and so on. Also see Harriss, "One Blues."

11. See also p. 1000.

12. See Bradley 140–44.

13. See Sherazi, who offers a comprehensive reading of the ways Severen reflects the complicated development of Ellison's narrative, characters, and political idiosyncrasies.

14. See Nadel 402–03.

# An Episodic Writing-as-Inquiry Approach to *Three Days before the Shooting . . .*

## Tracy Floreani

*Three Days before the Shooting . . .* is admittedly a daunting volume to include in any class. When people do attempt to teach Ralph Ellison's second, unfinished novel, they might opt for *Juneteenth* because of its recognizably contained form and relative coherence as a narrative. I would argue that, despite the intimidating stature of the 1,100-plus-page, inches-thick volume that is *Three Days*, an upper-level undergraduate or graduate seminar focused on Ellison can benefit much by its inclusion on the reading list, depending on the goal for including the second novel. If one wants to focus on understanding Ellison as a writer in conjunction with the story on its own terms, the more raw and incomplete nature of *Three Days* proves a revealing and intriguing study. The instructor must be willing, however, to allow the approach to the book to be as incomplete, fragmented, episodic, and searching as the text itself. This approach includes creating opportunities for student choice and collaboration along with a scaffolded series of reading and writing assignments that may ultimately develop students' comfort with the book and strengthen their understanding of the author's imaginative writing process.

## The Struggle Is Real

Those of us who regularly teach academic-writing-focused courses often emphasize writing as process, as a mode of thinking or inquiry or discovery as much as a means of showcasing acquired knowledge or interpretive skills. It seems odd, then, that when we teach texts by famous writers in literature courses, we typically use only their completed works as models for writing or as sources for analysis. Some reprints might have a page or two of draft manuscript to look at in comparison to the published version. Some students might be lucky enough to have access to good literary archives that take them a bit deeper into the process. On the whole, though, when we teach process in relation to famous writers it is usually through the biographical lens and as process toward the culmination of "infallible genius" (as Keyana Parks terms it in the previous essay). Focusing on story and process simultaneously is a challenging but rich approach that appeals both to students with a literary analysis focus and to those on a creative-writing track, who typically study and are supposed to learn from only fully revised, complete, published models of writing.

Most instructors will opt for either *Juneteenth* or *Three Days*—seldom (never?) both in one course. Indeed, *Juneteenth* captures the essence of the core narrative Ellison envisioned for his complex, epic second novel. Choosing *Three Days* provides similar possibilities in the classroom but offers another angle for those

174 WRITING-AS-INQUIRY APPROACH

who wish to focus on process and archive, as well. Not an easy book in terms of a cover-to-cover reading experience, its gift is as a sort of portable archive. I would argue that it is not a book intended only for scholars or advanced graduate students but a volume that we should invite more students to experience.[1] The collection of bits and pieces that stymied the writer and his posthumous editor John Callahan allows students to deeply understand the episodic nature of Ellison's writing process and to simultaneously grapple and empathize with the intellectual and artistic challenges he was attempting to work out. Maybe more than any other famous writer, Ellison could understand students' own struggles as writers—as they might put it, how "the struggle is real."

## *Reading Episodically*

Because Ellison's approach to writing was heavily episodic, a way to help students engage with this volume is to encourage them to approach it episodically, too, both in how they read within the book and how they write about it. For the instructor's own preparation, I recommend reading or rereading Cheryl Alison's essay "Writing Underground" (described in the previous essay) and Timothy Parrish's essay "Ralph Ellison's *Three Days*: The Aesthetics of Political Change," which provides really helpful insights into the novel's goals and history as well as ways to think about how to embrace the second novel for its incompleteness— not in spite of it. Melanie Masterton Sherazi's article "The Posthumous Text and Its Archive: Toward an Ecstatic Reading of Ralph Ellison's Unbound Novel" also offers a useful overview and reframing of perspective that encourages readers to consider the pieces of writing as "unbound" rather than "unfinished." (Instructors may want to share these pieces of criticism with students further into their study of the book, too.) To set some groundwork for students' reading, it helps to delineate the book's overall narrative structure—how Welborn McIntyre's narrative voice frames the mystery of Sunraider/Bliss and Hickman— and to offer brief character sketches to provide a very basic anchoring synopsis along these lines: McIntyre is a reporter in Washington, DC, whose perspective we follow as he tries to understand the assassination attempt on the racist United States senator Adam Sunraider. When an African American man called Hickman shows up at Sunraider's hospital, the mystery deepens. The story weaves in and out of McIntyre's, Hickman's, and Sunraider's (unconscious) perspectives, moving back and forth from present to various past scenes—and through various settings in the United States—as we learn more and more detail about Sunraider's abandonment as a child of unknown racial origin (then known by the name Bliss), taken in as a child-preacher protégé of Hickman. All other scenes and minor characters in the book revolve around the constellation of these core characters and the mystery of who Sunraider really is and who wants to kill him.

With the essentials of the story in place, the focus can then reorient toward working to understand the story, thinking of it as an existing narrative, but one that is still evolving. Students should not expect definitive answers to some of their questions and confusions. In approaching a text that is inherently in progress, encourage them to try to read with an enjoyment of a behind-the-scenes view, or for experiences of the story more than mastery of it. A helpful analogy might be one of watching uncut and unedited footage for a film that is still being completed. We get to look over the shoulder of the cinematographer as it is being filmed and imaginatively consider what it might look like when it all comes together. (The scenes in which Bliss/Sunraider experiences and makes films reinforce this analogy and also highlight Ellison's interest in both visual culture and the potential of film for delivering national narratives.) Callahan and Adam Bradley's introduction to the *Three Days* volume is probably sufficient for establishing students' understanding of how Ellison's process centered on episode, scene, key concepts, and character voice as much as on (sometimes even taking precedence over) the narrative arc. Another useful resource for students in the early days of working with the novel is the twenty-eight-minute documentary piece "USA: The Novel—Ralph Ellison on Work in Progress 1966," produced by National Educational Television and available through the Oklahoma Historical Society Film and Video Archives channel on *YouTube*. I recommend having students watch it at home as an overview of Ellison's own views on the book in progress, with an ear toward how he talks about "incidents" that link together a whole narrative, how the novelist might engage with the project of capturing the national character, and how he reads the voices of Hickman and Bliss.[2] For those who would like students to explore more ancillary texts on Ellison's process after they have studied *Invisible Man* and as they read *Three Days*, portions of Bradley's *Ralph Ellison in Progress* prove useful, as well as some select letters in which Ellison writes to others about his ideas for the book.[3]

I prefer not to delay too long with setup before their diving into reading *Three Days*, offering just enough preparation to orient students on what to expect and whet their appetites. I schedule reading assignments from the volume in short segments, then set the reading on pause periodically so that we can reread pieces together, stopping to dwell on details. This way of reading mimics Ellison's own tendency to return to "incidents" repeatedly, to attend to them with detail and precision. One can assign segments out of sequence, if preferred, as an entry point and as a means of signaling that the volume need not be read beginning to end and tackled as a whole—right away or maybe even at all. Beginning with one or two of the segments that were published as stand-alone pieces (beginning on p. 1003 at the back of the volume) works well as an orientation to new characters and approaches, to divorce students from Invisible Man as the only protagonist through whom Ellison's vision is to be understood. My preferred method, however, is to begin with the prologue and about half of book 1 (the McIntyre segment) as a way of trying to approach the volume as an inchoate novel rather than as short fiction, but either approach can work. An episodic approach helps students to slow down the way they are attempting to process the reading and to handle the kind of breathless quality with which the narrative rolls from

176 WRITING-AS-INQUIRY APPROACH

one detail-dense scene to another, from one layered memory or story-within-a-story to the next (especially in book 2). Reading long segments of the narrative can be both mesmerizing and exhausting, so pausing to dwell in detail can also facilitate students' understanding of the whole. In this I go against Callahan's self-admonition in his essay that begins the *Invisible Man* section of this volume, in which he considers his misguided attempts to explicate individual scenes in *Invisible Man* rather than understand them as pieces of a larger picaresque whole. For *Three Days*, because the whole is not yet extant, the explication of scenes, I demonstrate later in this essay, can help students to understand the potential direction of the massive collection of drafts and pieces. That said, since the picaresque tradition relies on loosely connected episodes, one can certainly invoke the picaresque element of the first novel as a way of helping students make sense of *Three Days* as a sort of picaresque, too.

Regardless of how the reading assignments are sequenced, I encourage students to call on their understanding of *Invisible Man* occasionally, to reflect on what they've come to understand about Ellison as a writer, but also not to rely too heavily on a direct point of comparison between the two books (at least not yet), so as not to slip into thinking about *Three Days* as a failed sequel to the famous first novel. Instead, I encourage them to think of their understanding of the first novel as simply informing their reading of *Three Days*, enlightened as they have become about Ellison's overarching intellectual and artistic interests. In any case, the reading assignments and some subsequent analysis via discussion should occur before students write anything formal for this unit. This allows them to get a sense of the narrative frame through McIntyre's eyes and the central Sunraider/Bliss and Hickman characters and story elements.

The classroom conversations in the early stages might run along broader lines as a way to ground the sprawling text: how the outsider narrator fits within the Western tradition of similar narrative structures (*The Great Gatsby*, *The Heart of Darkness*), what that narrator's perspective does to mediate the Sunraider/Hickman story and the audience's perceptions of those characters, how McIntyre's own story contains implicit commentary on interracial and gendered relationships, how the narrative in these sections establishes conflict and the pacing of the plot, and so on. With some grounding in the intended narrative, students can soon begin to delve together into specific scenes and object lessons and eventually link those to the broader thematic concerns. This delving might first take the form of casual, small-group explorations of specific scenes or symbols they find intriguing, perhaps with informal, one-page written follow-ups to help students process ideas further and condition their interpretive eye as they read over the next few weeks more deeply into book 1, and later book 2 and "Bliss's Birth." Throughout the reading, it is helpful to remind them to embrace the incompleteness of the whole rather than get frustrated by it, to consider it akin to an ongoing epic.[4] Parrish's description of the multiple, incomplete versions of the scenes the book comprises as analogous to the multiple versions of a song that a performer might record or perform over the course of a career proves instructive in this regard, too, as does his thinking of the book as an "unending" story because it dwells within the "unending American present" ("Ralph Ellison's *Three Days*" 216).

Once students have a sense of the storylines and characters, I model a more formalized analysis using one specific episode. By zeroing in on one or two symbolic objects, actions, or scenes as a focus for these first formalistic close readings, students will come to see how the specific elements at work within a scene allow it to function as a microcosmic container of complex ideas. Soon they will feel more comfortable delving into writing about some of the possible symbolic connotations elsewhere in the volume. One way to help them feel comfortable with this approach is to again call on their familiarity with *Invisible Man*. After all, as Parrish argues, "there is a sense that regardless of the form in which he was writing [. . . Ellison] was always telling a version of the same story" ("Ralph Ellison's *Three Days*" 194). Start with a quick, conversational object lesson exploration of, for example, the connotations of Invisible Man's briefcase. The presumption is that Ellison's treatment of material signifiers is one of the features of his creative expression and that "everything he wrote reflects on everything else he wrote" (Parrish 195). A similar object lesson can then be applied to the unfinished novel.

The famous "Cadillac Flambé" scene works well for the modeling exercise, since the connotations of the Cadillac as an icon of midcentury American success are clear to students, as are the destructive gestures and location at which LeeWillie Minifees burns the car. This type of close reading may seem old-school to instructors who tend to focus more on theoretical approaches, but close reading helps students dig into deep connotations within the figurative language that are key to a precise—one might say perfectionistic—writer like Ellison. They will have sometimes read past details in their first encounters with the long volume, so this exercise encourages them to slow down through rereading and consider how complete some of the scenes actually were in the pieces of the larger structure Ellison was assembling. Furthermore, through the details of the symbolic, students may feel more comfortable trying to access the larger cultural theories and questions posited within the prose. That is, by working with the story through an inductive mode, students can become more comfortable tackling and theorizing about the inchoate novel as a whole, about the extent to which the novel-in-progress articulates an understanding of "the nation whose abiding and shifting identity [Ellison] was so intent upon rendering in fiction" (Callahan and Bradley xxvii).

I would argue that once students understand Ellison's compositional approach and have worked with some of these episodes individually, they can engage in a similar process alongside the author as they attempt to assemble pieces of the larger narrative's purpose for themselves. Because the book in its fragmented form verges into postmodernism in many of its gestures (though Ellison would not likely describe his writing as postmodern), the unfinished book's implicit invitation to readers to engage in making meaning seems quite appropriate.

178    WRITING-AS-INQUIRY APPROACH

Logically, *Three Days* belongs toward the end of an Ellison-focused course, and while students will likely have studied by then a lot of contextual materials and various works by Ellison, I discourage them from buckling under the pressure of having to synthesize all they have studied into some kind of massive, culminating, research-based seminar paper on *Three Days*; rather, I encourage them to consider how all their study of Ellison up to this point informs their thinking and reading within the volume and allows them to continue in a mode of inquiry as a means of further deepening their study in progress, in an echo of Ellison's work in progress.

## *Writing Episodically and Inquisitively*

The rest of this essay walks through an approach that focuses on a scaffolded sequence of shorter written assignments requiring students not to show mastery of the subject but to use writing as an inquisitive tool. Developing a potential model based on my own experiences teaching the book, I detail below some possibilities for guiding students through a series of focused micro-essays over several weeks and then integrating those smaller pieces into a larger essay that allows them, through a gradual, episodic method, to successfully grapple with the larger narrative.

This kind of detailed explication of scenes or symbols happens pretty naturally within class discussions, but, again, I find it helpful for them to think about how to move through reading, discussion, sketching ideas in writing, and then building intentionally toward more sophisticated analytical writing by means of process writing itself. This is inquiry-based writing, writing used as an instrument for thinking.[5] Some students do this on their own as part of their note-taking or journaling, but by requiring it as part of the course assignment structure, my intent is not to create busywork or undermine their existing abilities to write sophisticated term papers but to help them find a "way in" that is low stakes so that they can continue to develop their understanding of Ellison's craft and intellectual views before trying to develop a higher-stakes term paper about a story that seems to have defied, at times, its creator's own full understanding. I want them to use the page to carefully document their thinking and take interpretive risks before attempting a full formal analysis. Of course, these pieces require an engaged conversation on the part of the instructor, too, who brings a level of expertise to bear on their inquiries. In my experience, the focused interpretation required by these short writings affords the students a lot of opportunity for original thought that, I would argue, can even lead to the instructor learning more about the book that many of us are still working to fully understand, and setting aside one's own sense of needing complete mastery of a text before teaching it can make space for some really rich conversations in decentered, collaborative learning. Furthermore, allowing students to follow the details that they find most intriguing, mysterious, or compelling typically sets them up for successful interpretations, and the

Tracy Floreani    179

discursive feedback loop built into the scaffolded assignment structure ultimately leads to higher-quality term papers at the end of the unit. In short, requiring, and the instructor responding to, shorter pieces in this mode is a worthwhile expenditure of energy for both students and instructor.

I have students start writing one short, focused piece each week after they have gotten enough sense of the work through their reading. (I begin requiring writings when they are about halfway through book 1.) This allows them to start documenting some of their ideas from their reading and discussions, and the exploratory writing begins to push their subsequent reading to become deeper and more attentive. I have used this type of approach—short, focused, more-frequent writings that build into something bigger—in literature classes for several years now. It goes against much of what students have been taught to do in literature papers, and they find the exercise both challenging and liberating. I've called these assignments various things, such as "micro-essays" or "object lessons." To set up the prompt, explain not just the what and how but also the why of the assignment and put in writing the goals and expectations of writing-as-inquiry versus writing-as-argument. To encourage their risk-taking, also articulate the grading approach in ways that will alleviate their impulse to write theme-focused or thesis-driven analysis. I tell them I will look for nothing more than a clear through line in the essay, which should be no more than two pages and should contain deep, detailed, and thoughtful exploration of the symbolic element; some summary or a brief attempt to link the specific piece to the larger ideas in the story; and clear, well-edited writing (with a reminder that "exploratory" does not mean unedited, first-brain-dump writing). I require that they choose just one very specific element from anywhere in the book, as long as it's not an object we already analyzed together (e.g., the Cadillac): an object, an animal, an action, a minor character, a specific setting, a specific scene or piece of a scene, the text of a speech, a dream sequence. Then I ask them to write a really detailed reading of that element in terms of symbolic potential, to dig in and explore all the possible ways of interpreting that element—even if an interpretation seems silly—and explore as precisely and thoroughly as possible the nuances of the language Ellison uses to depict whatever it is they have chosen to focus on. Another way in is to use inquiry in a literal sense by having each student develop a question—and then attempt to answer that question—about the details they are interested in: What does that floating head in the jar represent? What does it mean that Bliss thinks his mother is the actress Mary Pickford? Why is there a coffin in the Jessie Rockmore scene?

They will write several of these short pieces, and they need not be related to one another in any way. Students might want to start with one that feels safe and clearly manageable in terms of symbolism (e.g., the Lincoln Memorial) and use another micro-essay to explore a detail that surprises and confounds them, such as the floating head preserved in a jar or McIntyre's uncontrollable laughter (Ellison, *Three Days* 188, 135). What is most important in the instructor's marking of these short writings is not how they contribute to the course grade but some

180 WRITING-AS-INQUIRY APPROACH

conversations about the ideas, which interpretations succeed, which need work, which might be built upon further in future. Ultimately, they will be using these short, individual pieces in an inductive mode toward a larger analysis.

Alternatively, some instructors and students might have a natural inclination toward the deductive. I try to model both approaches, to accommodate the various styles of thinking and approaching writing. For instance, one of my students picked up pretty quickly on how frequently birds—real, metaphorical, folkloric—are mentioned in the book (over two hundred times).[6] Admittedly, I had noticed a few references to birds but hadn't given them much thought. After the student mentioned their observation about birds to the class, several of them took the importance of birds as a given, started actively looking for birds, worked at noticing them with more intention while reading, and considered the functions of these birds within various scenes and differing or parallel connotations of the birds (e.g., buzzards versus doves). The result for a few of the students was to choose to write their exploratory essays on specific scenes in which birds feature, to just hang out with the flock for a bit and see where it led them. Other larger motifs that could instigate detailed exploration are father figures; public speechmaking; the setting of Washington, DC; scenes of chaos or groups of people in disorder; or representations of the unconscious mind.[7]

Once students have written and received feedback on these short inquiries, they simply need to find ways to link those scenes. I tend to hold off on giving them a prompt for the larger term paper (though I do let them know it will be coming) so that they can focus on the details of the moment and not worry yet about what the larger analysis will look like. There are various approaches to helping them sit down with the pieces and assemble a whole, whether through one-on-one conversations or in peer-group form.

Here is an example of working inductively with the short pieces toward a larger analysis: Say a student wrote a detailed explication of the nun in drag at the jazz club (in the McIntyre section, bk. 1, ch. 10), one about the raucous scene at Jessie Rockmore's (bk. 1, ch. 12), and one about the first time Bliss sees the tiny coffin he is to use in his resurrection act (bk. 2, 249–53). Each scene is interesting in its own right, has its place in the narrative, and can be threaded together through a couple of different motifs, such as violence and chaos, or resurrection and revelation, or the idea of costuming and performance.[8] Maybe only two of these ultimately work well together, so they might drop one—the scene at the jazz club—and choose another scene or detail that fits with the motif they are now seeing more clearly as one of interest to them, resurrection and revelation. They can then build on this idea by writing one or two more short analyses of scenes that can come together for a whole essay on this topic. This kind of exercise eventually could also be used to bridge texts, such as a comparative analysis of the aging exotic dancer at Rockmore's and the dancer in the "battle royal" scene in *Invisible Man*, or of specific depictions of Bliss Proteus Rinehart and Bliss/Sunraider, examining carefully what these paired characters seem to say about Ellison's ideas on performance and power.

Another student might be particularly interested in a specific character, like Laura, or McIntyre, or young Bliss/Sunraider as a filmmaker. So they might have written in detail about scenes that specifically feature a character and can later examine what motifs or thematics link them—perhaps the ideas of playing witness for McIntyre, or the pressures of race, family, and romance for Laura. This kind of isolation of scenes, zooming in and zooming out, can ultimately reveal more about these characters. The next step would be to then apply their deepened understanding of the character to their larger function within the story-in-the-making. What is their literal function within the story? What is their allegorical function? How might they represent something about race? about the nation?

To help students ground their larger analyses, I like to use one quotation that captures the big idea and pose it as a question that they must attempt to answer with the pieces they have already written. Some examples:

> How do these scenes or elements contribute to Ellison's goal of "rendering" the "abiding and shifting identity" of the United States? (Callahan and Bradley xxvii)
> How do these scenes "identif[y] and explore the paradoxes and contradictions" inherent in American national identity? (Parrish, "Ralph Ellison's *Three Days*" 198)
> How do these scenes illustrate Ellison's idea that "the evasion of identity is another characteristically American problem"? (*Selected Letters* 360)
> How do these work toward fulfilling Ellison's idea for the provisional title, *USA: The Novel*?

Were one of these questions offered as prompt at the beginning of studying *Three Days*, and were it framed in terms of how "the novel" accomplishes the idea in question, the assignment might be overwhelming. However, asking students to imaginatively work alongside Ellison, getting lost in details and "incidents," they grow more comfortable with his writing process and, consequently, come to perceive the (provisional) whole composed of these parts.

NOTES

1. When I first taught *Three Days*, the interdisciplinary seminar class comprised twelve juniors and seniors, only four of whom were English majors or minors. They all managed the text quite well with the method I lay out in this essay.

2. In the footage from 1966, Ellison mentions wanting to publish the book within the next year. Whether or not the instructor wants to include in-depth content about the 1967 house fire that set back the novel's progress is a matter of choice—it's certainly an incident that students are curious about. I tend to talk about it if students are interested but play down its role, as I am not a fan of psychoanalyzing authors, and people tend to invest a lot in the incident in ways that draw attention away from the novel's ultimate aim.

## 182 WRITING-AS-INQUIRY APPROACH

3. For example, from the *Selected Letters*, the letter to Morteza Sprague, 19 May 1954 (360); the Sept. 1954 "Statement of Plan" letter with the original overview for the novel that Ellison submitted as part of an application to the Guggenheim Foundation (371–72); and the letter to Albert Murray updating him on progress and characters, dated 2 April 1960 (583–84).

4. Book 1 is much easier for students to read because of its clearly marked chapters, so spending time getting situated in book 1 is helpful preparation for the stream-of-consciousness thrill ride of book 2 (which Marc Conner sees in kinship with James Joyce's *Ulysses*). For analyses of the second novel in terms of the Western canon, see the essays by Sundquist, Conner, and Parrish in *The New Territory* (Conner and Morel).

5. Most published work on inquiry-based writing methods is geared toward first-year composition and creative-writing pedagogy; little has been written on applying that technique within literature analysis, but those unfamiliar with writing-as-inquiry concepts that are common in composition studies can easily find sources through academic-database searches.

6. The e-book version of *Three Days* is quite helpful to students when they start writing, since they can easily search for and locate scenes and identify motifs in the large volume.

7. On the father-figure motif, see Hill, "Politics." On this type of assignment, however, I typically encourage students to work out their own ideas on the motifs they notice before integrating secondary source research.

8. On violence and chaos, see the editors' note to "McIntyre at Jessie Rockmore's" (*Three Days* 927–28).

# NOTES ON CONTRIBUTORS

**Clark Barwick** is teaching professor of communication and associate director of the Faculty Academy on Excellence in Teaching (FACET) at Indiana University, Bloomington. He has published widely on African American literature and the pedagogies of race, and he is a two-time recipient of the IU Trustees Teaching Award.

**Sterling Lecater Bland, Jr.,** is professor in the departments of English, Africana studies, and American studies at Rutgers University, Newark. His teaching and research interests include nineteenth-century American literature, Black literature and culture, narrative theory, and jazz studies. His most recent book is *In the Shadow of Invisibility: Ralph Ellison and the Promise of American Democracy* (2023). He is the author or editor of *Voices of the Fugitives: Runaway Slave Stories and Their Fictions of Self-Creation* (2000); *Understanding Nineteenth-Century Slave Narratives* (2016); "Narration on the Lower Frequencies in Ralph Ellison's *Invisible Man*," which appears in *Narrative, Race, and Ethnicity in the United States*; and "Aesthetics of Democracy," which appears in *Ralph Ellison in Context*. Most recently, his essays have appeared in the journals *MELUS*, *American Studies*, and *South Atlantic Review*.

**J. J. Butts** is professor of English at Simpson College and teaches courses on race and ethnicity in American literature and film. He is the author of *Dark Mirror: African Americans and the Federal Writers' Project* (2021) and has published several essays exploring African American narratives and the development of welfare state liberalism.

**Keith Byerman** is professor of English at Indiana State University, where he teaches courses in African American literature and culture, Southern literature, gender studies, and folklore. His research is primarily in modern and contemporary African American writing, and he has published seven books on the subject, including *Seizing the Word: History, Art, and Self in the Work of W. E. B. Du Bois* (2010), *Remembering the Past in Contemporary African American Fiction* (2005), *The Art and Life of Clarence Major* (2016), and two volumes on the writer John Edgar Wideman.

**John F. Callahan** is the Odell Professor of Humanities at Lewis and Clark College. He has been the editor or author of numerous volumes related to African American and twentieth-century literature. As Ralph Ellison's literary executor, Callahan worked as the primary editor of the posthumously released Ellison novel *Juneteenth* (1999) and of *The Selected Letters of Ralph Ellison* (2019).

**Paul Devlin** is the editor of *Ralph Ellison in Context* (2021), among other books, and coeditor of *Albert Murray: Collected Essays and Memoirs* (2016) and *Albert Murray: Collected Novels and Poems* (2018). He is associate professor of English at the United States Merchant Marine Academy and the book review editor for the journal *African American Review*.

**Martha Greene Eads** serves as professor of English at Eastern Mennonite University. She previously taught at the North Carolina Correctional Center for Women and at Valparaiso University. Her most recent work explores intersections of theology and trauma studies in contemporary drama and fiction. Her essays have appeared in *Appalachian*

184 NOTES ON CONTRIBUTORS

*Journal, Christianity and Literature, The Cresset, Modern Drama, The Southern Quarterly*, and *Theology*, as well as in *Approaches to Teaching Virginia Woolf's Mrs. Dalloway* (2009).

**Tracy Floreani** is the author of *Fifties Ethnicities: The Ethnic Novel and Mass Culture at Midcentury* (2013). She has written several book chapters on Ralph Ellison and on Fanny McConnell Ellison and is completing a biography of Fanny. In 2014 she hosted a national symposium in honor of Ralph Ellison's centenary in his hometown of Oklahoma City. She coedited *The Ralph Ellison Issue* (2015), a special issue of *American Studies (AMSJ)* that evolved from the symposium. A specialist in multiethnic American literature, she has held multiple leadership positions in the Society for the Study of the Multiethnic Literature of the US (MELUS). She currently teaches at Oklahoma City University, where she also directs much of the university's public humanities programming.

**Barbara Foley** is distinguished professor emerita of English at Rutgers University, Newark. She has published widely in the fields of Marxist theory, African American literature, and the literature of the left and is the author of six books, including *Radical Representations: Politics and Form in U.S. Proletarian Fiction, 1929–1941* (1993), *Spectres of 1919: Class and Nation in the Making of the New Negro* (2003), *Wrestling with the Left: The Making of Ralph Ellison's* Invisible Man (2010), and *Jean Toomer: Race, Repression, and Revolution* (2014). She is the former president of the Radical Caucus of the Modern Language Association and is currently vice president of the Marxist journal *Science and Society*, where she serves on the manuscript committee and the editorial board.

**Alvin J. Henry** is associate professor of Asian American studies at San Diego State University and founding director of SDSU's Asian American studies program. He is also launching a career bridge program for humanities and social science majors. He is a specialist in queer of color critique and Asian American and African American studies and is the author of *Black Queer Flesh: Rejecting Subjectivity in the African American Novel* (2020).

**Jake Johnson** is assistant professor of musicology at the University of Oklahoma. He is the author of *Mormons, Musical Theater, and Belonging in America* (2019) and *Lying in the Middle: Musical Theater and Belief at the Heart of America* (2021) and is editor of *The Possibility Machine: Music and Myth in Las Vegas* (2023). He also keeps a robust vocal coaching studio and remains in demand throughout the country as a recital partner, collaborative pianist, and musical director.

**Sherry Johnson** tells stories that engage memory and Black writing between Canada and the United States. She is a writer, researcher, and scholar of literature, particularly at the intersection of Black women's lives and their writing, critical cultural studies, and the digital humanities. An associate professor and graduate program administrator, she teaches courses in African American literature, multicultural American literature, neo–slave narratives, and critical approaches to literary study.

**Aimée Myers** is associate professor of literacy and learning at Texas Woman's University. She has taught courses in the Departments of Teacher Education, Multicultural Women's and Gender Studies, and English, Speech, and Foreign Languages. Her research focuses on culturally responsive and sustaining practices, and her current project with

## NOTES ON CONTRIBUTORS 185

refugee and immigrant high school students supports Chicana feminist *testimonio* pedagogy. Her work has been presented internationally and nationally, most recently at the International Conference on Urban Education, the National Council of Teachers of English, and the National Association of Multicultural Educators. She previously worked as a secondary English teacher and developed English curriculum and research-based classroom instruction resources for the K20 Center for Educational and Community Renewal.

**Keyana Parks** is assistant professor of English at the University of Massachusetts, Boston. Her research and teaching interests include twentieth- and twenty-first-century African American literature, humor, satire, and Black women's writing and feminism. Her work appears in *Greater Atlanta: Black Satire after Obama*, forthcoming from the University Press of Mississippi, and in *Post45 Contemporaries*. She is currently working on a manuscript entitled "The Real Absurd: Black Women Writers and the Satiric Mode."

**Agnieszka Tuszynska** is associate professor of English at Queensborough Community College, City University of New York, where she teaches courses in African American literature and writing. She has also taught incarcerated students, volunteering for college-level education programs in prisons in Illinois and New York since 2009. Her research focuses on African American literature of the Jim Crow era and the Harlem Renaissance, with special focus on recovering overlooked or forgotten writing and writers. Her work has appeared in *MELUS*, *English Language Notes*, *CLA Journal*, and *Dialogues in Social Justice*. She is currently working on a critical biography of the African American writer Willard Motley, author of the best-selling 1947 novel *Knock on Any Door*.

**Kirin Wachter-Grene** is assistant professor of liberal arts at the School of the Art Institute of Chicago. She serves on the editorial board of *The Black Scholar* and is the guest editor of the journal's fiftieth anniversary issue, *At the Limits of Desire: Black Radical Pleasure*, and the double follow-up issue *Edgeplay: Black Radical Pleasure II*. Her work has appeared in *African American Review*, *The Black Scholar*, *Callaloo*, *Feminist Formations*, and *Legacy*, as well as various edited collections, and is forthcoming in *Social Text*, *Palimpsest*, *Cultural Critique*, and *Post45*. Her monograph *Black Kenosis: The Erotic Undoing of African American Literature* is forthcoming from Fordham University Press.

# SURVEY PARTICIPANTS

Tiffany Boyd Adams, *Independent Scholar*
Clark Barwick, *Indiana University, Bloomington*
Sterling Lecater Bland, Jr., *Rutgers University, Newark*
J. J. Butts, *Simpson College*
Matthew Calihman, *Missouri State University*
Jualynne E. Dodson, *Michigan State University*
Martha Greene Eads, *Eastern Mennonite University*
Niza Fabre, *Ramapo College*
Barbara Foley, *Rutgers University, Newark*
Alvin J. Henry, *San Diego State University*
A Yẹmisi Jimoh, *University of Massachusetts, Amherst*
Kelly Latchaw, *University of North Alabama*
Allen M. McFarlane, *New York University*
Joseph R. Millichap, *Western Kentucky University (emeritus)*
Nilüfer Özgür, *Kırklareli University, Turkey*
Roy Rosenstein, *American University of Paris*
Jolie A. Sheffer, *Bowling Green State University*
Pierre A. Walker, *Salem State University*

# WORKS CITED

Abdurraqib, Hanif. *A Little Devil in America: Notes in Praise of Black Performance.* Random House, 2021.

Abes, Elisa S., et al. "Reconceptualizing the Model of Multiple Dimensions of Identity: The Role of Meaning-Making Capacity in the Construction of Multiple Identities." *Journal of College Student Development*, vol. 48, no. 1, 2007, pp. 1–22.

Adelman, Rebecca. "'When I Move, You Move': Thoughts on the Fusion of Hip-Hop and Disability Activism." *Disability Studies Quarterly*, vol. 25, no. 1, 1 Dec. 2005, https://doi.org/10.18061/dsq.v25i1.526.

Alexander, Bryant Keith. "The Outsider (or *Invisible Man* All Over Again): Contesting the Absented Black Gay Body in Queer Theory (with Apologies to Ralph Ellison)." *The Image of the Outsider in Literature, Media, and Society*, edited by Will Wright and Steven Kaplan, U of Southern Colorado, 2002, pp. 308–15.

Alim, H. Samy, and Django Paris, editors. *Culturally Sustaining Pedagogies: Teaching and Learning for Justice in a Changing World.* Teachers College Press, 2017.

Alison, Cheryl. "Writing Underground: Ralph Ellison and the Novel." *Twentieth-Century Literature*, vol. 63, no. 3, Sept. 2017, pp. 329–58.

Althusser, Louis. *On the Reproduction of Capitalism: Ideology and Ideological State Apparatuses.* Translated by G. M. Goshgarian, Verso Books, 2014.

"Americans with Disabilities Act of 1990, As Amended." *ADA*, 8 Nov. 2023, www.ada .gov/law-and-regs/ada/.

"Amiri Baraka—AM/TRAK." *YouTube*, uploaded by Sean Bonney, 20 Sept. 2011, www.youtube.com/watch?v=71i6tCHGUYo.

Anderson, Paul Allen. "Ralph Ellison's Music Lessons." Posnock, pp. 82–103.

Archer, Margaret S. *Being Human: The Problem of Agency.* Cambridge UP, 2000.

Armstrong, Louis. "(What Did I Do to Be So) Black and Blue." *Satch Plays Fats: A Tribute to the Immortal Fats Waller,* Sony Music Entertainment / Columbia Records, 2000.

Atcho, Claude. *Reading Black Books: How African American Literature Can Make Our Faith More Whole and Just.* Baker Publishing Group, 2022.

Baldwin, James. *Collected Essays.* Edited by Toni Morrison, Library of America, 1998.

———. *The Fire Next Time. Collected Essays*, pp. 291–347.

———. "Going to Meet the Man." *Going to Meet the Man*, by Baldwin, Vintage, 1995, pp. 227–49.

———. "Sonny's Blues." *Early Novels and Stories*, edited by Toni Morrison, Library of America, 1998.

Banks, James A. "Multicultural Education: Historical Development, Dimensions, and Practice." *Review of Research in Education*, vol. 19, no. 1, 1993, pp. 3–49.

Baraka, Amiri. *Blues People: Negro Music in White America.* 1963. Harper Perennial, 1999.

———. "The Screamers." *The LeRoi Jones/Amiri Baraka Reader,* edited by William J. Harris, Basic Books, 1999, pp. 171–76.

190 WORKS CITED

Baynton, Douglas C. "Disability and the Justification of Inequality in American History." *The Disability Studies Reader*, edited by Lennard J. Davis, 5th ed., Routledge, 2017, pp. 17–35.

Beatty, Paul, editor. *Hokum: An Anthology of African-American Humor*. Bloomsbury, 2006.

———. *The Sellout*. Farrar, Straus and Giroux, 2015.

Beavers, Herman. "The Noisy Lostness: Oppositionality and Acousmatic Subjectivity in *Invisible Man*." Conner and Morel, pp. 75–98.

Bell, Christopher. "Introducing White Disability Studies: A Modest Proposal." *The Disability Studies Reader*, edited by Lennard J. Davis, 2nd ed., Routledge, 2006, pp. 275–82.

Bellow, Saul. *Henderson the Rain King*. 1959. Penguin, 2012.

*The Bible*. King James Version, *Bible Gateway*, www.biblegateway.com/versions/King -James-Version-KJV-Bible/.

Biss, Eula. "Time and Distance Overcome." *Notes from No Man's Land: American Essays*, by Biss, Graywolf Press, 2018, pp. 3–13.

Blair, Sara. "Ellison, Photography, and the Origins of Invisibility." Posnock, pp. 56–81.

———. *Harlem Crossroads: Black Writers and the Photograph in the Twentieth Century*. Princeton UP, 2007.

Blake, Susan L. "Ritual and Rationalization: Black Folklore in the Works of Ralph Ellison." *PMLA*, vol. 94, no. 1, 1979, pp. 121–36.

Blakemore, Erin. "Gay Conversation Therapy's Disturbing Nineteenth-Century Origins." *History*, A&E Television Networks, 28 June 2019, www.history.com/ news/gay-conversion-therapy-origins-19th-century.

Bland, Sterling Lecater, Jr. "Being Ralph Ellison: Remaking the Black Public Intellectual in the Age of Civil Rights." Calihman et al., pp. 52–62.

———. *In the Shadow of Invisibility: Ralph Ellison and the Promise of American Democracy*. Louisiana State UP, 2023.

Boster, Dea H. *African American Slavery and Disability: Bodies, Property and Power in the Antebellum South, 1800–1860*. Routledge, 2013.

Botcharova, Olga. "Implementation of Track Two Diplomacy: Developing a Model of Forgiveness." *Forgiveness and Reconciliation: Religion, Public Policy, and Conflict Transformation*, edited by Raymond J. Helmick and Rodney L. Petersen, Templeton Foundation Press, 2001, pp. 279–304.

Bradley, Adam. *Ralph Ellison in Progress: From* Invisible Man *to* Three Days before the Shooting . . . . Yale UP, 2010.

Brown, Sterling A. *The Collected Poems of Sterling Brown*. Edited by Michael S. Harper, TriQuarterly, 1996.

Butler, Robert. "*Invisible Man* and the Politics of Love." Conner and Morel, pp. 39–54.

Butts, J. J. *Dark Mirror: African Americans and the Federal Writers' Project*. Ohio State UP, 2021.

Byerman, Keith. "'I Did Not Learn Their Names': Female Characters in the Short Fiction of Ralph Ellison." Calihman et al., pp. 101–14.

## WORKS CITED

Calihman, Matthew, and Gerald Early. Introduction. *Approaches to Teaching Baraka's Dutchman*, edited by Calihman and Early, Modern Language Association of America, 2018, pp. 19–25.

Calihman, Matthew, et al., editors. *The Ralph Ellison Issue*. Special issue of *American Studies*. Vol. 54, no. 3, 2015, journals.ku.edu/amsj/issue/view/618.

Callahan, John F. "Chaos, Complexity, and Possibility: The Historical Frequencies of Ralph Waldo Ellison." *Black American Literature Forum*, vol. 11, no. 4, winter 1977, pp. 130–38.

———. General Introduction. Ellison, *Selected Letters*, pp. 3–14.

———. *In the African-American Grain: Call-and-Response in Twentieth-Century Black Fiction*. U of Illinois P, 1990.

———. Introduction. Ellison, *Flying Home*, pp. ix–xxxviii.

———. Introduction. Ellison, *Juneteenth*, pp. xix–xxx.

———, editor. *Ralph Ellison's* Invisible Man: *A Casebook*. Oxford UP, 2004. Casebooks in Criticism.

Callahan, John F., and Adam Bradley. General Introduction. Ellison, *Three Days*, pp. xv–xxix.

Capeci, Dominic J. *The Harlem Riot of 1943*. Temple UP, 1977.

Cerda-Jara, Michael, et al. "Criminal Record Stigma in College-Educated Labor Market." *Institute for Research on Labor and Employment*, U of California, Berkley, 19 May 2020, irle.berkeley.edu/publications/student-publication/criminal-record-stigma-in-the-college-educated-labor-market/.

Chauncey, George. *Gay New York: Gender, Urban Culture, and the Making of the Gay Male World, 1890–1940*. Basic Books, 1995.

Cheng, Anne Anlin. "Ralph Ellison: Melancholic Visibility and the Crisis of American Civil Rights." *Journal of Law, Philosophy and Culture*, vol. 5, no. 1, 2010, pp. 119–39.

Chude-Sokei, Louis. *The Last "Darky": Bert Williams, Black-on-Black Minstrelsy, and the African Diaspora*. Duke UP, 2006.

Cifu, David X., et al. "The History and Evolution of Traumatic Brain Injury Rehabilitation in Military Service Members and Veterans." *American Journal of Physical Medicine and Rehabilitation*, vol. 89, no. 8, 2010, pp. 688–94.

Cloutier, Jean-Christophe. *Shadow Archives: The Lifecycles of African American Literature*. Columbia UP, 2019.

Coates, Ta-Nehisi. *Between the World and Me*. Random House, 2015.

Coltrane, John. *My Favorite Things*. Atlantic Catalog Group, 1990.

Conner, Marc C. "Father Abraham: Ellison's Agon with the Fathers in *Three Days before the Shooting . . . .*" Conner and Morel, pp. 167–93.

Conner, Marc C., and Lucas E. Morel, editors. *The New Territory: Ralph Ellison and the Twenty-First Century*. UP of Mississippi, 2016.

Couloute, Lucius. *Nowhere to Go: Homelessness among Formerly Incarcerated People*. Prison Policy Initiative, Aug. 2018, www.prisonpolicy.org/reports/housing.html.

## 192   WORKS CITED

Crable, Bryan. *Ralph Ellison and Kenneth Burke: At the Roots of the Racial Divide.* U of Virginia P, 2012.

Craigie, Terry Ann, et al. *Conviction, Imprisonment, and Lost Earnings: How Involvement with the Criminal Justice System Deepens Inequality.* Brennan Center for Justice, 15 Sept. 2020, www.brennancenter.org/our-work/research -reports/conviction-imprisonment-and-lost-earnings-how-involvement-criminal.

Crouch, Stanley. "Howling Wolf: A Blues Lesson Book." *Black World*, vol. 20, no. 2, 1970, pp. 60–64.

Devi, Mahashweta. "Arjun." Translated by Miridula Nath Chakraborty, 1984. *Lotus Singers: Short Stories from Contemporary South Asia*, edited by Trevor Carolan, Cheng and Tsui, 2011, pp. 11–20.

Devlin, Paul, editor. *Ralph Ellison in Context.* Cambridge UP, 2021.

*Diagnostic and Statistical Manual of Mental Disorders.* 3rd ed., American Psychiatric Association, 1980.

Dobbs, Cynthia. "Mapping Black Movement, Containing Black Laughter: Ralph Ellison's New York Essays." *American Quarterly*, vol. 68, no. 4, 2016, pp. 907–29, https://doi.org/10.1353/aq.2016.0072.

Dostoyevsky, Fyodor. Notes from Underground *and* The Double. Translated by Ronald Wilks, Penguin Classics, 2009.

Doyle, Mary Ellen. "In Need of Folk: The Alienated Protagonists of Ralph Ellison's Short Fiction." *CLA Journal*, vol. 19, no. 2, 1975, pp. 165–72.

Du Bois, W. E. B. *The Souls of Black Folk.* 1903. Library of America, 2009.

Early, Gerald. "Jazz and the African American Literature Tradition." *TeacherServe*, National Humanities Center, nationalhumanitiescenter.org/tserve/freedom/ 1917beyond/essays/jazz.htm. Accessed 25 Sept. 2020.

Edwards, Erica R. *Charisma and the Fictions of Black Leadership.* U of Minnesota P, 2012.

Eidsheim, Nina Sun. "Race and the Aesthetics of Vocal Timbre." *Rethinking Difference in Music Scholarship*, edited by Olivia Bloechl et al., Cambridge UP, 2015.

———. *Sensing Sound: Singing and Listening as Vibrational Practice.* Duke UP, 2015.

Eliot, T. S. *The Complete Poems and Plays, 1909–1950.* Harcourt Brace, 1980.

———. *Four Quartets.* Eliot, *Complete Poems*, pp. 117–48.

———. "Tradition and the Individual Talent." 1919. *Poetry Foundation*, www.poetry foundation.org/articles/69400/tradition-and-the-individual-talent.

———. *The Waste Land.* Eliot, *Complete Poems*, pp. 37–55.

Ellis, Jonathan, editor. *Letter Writing among Poets: From William Wordsworth to Elizabeth Bishop.* Edinburgh UP, 2015.

Ellison, Fanny McConnell. Letter to her mother. 17 Oct. 1951. Ralph Ellison papers, Manuscript Division, Library of Congress, part 2, box 4.

Ellison, Ralph. "Adventures of an Unintentional New Yorker." Ralph Ellison papers, Manuscript Division, Library of Congress, part 1, box 95.

———. "All of Harlem Was Awake." *New York Post*, 2 Aug. 1943. *Reporting Civil Rights*, compiled by Clayton Carson et al., vol. 1, Library of America, 2003, pp. 50–51.

## WORKS CITED

———. *The Collected Essays of Ralph Ellison*. Edited by John F. Callahan, Modern Library, 2003.

———. *Conversations with Ralph Ellison*. Edited by Maryemma Graham and Amritjit Singh, UP of Mississippi, 1995.

———. *Flying Home and Other Stories*. Edited by John F. Callahan, 2nd ed., Vintage International, 2012.

———. *Going to the Territory*. 1986. Vintage, 1995.

———. "The Great Migration." *New Masses*, vol. 41, no. 9, 2 Dec. 1941, pp. 23–24.

———. "Harlem Is Nowhere." *Harper's Magazine*, Aug. 1964, harpers.org/archive/1964/08/harlem-is-nowhere/.

———. *Invisible Man*. 1952. Vintage International, 2012.

———. *Juneteenth*. Edited by John F. Callahan, Random House, 1999.

———. *Juneteenth*. Edited by John F. Callahan, revised ed., Vintage International, 2021.

———. "The Negro and the Second World War." Sundquist, pp. 233–40.

———. "Out of the Hospital and under the Bar." *Soon, One Morning: New Writing by American Negroes, 1940–1962*, edited by Herbert Hill, Random House, 1963, pp. 242–90.

———. *Photographer*. Edited by Michal Raz-Russo and John F. Callahan, Steidl, 2023.

———. *The Selected Letters of Ralph Ellison*. Edited by John F. Callahan and Marc C. Conner, Random House, 2019.

———. *Shadow and Act*. 1964. Vintage International, 1995.

———. *Three Days before the Shooting* . . . . Edited by John F. Callahan and Adam Bradley, Modern Library, 2011.

Everett, Percival. *Erasure*. Graywolf Press, 2011.

*F.B. Eyes Digital Archive*. Washington U in St. Louis, digital.wustl.edu/fbeyes/. Accessed 15 June 2022.

Feld, Steven. "Waterfalls of Song: An Acoustemology of Place Resounding in Bosavi, Papua New Guinea." *Senses of Place*, edited by Feld and Keith H. Basso, School of American Research Press, 1996, pp. 91–135.

Ferguson, Roderick A. *Aberrations in Black: Toward a Queer of Color Critique*. U of Minnesota P, 2004.

Fitzgerald, Ella. "Take the 'A' Train." *Ella Fitzgerald Sings the Duke Ellington Songbook*, Essential Jazz Classics, 2006.

Foley, Barbara. "Becoming 'More Human': From the Drafts of Ralph Ellison's *Invisible Man* to *Three Days before the Shooting* . . . ." *African American Review*, vol. 48, nos. 1–2, 2015, pp. 67–82.

———. *Wrestling with the Left: The Making of Ralph Ellison's* Invisible Man. Duke UP, 2010.

Foucault, Michel. *Discipline and Punish: The Birth of the Prison*. Translated by Alan Sheridan, Vintage, 1977.

Freire, Paulo. *Pedagogy of the Oppressed*. 1968. Bloomsbury, 2018.

Gallagher, Kelly. *In the Best Interest of Students: Staying True to What Works in the ELA Classroom*. Stenhouse Publishers, 2015.

Garland-Thomson, Rosemarie. *Extraordinary Bodies: Figuring Physical Disability in American Culture and Literature.* Columbia UP, 1997.

Garvey, Marcus. "Africa for the Africans." Sundquist, pp. 182–92.

Germana, Michael. *Ralph Ellison, Temporal Technologist.* Oxford UP, 2018.

Ghatage, Rohan. "Rethinking the Aesthetic in Ralph Ellison's *Three Days before the Shooting . . . .*" *MELUS*, vol. 48, no. 3, 2023, pp. 25–49.

"The Gift." *Jazz*, directed by Ken Burns, episode 2, Public Broadcasting Service, 2001.

Glaude, Eddie S., Jr. *Begin Again: James Baldwin's America and Its Urgent Lessons for Our Own.* Crown Books, 2020.

"Gold Standard PBL: Essential Project Design Elements." *PBL Works*, Buck Institute for Education, www.pblworks.org/what-is-pbl/gold-standard-project-design. Accessed 19 Oct. 2021.

Gramsci, Antonio. *Selections from the Prison Notebooks of Antonio Gramsci.* Edited and translated by Quintin Hoare and Geoffrey Nowell Smith, International Publishers, 1971.

Greenberg, Cheryl. "The Politics of Disorder: Reexamining Harlem's Riots of 1935 and 1943." *Journal of Urban History*, vol. 18, no. 4, 1992, pp. 395–441.

Greif, Mark. *The Age of the Crisis of Man: Thought and Fiction in America, 1933–1973.* Princeton UP, 2015.

Griffin, Farah Jasmine. *Read until You Understand: The Wisdom of Black Life and Literature.* W. W. Norton, 2022.

———. *"Who Set You Flowin'?": The African-American Migration Narrative.* Oxford UP, 1995.

Ha, Hyo-seol. "'I Should Have Gone to Mary's': Filling the Void in Ralph Ellison's *Invisible Man.*" *Gender Forum*, vol. 50, 2014, pp. 39–55.

Hardin, Michael. "Ralph Ellison's *Invisible Man*: Invisibility, Race, and Homoeroticism from Frederick Douglass to E. Lynn Harris." *The Southern Literary Journal*, vol. 37, no. 1, 2004, pp. 96–120.

Harper, Michael S. "Brother John." *Dear John, Dear Coltrane*, by Harper, U of Pittsburgh P, 1970, pp. 3–4.

———. "Here Where Coltrane Is." *History Is Your Own Heartbeat*, by Harper, U of Illinois P, 1971, p. 32.

Harriss, M. Cooper. "One Blues Invisible: Civil Rights and Civil Religion in Ralph Ellison's Second Novel." *African American Review*, vol. 47, nos. 2–3, summer-fall 2014, pp. 250–51.

———. *Ralph Ellison's Invisible Theology.* New York UP, 2017.

Hayes, Terrance. "How to Draw an Invisible Man." *How to Be Drawn*, by Hayes, Penguin, 2015, pp. 38–39.

———. "How to Draw an Invisible Man." Calihman et al., pp. 185–86.

Henry, Alvin J. *Black Queer Flesh: Rejecting Subjectivity in the African American Novel.* U of Minnesota P, 2020.

Herndon, Angelo. *Let Me Live.* Random House, 1937.

Hill, Lena M. "The Politics of Fatherhood in *Three Days before the Shooting . . . .*" Conner and Morel, pp. 142–66.

———. *Visualizing Blackness and the Creation of the African American Literary Tradition*. Cambridge UP, 2014.

Hill, Lena M., and Michael D. Hill. *Ralph Ellison's* Invisible Man: *A Reference Guide*. Greenwood Press, 2008.

Hirsch, Jerrold. "Cultural Pluralism and Applied Folklore: The New Deal Precedent." *The Conservation of Culture: Folklorists and the Public Sector*, edited by Burt Feintuch, UP of Kentucky, 1988, pp. 46–67.

Hoeveler, Diane Long. "Game Theory and Ellison's *King of the Bingo Game*." *Journal of American Culture*, vol. 15, no. 2, 1992, pp. 39–42.

Hollander, Jocelyn A., and Rachel L. Einwohner. "Conceptualizing Resistance." *Sociological Forum*, vol. 19, no. 4, 2004, pp. 533–54.

Holmes, Richard. *The Age of Wonder: How the Romantic Generation Discovered the Beauty and Terror of Science*. Pantheon, 2009.

Horne, Gerald. *The Color of Fascism: Lawrence Dennis, Racial Passing, and the Rise of Right-Wing Extremism in the United States*. New York UP, 2006.

Hudson, Hosea. *Black Worker in the Deep South: A Personal Account*. International Publishers, 1991.

Hughes, Langston. *The Collected Poems of Langston Hughes*. Edited by Arnold Rampersad and David Roessel, Vintage, 1995.

Jackson, Lawrence. *The Indignant Generation: A Narrative History of African American Writers and Critics, 1934–1960*. Princeton UP, 2011.

———. *Ralph Ellison: Emergence of Genius*. Wiley, 2002.

———. "Ralph Ellison, Sharpies, Rinehart, and Politics in *Invisible Man*." *The Massachusetts Review*, vol. 40, no. 1, 1991, pp. 71–95.

Jamieson, Egbert, and Francis Adams. *The Municipal Code of Chicago: Comprising the Laws of Illinois Relating to the City of Chicago, and the Ordinances of the City Council*. Chicago, 1881.

Jarrett, Gene Andrew, editor. *The Wiley Blackwell Anthology of African American Literature*. Wiley Blackwell, 2015.

Jefferson, Thomas. *Notes on the State of Virginia*. 1788. *Documenting the American South*, U of North Carolina at Chapel Hill, 2006, docsouth.unc.edu/southlit/jefferson/jefferson.html.

Johnson, James Weldon. *Along This Way. Writings*, edited by William L. Andrews, Library of America, 2004, pp. 125–606.

Johnson, Marilynn S. "Gender, Race, and Rumours: Re-examining the 1943 Race Riots." *Gender and History*, vol. 10, no. 2, 1998, pp. 252–77.

Johnson, Paula B., et al. "Black Invisibility, the Press, and the Los Angeles Riot." *American Journal of Sociology*, vol. 76, no. 4, 1971, pp. 698–721.

Johnson, Walter. "Slavery, Reparations, and the Mythic March of Freedom." *Raritan*, vol. 27, no. 2, 2007, pp. 41–67.

Jones, Susan R., and Marylu K. McEwen. "A Conceptual Model of Multiple Dimensions of Identity." *Journal of College Student Development*, vol. 41, no. 4, 2000, pp. 405–14.

Kafer, Alison. *Feminist, Queer, Crip*. Indiana UP, 2013.

## WORKS CITED

Kafka, Franz. "The Silence of the Sirens." 1931. *The Great Wall of China: Stories and Reflections*, by Kafka, translated by Willa Muir and Edwin Muir, Schocken Books, 1946.

Kelley, Robin D. G. *Freedom Dreams: The Black Radical Imagination*. Revised and expanded ed., e-book ed., Beacon Press, 2022.

Kent, George E. "Ralph Ellison and the Afro-American Folk and Cultural Tradition." *The Critical Response to Ralph Ellison*, edited by Robert J. Butler, Greenwood Press, 2000, pp. 51–57.

Kim, Daniel Y. *Writing Manhood in Black and Yellow: Ralph Ellison, Frank Chin, and the Literary Politics of Identity*. Stanford UP, 2005.

King, Bradley Ray. "Ralph Ellison's Melville Masks." *REAL*, vol. 30, no. 1, 2014, pp. 127–47.

Kittler, Friedrich A. *Gramophone, Film, Typewriter*. Translated by Geoffrey Winthrop-Young and Michael Wutz, Stanford UP, 1999.

Ladson-Billings, Gloria. "The Importance of 'White Students Having Black Teachers': Gloria Ladson-Billings on Education." Interview by Larry Ferlazzo. *Education Week*, 20 Feb. 2018, www.edweek.org/education/opinion-the-importance-of-white -students-having-Black-teachers-gloria-ladson-billings-on-education/2018/02/.

———. "Toward a Theory of Culturally Relevant Pedagogy." *American Educational Research Journal*, vol. 32, no. 3, 1995, pp. 465–91.

Lederach, John Paul. "The Meeting Place." U of Colorado, Conflict Research Consortium, 1997, www.intractableconflict.org/www_colorado_edu_conflict/transform/ jplchpt.htm.

Lee, Chang-rae. *Native Speaker*. Riverhead Books, 1995.

Lee, Spike. *Bamboozled*. New Line Home Entertainment, 2001.

Lieberman, Jennifer L. "Alternating Currents: Electricity, Humanism, and Resistance." Devlin, pp. 127–36.

———. "Ralph Ellison's Technological Humanism." *MELUS*, vol. 40, no. 4, 2015, pp. 8–27.

Lucy, Robin. "'Flying Home': Ralph Ellison, Richard Wright, and the Black Folk during World War II." *The Journal of American Folklore*, vol. 120, no. 477, 2007, pp. 257–83.

Lupo, Lindsey. *Flak-Catchers: One Hundred Years of Riot Commission Politics in America*. Lexington Books, 2011.

*Marcus Garvey: Look for Me in the Whirlwind*. Directed and produced by Stanley Nelson. *American Experience*, Public Broadcasting Service, 12 Feb. 2001.

Masterton Sherazi, Melanie. "The Posthumous Text and Its Archive: Toward an Ecstatic Reading of Ralph Ellison's Unbound Novel." *MELUS*, vol. 42, no. 2, 2017, pp. 6–29.

Maus, Derek C. "'Mommy, What's a Post-Soul Satirist?': An Introduction." Maus and Donahue, pp. xi–xxiii.

Maus, Derek C., and James J. Donahue, editors. *Post-Soul Satire: Black Identity after Civil Rights*. UP of Mississippi, 2014.

Maxwell, William J. "'Creative and Cultural Lag': The Radical Education of Ralph Ellison." Tracy, pp. 59–84.

## WORKS CITED     197

———. *F.B. Eyes: How J. Edgar Hoover's Ghostreaders Framed African American Literature*. Princeton UP, 2015.

McKay, Claude. "Harlem Runs Wild." Sundquist, pp. 222–25.

McNeill, Katherine L., and Joseph Krajcik. "Inquiry and Scientific Explanations: Helping Students Use Evidence and Reasoning." *Science as Inquiry in the Secondary Setting*, edited by Julie Luft et al., National Science Teaching Association, 2008, pp. 34–42.

McPherson, William D., and J. Oliver. "The Scourged Back." Circa 1863. African American History Photographs, Print Department, Library Company of Philadelphia, digital.librarycompany.org/islandora/object/digitool:127246.

McSweeney, Kerry. *Invisible Man: Race and Identity*. Twayne, 1988.

Melville, Herman. *Benito Cereno. The Piazza Tales*, by Melville, New York, 1856. *Project Gutenberg*, 18 May 2005, www.gutenberg.org/files/15859/15859-h/15859-h.htm.

Miller, D. Quentin. *The Routledge Introduction to African American Literature*. Routledge, 2016.

Miller, Reuben Jonathan, and Amanda Alexander. "The Price of Carceral Citizenship: Punishment, Surveillance, and Social Welfare Policy in an Age of Carceral Expansion." *Michigan Journal of Race and Law*, vol. 21, no. 2, 2016, pp. 291–314, https://doi.org/10.36643/mjrl.21.2.price.

Mills, Nathaniel. "Playing the Dozens and Consuming the Cadillac: Ralph Ellison and Civil Rights Politics." *Twentieth-Century Literature*, vol. 61, no. 2, 2015, pp. 147–72.

Morel, Lucas E., editor. *Ralph Ellison and the Raft of Hope: A Political Companion to Invisible Man*. UP of Kentucky, 2004.

Morrell, Ernest. "Toward Equity and Diversity in Literacy Research, Policy, and Practice: A Critical, Global Approach." *Journal of Literacy Research*, vol. 49, no. 3, 2017, pp. 454–63.

Morrison, Toni. Letter to Ralph Ellison. 6 June 1972. Ralph Ellison papers, Manuscript Division, Library of Congress, part 2, box 65.

———. *Playing in the Dark: Whiteness and the Literary Imagination*. Random House, 1992.

Muhammad, Gholdy. *Cultivating Genius: An Equity Framework for Culturally and Historically Responsive Literacy*. Scholastic, 2020.

Muhammad, Gholnecsar E., and LaTasha T. Mosley. "Why We Need Identity and Equity Learning in Literacy Practices: Moving Research, Practice, and Policy Forward." *Language Arts*, vol. 98, no. 4, 2021, pp. 189–96.

Murray, Albert. *Albert Murray: Collected Essays and Memoirs*. Edited by Henry Louis Gates, Jr., and Paul Devlin, Library of America, 2016.

———. "The Omni Americans." *The Urban Review*, vol. 3, no. 6, June 1969, pp. 38–45.

———. Preface. Murray and Callahan, pp. xix–xxiiii.

Murray, Albert, and John F. Callahan, editors. *Trading Twelves: The Selected Letters of Ralph Ellison and Albert Murray*. Vintage Books, 2001.

Nadel, Alan. "Ralph Ellison and the American Canon." *American Literary History*, vol. 13, no. 2, 2001, pp. 393–404.

WORKS CITED

Naison, Mark. *Communists in Harlem during the Depression*. Grove Press, 1983.

Neal, Larry. "Ellison's Zoot Suit." Callahan, *Ralph Ellison's* Invisible Man, pp. 81–108.

Nguyen, Viet Thanh. *The Sympathizer*. Grove Press, 2015.

Noh, Jeff. "Ralph Ellison's Computer Memory." *Contemporary Literature*, vol. 62, no. 4, 2021, pp. 527–57.

O'Meally, Robert G. *The Craft of Ralph Ellison*. Harvard UP, 1980.

———, editor. *Living with Music: Ralph Ellison's Jazz Writings*. Modern Library, 2002.

———, editor. *New Essays on* Invisible Man. Cambridge UP, 1988.

———. "On Burke and the Vernacular: Ralph Ellison's Boomerang of History." *History and Memory in African American Culture*, edited by Geneviève Fabre and O'Meally, Oxford UP, 1994, pp. 244–60.

Omi, Michael, and Howard Winant. *Racial Formation in the United States: From the 1960s to the 1990s*. 2nd ed., Routledge, 1994.

Orem, Sarah. "(Un)Necessary Procedures: Black Women, Disability, and Work in *Grey's Anatomy*." *African American Review*, vol. 50, no. 2, 2017, pp. 169–83, https://doi.org/10.1353/afa.2017.0020.

Ostendorf, Bernhard. "Ralph Ellison's 'Flying Home': From Folk Tale to Short Story." *Journal of the Folklore Institute*, vol. 13, no. 2, 1976, pp. 185–99.

Parr, Susan Resneck, and Pancho Savery, editors. *Approaches to Teaching Ellison's* Invisible Man. Modern Language Association of America, 1989.

Parrish, Timothy. *Ralph Ellison and the Genius of America*. U of Massachusetts P, 2012.

———. "Ralph Ellison's *Three Days*: The Aesthetics of Political Change." Conner and Morel, pp. 194–217.

Patterson, Orlando. *The Privatization of Freedom in America: Its Meaning and Consequences. Scholars at Harvard*, scholar.harvard.edu/files/patterson/files/the_privatization_of_freedom_in_america.pdf. Accessed 15 Nov. 2023.

Petry, Ann. *The Street*. Houghton Mifflin, 1998

Pickens, Therí Alyce. *Black Madness :: Mad Blackness*. Duke UP, 2019.

Porter, Horace A. *Jazz Country: Ralph Ellison in America*. U of Iowa P, 2001.

Porter, J. D. "Ellison and Digital Humanities." Devlin, pp. 385–95.

Posnock, Ross, editor. *The Cambridge Companion to Ralph Ellison*. Cambridge UP, 2005.

Powell, Adam Clayton. "The Harlem Riot of 1943." Sundquist, pp. 226–32.

Proulx, Natalie. "Nine Teaching Ideas for Using Music to Inspire Student Writing." *The New York Times*, 10 May 2018, www.nytimes.com/2018/05/10/learning/lesson-plans/nine-teaching-ideas-for-using-music-to-inspire-student-writing.html.

*Ralph Ellison: An American Journey*. Directed by Avon Kirkland and Elise Robertson, *American Masters*, Public Broadcasting Service, 2002.

Rampersad, Arnold. *Ralph Ellison: A Biography*. Knopf, 2007.

Rankine, Claudia. *Citizen: An American Lyric*. Graywolf Press, 2014.

Raz-Russo, Michal, and Jean-Christophe Cloutier. *Invisible Man: Gordon Parks and Ralph Ellison in Harlem*. Steidl / Art Institute of Chicago / Gordon Parks Foundation, 2016.

## WORKS CITED   199

*Rear Window.* Directed by Alfred Hitchcock, Paramount Pictures, 1954.

Reger, Wibke. *The Black Body of Literature: Colorism in American Fiction.* Brill, 2008.

Rice, H. William. *Ralph Ellison and the Politics of the Novel.* Lexington Books, 2003.

*Richard Pryor: Live in Concert.* Performance by Richard Pryor, directed by Jeff Margolis, Long Beach, CA, 1979.

Rodgers, Richard, and Oscar Hammerstein II. *The Sound of Music: An Original Soundtrack Recording.* RCA Victor, 1984.

Rohrberger, Mary. "'Ball the Jack': Surreality, Sexuality, and the Role of Women in *Invisible Man.*" Parr and Savery, pp. 124–32.

Rohrwacher, Alice, director. *Happy as Lazzaro.* RAI Cinema, 2018.

Rudick, Nicole. "Nearly Seventy Years Later, 'Invisible Man' Is Still Inspiring Visual Artists." *The New York Times Style Magazine,* 11 June 2021, www.nytimes.com/2021/06/11/t-magazine/invisible-man-ellison-art.html.

Rutherford-Johnson, Tim. "Birtwistle Games, South Bank Centre." *The Rambler,* 1 Nov. 2004, johnsonsrambler.wordpress.com/2004/11/01/birtwistle-games-south-bank-centre/.

"Satire, N." *Oxford English Dictionary,* Oxford UP, 2013, www.oed.com/viewdictionaryentry/entry/171207.

Saunders, Catherine E. "Makers or Bearers of Meaning? Sex and the Struggle for Self-Definition in Ralph Ellison's *Invisible Man.*" *Critical Matrix,* vol. 5, no. 1, 1989, pp. 1–14.

Savery, Pancho. "'Not like an Arrow, but a Boomerang': Ellison's Existential Blues." Parr and Savery, pp. 65–74.

Schalk, Sami. "Interpreting Disability Metaphor and Race in Octavia Butler's 'The Evening and the Morning and the Night.'" *African American Review,* vol. 50, no. 2, 2017, pp. 139–51, https://doi.org/10.1353/afa.2017.0018.

Schweik, Susan. "Begging the Question: Disability, Mendicancy, Speech and the Law." *Narrative,* vol. 15, no. 1, 2007, pp. 58–70.

———. *Ugly Laws: Disability in Public.* New York UP, 2009.

Selisker, Scott. "'Simply by Reacting?': The Sociology of Race and *Invisible Man*'s Automata." *American Literature,* vol. 83, no. 3, 2011, pp. 571–96.

Sheffer, Jolie A. "*Invisible Man* by Ralph Ellison." *Digital Public Library of America,* 2017, dp.la/primary-source-sets/invisible-man-by-ralph-ellison. Primary source set.

Sherazi, Melanie Masterton. "The Posthumous Text and Its Archive: Toward an Ecstatic Reading of Ralph Ellison's Unbound Novel." *MELUS,* vol. 42, no. 2, 2017, pp. 6–29.

"Slavery, Race and the Origins of American Freedom." *YouTube,* uploaded by UW Video, 8 Nov. 2013, www.youtube.com/watch?v=xwLci-NTpqo&t=2s.

Smallwood, Stephanie. "Freedom." *Keywords for American Cultural Studies,* edited by Bruce Burgett and Glenn Hendler, New York UP, 2014, pp. 111–15.

———. "Slavery and the Framing of the African American Past: Reflections from a Historian of the Transatlantic Slave Trade." *The Future of the African American Past,* National Museum of African American History and Culture, May 2016,

## WORKS CITED

futureafampast.si.edu/blog/slavery-and-framing-african-american-past -reflections-historian-transatlantic-slave-trade.

Smethurst, James. *The African American Roots of Modernism: From Reconstruction to the Harlem Renaissance.* U of North Carolina P, 2011.

———. "'Something Warmly, Infuriatingly Feminine': Gender, Sexuality, and the Work of Ralph Ellison." Tracy, pp. 115–42.

Solnit, Rebecca. "Diary: In the Day of the Postman." *London Review of Books,* vol. 35, no. 16, 29 Aug. 2013, pp. 32–33.

*Sorry to Bother You.* Directed by Boots Riley, Significant Productions, 2018.

Spandler, Helen, and Sarah Carr. "The Shocking 'Treatment' to Make Lesbians Straight." *Wellcome Collection,* 22 Jan. 2020, wellcomecollection.org/articles/ XhWjZhAAACUAOpV2.

Spaulding, A. Timothy. "Embracing Chaos in Narrative Form: The Bebop Aesthetic in Ralph Ellison's *Invisible Man.*" *Callaloo,* vol. 27, no. 2, 2004, pp. 481–501.

Spielman, Rose M., et al. "Mental Health Treatment: Past and Present." *Psychology 2e,* by Spielman et al., e-book, OpenStax, 2020, openstax.org/books/psychology-2e/ pages/16-1-mental-health-treatment-past-and-present.

Spillers, Hortense. "Mama's Baby, Papa's Maybe: An American Grammar Book." *Diacritics,* vol. 17, no. 2, 1987, pp. 64–81.

Stein, Murray B., and Barbara O. Rothbaum. "175 Years of Progress in PTSD Therapeutics: Learning from the Past." *The American Journal of Psychiatry,* vol. 175, no. 6, 2018, pp. 508–16.

Stepto, Robert B. *From Behind the Veil: A Study of Afro-American Narrative.* 2nd ed., U of Illinois P, 1991.

Steward, Douglas. "The Illusions of Phallic Agency: *Invisible Man, Totem and Taboo,* and the Santa Claus Surprise." *Callaloo,* vol. 26, no. 2, 2003, pp. 522–35.

Stoever, Jennifer Lynn. *The Sonic Color Line: Race and the Cultural Politics of Listening.* New York UP, 2016.

Sundquist, Eric J. *Cultural Contexts for Ralph Ellison's* Invisible Man*: A Bedford Documentary Companion.* Bedford St. Martin's, 1995.

———. "Ralph Ellison in His Labyrinth." Conner and Morel, pp. 117–141.

Tate, Claudia. "Notes on the Invisible Women in Ralph Ellison's *Invisible Man.*" Callahan, *Ralph Ellison's* Invisible Man, pp. 253–66.

"Teaching Jazz as American Culture Lesson Plans." National Endowment for the Humanities Summer Institute, 5–29 July 2005, Center for the Humanities, Washington U in St. Louis, MO, wustl.app.box.com/s/ vp9wok27uaqdn9vd7mscxaftfmsfmalt.

Tracy, Steven C., editor. *A Historical Guide to Ralph Ellison.* Oxford UP, 2004.

Twain, Mark. *Adventures of Huckleberry Finn.* Edited by Thomas Cooley, Norton Critical Edition, W. W. Norton, 2021.

"A Typical Negro." *Harper's Weekly,* 4 July 1863, p. 429.

United States, Department of Agriculture. "Trends in U.S. Agriculture: Mechanization." *National Agricultural Statistics Service,* 4 May 2018, www.nass.usda.gov/ Publications/Trends_in_U.S._Agriculture/Mechanization/index.php.

WORKS CITED  201

United States, Supreme Court. *Brown v. Board of Education of Topeka*. 17 May 1954. *Westlaw*, Thomson Reuters, www.law.cornell.edu/supremecourt/text/347/483.

Urquhart, Troy A. "Ellison's King of the Bingo Game." *The Explicator*, vol. 60, no. 4, 2002, pp. 217–19.

"USA: The Novel—Ralph Ellison on Work in Progress 1966." Interview by National Educational Television, 1966. *YouTube*, uploaded by Oklahoma Historical Society Film and Video Archives, 29 May 2012, www.youtube.com/watch?v=LgC0zZ30kh8.

"Visualizing Jazz Scenes of the Harlem Renaissance." *TeacherVision*, 2022, www.teachervision.com/music-styles/visualizing-jazz-scenes-harlem-renaissance. Lesson plan.

Vygotsky, Lev S. *Mind in Society: The Development of Higher Psychological Processes*. Edited by Michael Cole et al., Harvard UP, 1978.

Waligora-Davis, Nicole A. "Riotous Discontent: Ralph Ellison's 'Birth of a Nation.'" *Modern Fiction Studies*, vol. 50, no. 2, 2004, pp. 385–410.

Walker, Anders. *The Burning House: Jim Crow and the Making of Modern America*. Yale UP, 2018.

Wall, Cheryl A. *On Freedom and the Will to Adorn: The Art of the African American Essay*. U of North Carolina P, 2018.

Warren, Kenneth W. "Chaos Not Quite Controlled: Ellison's Uncompleted Transit to *Juneteenth*." Posnock, pp. 188–200.

———. *So Black and Blue: Ralph Ellison and the Occasion of Criticism*. U of Chicago P, 2003.

Washington, Booker T. "Atlanta Exposition Address." Sundquist, pp. 33–38.

Watkins, Mel. *On the Real Side: A History of African American Comedy from Slavery to Chris Rock*. Chicago Review Press, 1999.

West, Hollie I. "Exploring the Life of a Not So Invisible Man." *Washington Post*, 19 Aug. 1973, sec. G.

Whitehead, Colson. *The Intuitionist*. Anchor Books, 2000.

Wilcox, Johnnie. "Black Power: Minstrelsy and Electricity in Ralph Ellison's *Invisible Man*." *Callaloo*, vol. 30, no. 4, 2007, pp. 987–1009.

Wilson, A. Bennett, Jr. "History of Amputation Surgery and Prosthetics." *Atlas of Limb Prosthetics: Surgical, Prosthetic, and Rehabilitation Principles*, edited by John H. Bowker and John W. Michael, American Academy of Orthopedic Surgeons, 2002. *The Orthotics and Prosthetics Virt7ual Library*, www.oandplibrary.org/alp/chap01-01.asp.

Wilson, August. *Gem of the Ocean*. 2003. Theatre Communications Group, 2006.

———. *Radio Golf*. 2005. Theatre Communications Group, 2007.

Wilson, Chelsee, et al. "Instructional Strategy: Bento Box." *Authentic Lessons for Twenty-First Century Learning*, K20 Center for Educational and Community Renewal, U of Oklahoma, 23 Apr. 2021, learn.k20center.ou.edu/strategy/1128.

Wilson, Kalpana. "Reclaiming 'Agency,' Reasserting Resistance." *IDS Bulletin*, vol. 39, no. 6, 2008, pp. 83–91.

Woolf, Virginia. *The Waves*. 1931. Oxford UP, 1992.

## 202 WORKS CITED

Wright, John S. "The Confederacy of Sages and the Agon of Black Power: Ellison's Hidden Heart." Calihman et al., pp. 63–82.

———. *Shadowing Ralph Ellison*. UP of Mississippi, 2010.

Wright, Richard. "Blueprint for Negro Writing." *New Challenge*, vol. 2, no. 1, 1937.

———. "The Ethics of Living Jim Crow." Wright, *Uncle Tom's Children*, pp. 1–15.

———. *Native Son*. 1940. Harper Perennial, 1998.

———. *Twelve Million Black Voices: A Folk History of the Negro in the United States*. 1941. Basic Books, 2002.

———. *Uncle Tom's Children*. 1938. HarperCollins, 2009.

Yaszek, Lisa. "An Afrofuturist Reading of Ralph Ellison's *Invisible Man*." *Rethinking History*, vol. 9, nos. 2–3, 2005, pp. 297–313.

Yates-Richard, Meina. "'What Is Your Mother's Name?': Maternal Disavowal and the Reverberating Aesthetic of Black Women's Pain in Black Nationalist Literature." *American Literature*, vol. 88, no. 3, 2016, pp. 477–507.

Yeats, William Butler. *The Collected Poems of W. B. Yeats*. Edited by Richard J. Finneran, rev. 2nd ed., Scribner, 1996.

Young, Kevin. "Slow Burn: The Letters of Ralph Ellison." *The New Yorker*, 9 Dec. 2019, pp. 68–73.